ADVANCED BRAND MANAGEMENT

MANAGING BRANDS IN A CHANGING WORLD

SECOND EDITION

ADVANCED
BRAND
MANAGEMENT

MANAGING BRANDS IN A CHANGING WORLD

PAUL TEMPORAL

WILEY

John Wiley & Sons (Asia) Pte. Ltd.

Other Wiley Editorial Offices

John Wiley & Sons, Inc., 111 River Street, Hoboken, NJ 07030, USA

John Wiley & Sons, Ltd., The Atrium, Southern Gate, Chichester, West Sussex PO19 8SQ, UK

John Wiley & Sons (Canada), Ltd., 5353 Dundas Street West, Suite 400, Toronto, Ontario
M9B 6H8, Canada

JohnWiley & Sons Australia Ltd., 42 McDougall Street, Milton, Queensland 4064,
Australia

Wiley-VCH, Boschstrasse 12, D-69469 Weinheim, Germany

Library of Congress Cataloging-in-Publication Data

ISBN: 9780470824498

Typset in 10.5pt/13.5pt, Berkeley-Medium by Thomson Digital

Printed in Singapore by Toppan Security Printing Pte. Ltd.
10 9 8 7 6 5 4 3 2 1

Contents

Acknowledgments

Contrary to popular belief, writing books gets harder, not easier, the more you progress. Readers have higher expectations, the number of books available increases, and pressures on time are more difficult to handle. To produce a book like this requires not just a lot of co-operation, but a lot of assistance and ideas from other people. I would like to take this opportunity to express my gratitude to some of the many people and organizations that have wholeheartedly given of their valuable time and energy during the writing of this, and the previous, edition of the book.

Aaron Boey
Abdullah Fazalbhoy
Bronwyn Coles
Catherine Hu
Danny Ng
Edward Chalk
Gary Moyer
Mark Fields
Nada Dugas
Natalie Croft
Nik Mustapha
Peter Snell
Stan Shih
Suhaimi Halim
Takahiro Ooi
Tom Maas
Tomomitsu Taue
Tunku Siti Raudzoh Tunku Ibrahim
Walter Cheung
Yusuke Horita

Acer
Aegis
Asia Market Intelligence
Brand Finance
Google
Hakuhodo Inc.
Interbrand
Lloyds Banking Group
Malaysia Airlines
Mazda
Mercedes-Benz
Millward Brown
MTV
Opus plc
Oxford University Press
Philips
Procter & Gamble
Synovate
Unilever Malaysia
WPP

I would like particularly to express my gratitude to my colleagues Ornuma Prayoonrattana, Lau Kong Cheen, Andrew Ong, and Denis Tan, for their hard work and support in helping me to revise the text, and for their devotion to our work. Thanks also to the ever-friendly Wiley team for their support—in particular, Janis Soo and Fiona Wong for managing the project so well, Robyn Flemming for great editing, and Nick Wallwork for the opportunity and guidance.

Preface

It has been more than seven years since the first edition of *Advanced Brand Management* was published, and many things have changed during that time which impact on the work of brand managers. While their role remains the same, brand managers now have to cope with a broader range of variables and pressures from the marketplace and consumers. The dynamic changes we have seen in world markets over the past decade have been especially challenging for brand managers. They include:

- the pursuit of speed, agility, and innovation as areas of strategic competitive advantage in a world characterized by a faster pace of change;
- the growth of the digital world and increased use of the Internet in building brands;
- greater emphasis on the projection of brand personality as a means of differentiation;
- the spread of branding in business-to-business markets and the public sector;
- the continued brand architecture trend away from product branding toward corporate branding;
- increased pressure from consumers on organizations to adopt better corporate social responsibility practices;
- the adoption of internal branding and employee engagement to enhance the customer experience; and
- the increased number of mergers, acquisitions, and alliances.

To illustrate these changes, I have made many adjustments to both the text and the case studies in this new edition of the book. All the chapters have been updated, and a completely new chapter is included on the growth of the digital world and the use of the Internet. There are a significant number of new case studies, including some brands whose mistakes offer insights from which we can learn.

Overall, the book has remained steadfast in its philosophy of, and approach to, brand management, but it now reflects the new challenges and opportunities facing practitioners in this highly exciting field.

As I complete this book the business world has changed again in a very negative way. Brand managers are now facing even more daunting challenges posed by the severe global economic recession. To survive in these harsh, adverse conditions, it is vitally important that brand managers apply their brand management skills with even more vigor and discipline.

I hope you enjoy reading this new edition, and get some ideas to take away and put into practice.

Paul Temporal, 2009

Introduction

Brands have never been more important than they are today. The accelerating rate of turbulent change, the volatility of economies and markets, the relentless progress of technologies and innovations, and increasing market fragmentation, have caused the destruction of many companies and their products that have failed to develop the lifeline of a strong brand. Though we are not far into the new century, already markets are littered with failures, physical and virtual, that could have survived had strong branding been in place.

We are in the world of parity where everything tends to be equal, and the world marketplace is a world of commodities. The availability of new technologies has enabled companies to easily replicate the products, systems, services, and processes of others, generating a huge strategic problem for businesses of differentiation. Added to this problem is the rapidly decreasing life cycle of products, in some cases now down to a matter of weeks.

Strong brands alleviate these problems. They differentiate companies and products from their competitors, make access to new markets and industries easier, provide returns on investment worth multiples of the value of the net assets of businesses through an endless stream of profits, and—best of all—have no life cycle if they are looked after and managed well.

Powerful brands, when nurtured and managed properly, give companies longevity, and the potential for immortality. Coca-Cola is over 120 years old, and Tide washing powder is well over 60 years old, but both are still leaders in their chosen markets, despite intensive competition. Powerful brands such as these would not have lasted so long without careful management, and it is brand management that this book is about.

Good brand management helps make strong brands and great customer relationships, but it is surprising that many companies still pay less attention to managing their brands than to managing other aspects of their business. One reason for this might be that in many parts of the world, including Asia and the Middle East, brand management is still fairly new to marketers. Branding itself is an ever-evolving concept, and the techniques associated with managing brands are constantly changing.

This book provides a guide to the various aspects of brand management, and includes examples of practice—both good and not-so-good— from around the world, in the hope that the reader will learn from the experiences of others. The book will provide you with answers to many of the main issues facing brand builders and managers, such as:

- Should the brand vision replace the corporate vision?
- Should the brand determine business strategy, or vice versa?
- What returns on investment do brands bring?
- How can the long-term and short-term demands of the business be accommodated in brand management?
- Should brands be proactive or reactive, strategic or tactical?
- How is it possible to gain a strong and sustainable brand position and differentiation in crowded markets?
- How are decisions made to reposition brands, revitalize them, or let them die?
- How are brands revitalized?
- How far can a brand be stretched, and what are the pitfalls to avoid?
- What roles do emotion and attitude play in brand management and development?
- What impact do new technologies have on brand management and consumer relationships?
- How is brand management different in the physical and virtual worlds?
- What options are available for organizing and structuring the brand management process?
- What role should the CEO play in brand building and management?
- How can we use limited budgets to best advantage?
- What trends are taking place in brand communications?
- How can we create a brand culture so that everyone lives the brand?

- How can we measure the success of our brand(s)?
- What tools and checklists are needed in brand management?

Just to give you a flavor of what is to come in the book, here is a light-hearted, but nevertheless accurate view of just a few of the decisions and situations that face those whose job it is to manage a brand.

A DAY IN THE LIFE OF A BRAND

"I'm a quite famous brand—well I like to think so. I'm available in most parts of the world and have pretty good market share and profitability in most markets. I've been around for quite a while (don't ask me my age), and hope that what they say about brands having no life cycles is true.

I have a brand manager who is very senior in the company here, and he reports to a brand management committee that includes other brand managers in our product brand portfolio, plus corporate marketing, and various others who seem to be determined to influence my future in some way. People think strong brands have it easy, but that's not the case. Here's a typical day that I have to go through.

8.00 am: Agency news. The worldwide advertising agency has got the boot, and has to re-pitch against the competition next month. Well, they've not done too badly, but I never thought they understood my personality very well. I hope the top guys give the new agency a thorough briefing—I seem to remember the last one wasn't too great.

9.00 am: Panic in the camp. Europe had a quality problem in the French factory the day before yesterday that hit the press. There were actually accusations that I was poisoning people! Why do the press always report the bad news? Discussions here (most of which I can't repeat) centered around what we *might* say. They are still talking—the phones are going beserk, and we still haven't replied to the public at all. This is going to get worse if Corporate Communications doesn't snap out of it.

Haven't they heard of crisis management? And what about my image? People trust me; I stand for top quality! I feel a headache coming on, and I suspect other heads will roll.

10.00 am: Good news at last. I have been valued in dollar terms and have made it into the top 20 brands in the world. I've been telling top management that I'm a strategic asset, not just a brand, but did they believe me? I restrained myself from saying, "I told you so."

11.00 am: Request from Asia to change my personality to fit the local culture. My BM said, "No way." Good for him. He replied that we have to be consistent with my brand character, but we can emphasize the more appropriate attributes in campaigns, and can use market communications to localize me a bit more.

12.30 pm: Lunch and indigestion. I was asked to co-brand with a drinks brand that appeals to an entirely different audience. Thanks, but no thanks. Despite promises of more sales, which has the sales force leaping up and down, my values just don't fit. I mean, really! Who wants to be seen arm-in-arm with a down-market product? Image is everything.

2.00 pm: My BM was put on the spot by the chief marketing officer (prompted by an outside consultant, I suspect), who has asked him what business I am in. To make it clear, he said: "Not the company business, the business of your *brand*." A great question, and a predictable answer from the BM of: "Let me give that some serious thought." I wonder how long he's got to come up with the answer, and where this will lead us.

2.30 pm: The rack. This is pure torture. They are having discussions about how far they can "stretch" me—or "extend the brand," as my BM puts it. Much talk of which target audience, why, will it work, what about my current positioning, etc. I feel most uncomfortable—like a patient being discussed by a group of specialists, some of whom are of doubtful origin and qualifications.

4.00 pm: Message from London asking HQ to refresh me as I'm looking a bit old-fashioned. Thanks a lot, guys—and what about yourselves? Well, I don't mind some new packaging if my fans like it, but let's be sensible and not do anything that is out of character. Evolution is OK—revolution is out. My BM says he will take a look at this.

4.30pm: Gloom all around. The markets have dropped further as the recession bites. People at the top want my talk time cut— "Reduce all A&P expenditure on all brands" came the imperative from on high. Argument ensues, with one camp saying: "Cutting down is good if we focus a lot more," and another saying: "If the competitors are going to be quiet, now is the time to spend more, create more market share, and be remembered as the brand that is always there for people." I kind of like that last argument, but I fear the cost-cutters will win. Courageously, the director of marketing supports my BM in asking that brand expenditure should remain and costs be slashed elsewhere.

6.00 pm: I was just about to call it a day when I heard that the proposed customer relationship management program for me has been given the go-ahead. Great! Now I can begin to get to know all my customers individually, and look after those who are high value and have been very loyal to me. I hope the team doesn't get too caught up in technology, and that they concentrate on how better relationships can really benefit consumers.

6.30 pm: Let's go out on a high note. I have to attend an event I've sponsored tonight, which will feature me on YouTube. See you tomorrow.

What is Brand Management?

Of course, not all matters of importance hit brand managers every day, like the above suggests, but these are typical important strategic issues that brand managers have to deal with over time. They also have to involve themselves in many other things as part of their work, but put very simply, brand management is a process that tries to take control over everything a brand does and says, and the way in which it is perceived. There is a need, therefore, to influence the perceptions of various target audiences to ensure that people see what you want them to see with respect to your brand. This means identifying clearly what your brand stands for, its personality, and how to position it so that it appears different from and better than competing brands. It involves integrated communications, and constant tracking of the brand and its competitors.

The overall aim of this process, naturally, is to increase the value of the brand over time, however that may be measured. Profitability will be one measure, market share another, volume of sales perhaps another, and the emotional associations of the brand with consumers yet another. These will be discussed as we go along. But one of the hardest parts of brand management is to achieve a balance between the short-term numbers given by top management to satisfy various stakeholders, and the long-term growth of the brand. For example, price-cutting might buy short-term market share, but at what cost to the brand's long-term image? For listed companies there is the need to perform to stock market requirements on a quarterly basis in terms of sales and profitability while maintaining, or even increasing, investment in the brands that deliver the results. There can therefore be conflicts of interest between the needs of the business and those of the brands.

As you will now have begun to see, brand management is a difficult job. What makes it more difficult is the fact that many of the elements that influence a brand's success are often outside the control of those responsible for its management, such as competitor moves, economic factors, and consumer trends. Proactivity and reactivity live side by side in the daily work of brand managers, and this is the very reason that makes brand management so exciting—brands live in ever-changing landscapes, full of opportunities and challenges.

There are also several dimensions of a more tactical nature that have to be given meticulous attention on a daily basis. Brand managers have to juggle constantly with many activities to ensure that that can affect the image of the brand in both the short and long term. The situation becomes more complex and difficult for those whose job it is to manage a corporate brand under which there may be several sub-brands and/or product brands, as consistency and autonomy of brands can conflict. All of these factors will be discussed in the book. Also discussed will be the culture of the company, whether the right brand culture has been put into place, and how to do this.

But it all starts with brand strategy. Every aspect of brand management should be driven by the strategy of the brand, whether corporate or product. Unfortunately, many companies don't have a clear brand strategy and end up with confused images and consumer perceptions of the brand. They concentrate on trying to control the outside elements without having clear guidelines upon which they can do this.

So, although there are many issues that I will address, it is appropriate to start the book with a look at the changing roles of brand management, brand strategy, and how the interaction between brands and businesses has changed in recent times.

The Changing Roles of Brand Management

There have been several developments over the last 30 years or so with respect to how businesses have changed their view of the customer, and how consumers have reacted. These changes have led to the emergence of brand management as an important and complex role. A short summary follows of how business relationships with consumers have evolved, and how the role of brand management has changed as a result.

Business Evolution and the Consumer

The Dreadful Days of Product Focus

Some of you may remember the early days of mass production, when companies developed products that they thought the public needed and would want to buy, produced them, and then threw them into the market with the conviction that sales would result. The consumer often responded by buying the products because they were new and enhanced their quality of life. Consumer-durable and fast-moving goods—such as refrigerators, televisions, and cosmetics—had triggered the insatiable appetite of the consumer for branded products. However, there were as many failures as there were successes during this time. Marketers hadn't really understood what consumers wanted, because *they hadn't asked them.* This approach to marketing has now largely disappeared, although sometimes when I meet with companies I may still have my doubts. Some Japanese companies, for instance, still have a mindset that says, "Let's develop a great product and then go out there and sell it to the consumer, who doesn't know what he wants."

The Emergence of Market Orientation

Marketers soon learned that it was a wise move to understand a little more about what customers had in mind. Mass marketing was still predominant, but marketers began to realize that not all markets were homogenous. They discovered that within categories such as washing powders, different people expected different types of product performance; for instance, some people wanted a heavy-duty detergent, while others wanted a product suitable for use with delicate fabrics. So, during the 1970s and early 1980s we saw the introduction of market segmentation and the growth of market research as an industry. For the brand manager, this meant the growth of product categories and many opportunities for brand extensions.

The Age of the Big Brands

The age of the big brands dates from the late 1980s, when powerful brands, led by experienced and senior brand managers, began to dominate their chosen markets. There has been a tremendous demand for luxury brands during this time, with some brands, such as Nike, becoming global players. The whole world has now become more brand-conscious. Research studies claim that children become brand-conscious from as young as four years of age. Even in the less-developed and underdeveloped countries, the big brands have a presence and are the focus of consumer attention. However, the fragmentation of markets referred to above has led brand management into the complex world of mass customization, and there has been a strong movement away from pure, generic products manufactured to suit mass markets. Brand management has now turned its attention to customizing generic products to the needs of different market segments, and this has led to a proliferation of products available to consumers, with tremendous profits for those companies that understand these complex markets correctly.

The Realization of Brand Value

It is now widely acknowledged that brands, if created, developed, and managed well, can achieve spectacular financial results. If we look at the market capitalization of well-branded companies versus relatively unbranded companies in both the United States and the United Kingdom (the S&P and FTSE markets, respectively), and many other markets around the world, we see that around 70 percent or more of market capitalization isn't represented by the net asset value of the companies concerned. There is a huge gap between market capitalization and net tangible assets, and this unexplained value is represented by intangible assets, a significant part being the value of brands themselves. Other intangible items include patents, customer lists, licenses, know-how, and major contracts, but the value of the brand itself is increasingly becoming the biggest item. Brand names are often worth multiples of the value of the actual businesses. As a result, brands are often bought and sold for considerable amounts of money, which represent not so much the tangible assets belonging to the company, but the expectation of the brand's level of sales into the foreseeable future.

A strong corporate brand name brings with it additional financial strength which can be measured and used in many ways. They include:

- *Mergers and acquisitions*: Brand valuation plays a major part in these undertakings. Potential acquirers of branded goods companies, together with their investors and bankers, find comfort in the knowledge that the price being paid for a company can be substantiated by reference to the value of the specific intangible, as well as tangible, assets being acquired.
- *External investor relations*: For some major companies, building a portfolio of world-class brands is a central objective. Brand valuation can be used to provide hard numbers in what is often a soft argument.
- *Internal communications*: Brand valuation can help explain performance and be used as a means of motivating management. The use of internal royalty rates based on brand value can also make clear to a group of companies the value of the corporate assets they are being allowed to use.
- *Marketing budget allocation*: Brand valuation can assist in budgeting decisions, providing a more systematic basis for decision making.

- *Internal marketing management*: Strategic use of brand valuation techniques allows senior management to compare the success of different brand strategies and the relative performance of particular marketing teams.
- *Balance sheet reporting*: In certain parts of the world, acquired brands are now carried as intangible assets and amortized.
- *Licensing and franchising*: Accurate brand valuation allows a realistic set of charges to be created for the licensing and franchising of brand names.
- *Securitized borrowing*: Companies such as Disney and Levi Strauss have borrowed major sums against their brand names.
- *Litigation support*: Brand valuations have been used in legal cases to defend the brand value, such as in the case of illicit use of a brand name or receivership.
- *Fair trading investigations*: Brand valuation has been used to explain to non-marketing audiences the role of brands, and the importance their value has for the companies that spend so much to acquire and maintain them.
- *Tax planning*: More and more companies are actively planning the most effective domicile for their brand portfolios with branded royalty streams in mind.
- *New product and market development assessment*: New business strategies can be modeled using brand valuation techniques to make judgments on, for example, best brand, best market extension, and best consumer segment.

Brand Value versus Brand Equity

Brand value and brand equity are often confused. When we talk about *brand value*, we mean the actual financial worth of the brand. The term *brand equity*, on the other hand, is often used in referring to the descriptive aspects of a brand—whether symbols, imagery, or consumer associations—and to reflect its strength in terms of consumer perceptions. It represents the more subjective and intangible views of the brand as held by consumers, and is somewhat misleading, as the word *equity* has a financial origin.

There are several dimensions of brand equity, as opposed to brand value. Some of these key aspects of brand performance or strength are:

- *Price premium*—the additional price that consumers will pay for the brand compared to other offers.
- *Satisfaction/loyalty*—levels of satisfaction with the brand that help determine loyalty and prevent price sensitivity.
- *Perceived quality*—relative to other brands.
- *Leadership*—in terms of market leadership, connected to market share.
- *Perceived value*—a value-for-money concept linked not just to tangible items such as quality, but also to intangible factors.
- *Brand personality*—the attributes of the brand's character that differentiate it from others.
- *Mental associations*—the most important one being trust.
- *Brand awareness and recognition*—key measures of brand strength concerned with how well the brand is known in the market.
- *Market share*—volume and, in some cases, perceived positioning.
- *Market price*—premiums enjoyed by the brand.
- *Distribution coverage*—including percentage share.

There is no absolute score for these dimensions, but this mix of attitudinal, behavioral, and market measures of brand equity should be the focus for good brand management practice. What is interesting with this list is that it contains a mixture of what I would see as some of the drivers of both brand value and brand equity. Calculating brand value is, of course, a very specialized area, and the key drivers of brand performance are not all contained in the above list; however, there is a substantial overlap. For those readers interested in establishing the financial value of brands, some brand valuation methodology is outlined in detail in Chapter 9.

So, although there is a difference in terminology, it appears that there is a connection between brand value and brand equity, because many of the components of brand equity have been found to be the drivers of brand value. While we don't need to go into detail here about the methodologies involved in calculating brand equity and brand value, companies wishing to achieve spectacular rates of return on investment should be concentrating on building up the strength of their corporate brand name in their chosen markets. And the only way to do this is to concentrate on providing consumers with the best possible brand experience. This is where strong brand management is essential.

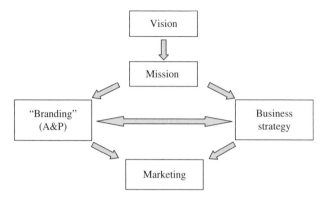

Figure 1.1 Brand link to corporate strategy in the 20th century

Brands Driving Business Strategy

Branding has been so successful that companies are now replacing corporate visions and missions with brand visions and missions. Figure 1.1 shows what I believe to be the old, 20th-century, business model. With this business strategy, companies developed corporate visions and missions that, while they looked impressive when mounted along the corridor walls, were largely ignored by anyone other than top management, who used them to drive the business forward. Branding merely provided support, usually in the form of advertising and promotion (A&P).

This business process has now changed. In the 21st century, the model being used by successful brands is to develop a vision and mission for the *brand*, and to let this drive the business strategy and all related activities, as shown in Figure 1.2. You will notice that business strategy leads directly into customer relationship strategy, and then the marketing activities. This concentration on relationships is explained in further detail below.

Greater Focus on the Brand–Consumer Relationship

Using this view of the consumer world—that is, focusing on how brands relate to consumers—the latest and most profitable strategies are those that strengthen the relationship of the brand with consumers, and then use this as the basis to drive the business forward and build brand value.

Figure 1.2   Brand link to corporate strategy in the 21st century

Consumer insight plays a vital role here. Examples of how branding has been affected by this new way of thinking are given in Chapter 2.

Brands—Fascists or Friends?

Occasionally, global brands are criticized by writers who argue that they are too powerful and not in the public interest. This argument is typified in the book *No Logo* by Naomi Klein, who suggests that branding is a somewhat anti-social activity. Taking an anti-globalization stance, Klein declares that brands have come to represent "a fascist state where we all salute the logo and have little opportunity for criticism because our newspapers, television stations, Internet servers, streets, and retail spaces are all controlled by multinational corporations." She goes on to say that the power and presence of advertising curtails choice, that brands are symbols of American power, and that they result in environmental damage, human rights abuses, and sweat-shop labor.

In its issue dated September 8–14, 2001, The Economist magazine led with an article arguing why brands are good for everyone. The article, entitled "Pro Logo®, The case for brands," argues that brands are becoming more vulnerable (and thus less powerful) and consumers more promiscuous (and thus more powerful). It further argues that brands enable consumers to express themselves and to enjoy the benefits of trust, self-expression, and new ways of enjoying their lives. Rather than promoting poor environmental and working conditions, brands are held captive by public opinion and are actively encouraged to help create a better world. The article makes the point, with some force, that, "far from being instruments of oppression, [brands] make firms accountable to consumers." To my mind, brand management is the conduit through which the psychological demands of consumers are delivered. If brand managers fail to satisfy these complex desires, then the brands they have responsibility for will cease to exist.

Brands That Care

It is my belief that the great brands of the future will be brands that care. They will be able to balance profitability with social responsibility. They will balance brand spirit with human spirit. They will be less unilateral in their actions and more altruistic. They will behave not as businesses, but as living entities that care for what happens in the world and for the people who live in it. Above all, they will focus on relationship building and bringing people together.

All of the above add up to a distinct shift in the role and status of brand management in the commercial world.

The Changing Role of Brand Management

Over the last couple of decades, there have been some discernible changes in the role of brand management and the activities of brand managers. Principally, they consist of the following changes in emphasis.

Change from an Industry to a Market Focus

One of the more obvious trends in business has been the move away from product-led to customer-led marketing. This change needs little explanation, but its impact on brand management in one sense has been to force managers to get closer to, and listen to, the customer. This has brought about many initiatives in market research, customer service, and quality management, and has also meant that brand managers are increasingly getting involved in new product development.

Change from Tactical Thinking to Strategic Thinking

Another change has been the move of corporate strategic thinking away from looking purely at how to grow the business within a specific industry, toward a mindset that looks at expansion across many industries and in multiple markets. This has led brand management to take a much more strategic view, and to become a more holistic activity, looking at how to project consistent identities and create consistent images in a variety of different situations. Brand managers still, however, have to fight the day-to-day tactical battles associated with shifting markets and competitive attacks.

Change from Local Market Focus and Analysis to Global Market Focus and Analysis

The economies of scale required to achieve world-class brands and the breakdown of market boundaries have meant that more companies are adopting a global focus, and that brand management now has to achieve the right balance between global identities and local adaptations. This trend has also led to the emergence of many more strategic alliances involving co-branding, in order to reduce the cost of global reach. In some cases, companies are now requiring brand managers to tailor brand offerings specifically to local markets. For instance, all advertising and promotion for Nestlé's Milo must show local sports, facilities, talent, and so on.

Change from Product Management to Category Management

Vicious competition in many markets, especially in fast-moving consumer goods, has given rise to the management of categories as opposed to individual products, with the brand manager looking at a multi-product portfolio and a complex set of positioning alternatives. This has been spurred in part by the fact that consumers think in terms of categories, such as shampoos, skincare products, and so on. There has also been a shift in power—again, especially in fast-moving consumer goods—from the brand manager to the retailer, and so brand managers must cope with the reality that their brands have to fit in with what the retailer would like to offer to the consumer. Brand managers must constantly assess what value their brands are providing to the retailer and the consumer in their chosen categories. Constant monitoring of competitive intruders is mandatory, as they may quickly erode the value a brand represents. Brand managers now have to view individual brands within a mix of several brands that satisfy both the consumer's desire for choice and the seller's need for profitability and a target audience.

As a result of this competition, the creation of new categories has now become important as some of the power brands crowd existing categories with their product line extensions. (Brand and line extensions are discussed in Chapter 4.) Smart companies are even changing the nature of categories. A great example is the energy drink Red Bull. Although not the first of its kind, the brand has dramatically changed and grown the market category for this kind of beverage, making it the number one energy drink for young, active people.

Change from Product Branding to Corporate Branding

There has been a marked change in direction, by companies around the world, away from concentrating on product branding and toward focusing on the corporate brand. Even the master of product branding, Procter & Gamble (P&G), is now putting much more strategic effort into leveraging its corporate brand name, as is its arch-rival Unilever. There are many reasons for this. It is an expensive exercise for a company to create and build brands independently, with little endorsement from the parent company. Product branding requires each brand to stand on its own and have its own investment, which in research and development (R&D) and A&P alone can be enormous. Without generous parental support, getting through the stages of brand awareness and acceptance in the marketplace can be highly resource-consuming. This is one reason why Unilever has reduced the number of its brands from 1,600 to approaching 400, its declared target.

While product branding continues to play an important part in brand strategy, there has been a marked trend toward corporate and umbrella branding, with even the traditional die-hard product brand organizations such as Procter & Gamble bringing the corporate brand more into the spotlight. P&G has made leveraging the corporate brand a global strategy, and throughout the world we are now seeing its initials used in support of product brands. One reason for this is that, for decades, P&G has been losing out on building the dollar value of the parent brand itself. In 2000, the market capitalization of the company declined, but if we look at the stock market indices around the world over the last 20 years, it is plain to see that heavily branded companies consistently outperform unbranded companies in terms of market capitalization. With corporate branding, most frequently seen where the company adds its name to the product brands it launches, there is the added value of trust and the shared synergies of the other investments needed. But one of the main determinants of this trend is the fact that brands can be valued in financial terms. Since adopting a strategy of leveraging the corporate brand, P&G has seen large increases in market capitalization.

Change from Branding Consumer Products to Business-to-Business (B2B) and Commodity Branding

There is a rising interest in branding many types of entity. The success of consumer product and corporate branding has led to an increase in B2B branding, and even the branding of commodities. Companies such as Accenture, IBM, BASF, and Hewlett-Packard (HP) have all carried out comprehensive branding initiatives. And in order to rise out of the commodity trap, basic commodity and trading entities have also begun to brand themselves, as the case study below illustrates.

CASE STUDY 1: THUNG KULA FARM

From Commodity Product to Premium Brand

Thung Kula Rong Hai—or "Thung Kula," for short—is an area approximately 500,000 acres in size covering five provinces in northeast Thailand. With no major rivers, the area is poorly irrigated and thus dry and barren. The Ministry of Agriculture and Co-operatives, in co-operation with other government agencies, has a mission to improve the quality of life of the 85,000 or so local farmers and their families. To this end, it has developed a five-year plan with the objective of increasing farming incomes through the promotion and export of the locally produced jasmine rice, which has a unique fragrance and taste, due to the high concentration of sodium and silica components in the soil. The project includes improving the area's irrigation systems and developing the infra-structure for farmers to produce high-quality rice to certified international standards such as GMP and ISO.

Farmers in the Thung Kula area have been encouraged to form themselves into six "co-operatives," each with its own mill, to produce jasmine rice for sale. The Ministry of Agriculture and Co-operatives has encouraged the development of one co-managed brand of jasmine rice that the farmers in the area can "own." This system enables the farmers to bypass the middlemen, who would normally buy their rice very cheaply, process it themselves in their own mills, and then sell the final product at a premium price under their own brands. Equipped with mod-ern rice mills, all certified to international standards of manu-facturing, the local farmers have instead been enabled to create and sell their own brand.

The farmers started the branding process by focusing on the fundamentals. Consumer research was conducted in order to understand consumers' consumption habits and attitudes toward brands. Over 100 key members of the six co-operatives were educated about the branding process and instructed in the key elements that contribute to building a great brand. Forty managers in total from all the co-operatives then got together to craft the brand strategy, starting with what they wanted their brand to stand for emotionally in the minds of consumers, and extending through to the brand personality and brand positioning.

The co-operatives stipulated which rice seeds farmers were to use, available from certified nurseries in the area, and agreed on uniform milling standards (for instance, a standard length and color of the grain). A team of quality control inspectors was assigned to check the quality of every batch of production from each of the six mills. These and other measures resulted in a great-quality, standard product that delivered on the brand promise. In return, the co-operatives agreed to buy only from their co-operative members.

The rice was marketed under the brand name "Thung Kula Farm." The name evoked the heritage of the land, while also referring to the farmers' decision to join forces to create their own brand. Confident of the high quality and unique fragrance of the product, the farmers then positioned their brand head-on with premium-grade jasmine rice from other parts of the country, and with other big brand names produced by the middlemen, with the goal of exporting the brand in the future.

Understanding how consumers develop an emotional connection with brands, Thung Kula Farm has escaped the commodity trap and become a symbol of love and care. The farmers' own love for their product, as evidenced by the care they take in its production, is seen by consumers as extending to their love for their families, as evidenced by their selection of this particular brand of high-quality rice.

In the selection of packaging for their product, the farmers decided to move away from the traditional rice bag to the modern-day 5kg package suitable for today's housewives. The gold and purple packaging design, colors not traditionally used for commodity rice products, reinforces the product's "elegant" brand personality. The "caring" personality of the brand was portrayed through special package design for ease of handling and to avoid the use of extra plastic bags (care for the earth). Every touchpoint of the Thung Kula Farm brand has been managed to ensure that customers have only great experiences with the brand.

This has been a good beginning for a brand co-managed by a group of farmers; and from a marketing point of view, the business has a unique competitive advantage. The bigger brands of packaged rice normally have to buy their raw produce from rice fields all over the country, which results in a product of variable quality. By contrast, the farmers of the Thung Kula area are able to bring to market a high-quality product, with a unique fragrance, whose consistency is second to none. And consistency in product quality is at the heart of success for any business and brand.

Despite these advantages, Thung Kula Farm faces quite a few challenges over the long term. One of the key challenges will be the farmers' ability to market and distribute their product. Traditionally, the middlemen to whom they sold their product performed these functions. In addition to sharpening their trading skills, they need to learn how to build business connections with modern trade channels.

Investment in the brand is another key challenge. In order to compete with big brand names in the market, Thung Kula Farm needs to invest in its brand, from creating awareness to enhancing loyalty and trust, particularly in the first few years following its launch. The responsible government agencies may need to provide some support in this area. Finally, the ultimate challenge will be the unity of the six co-operatives. They must work together as one team with one vision if they are to consistently manage customers' experiences with the brand. This will be a long-term journey, but the brand is likely to be successful, driven by loyalty and trust from happy customers.

Change from Product Responsibility to Customer Relationship Responsibility

Another interesting development has been the move away from the management of product(s) to the management of customer relationships, signified by the fact that some companies are now giving brand managers responsibility for specific groups of customers, across an entire product range. In this respect, *brand* management is becoming *customer* management. Customer relationship management, as a discipline, is now regarded as a necessary part of the brand manager's skill repertoire. This topic is dealt with in detail in Chapter 7.

Change from Managing the Physical Brand World to Both Physical and Virtual Brand Worlds

The onset of Web 2.0 (the new digital Internet revolution) has forced traditional brand companies to enhance their established Internet branding strategies. The virtual world raises additional problems for the brand manager, especially in terms of providing consumers with a consistent brand experience. The Internet world is complex and extremely volatile, but the rewards can be huge. The rules of branding in the virtual world are somewhat different from those that apply in the physical world; nevertheless, it is a "must have." It is true to say now that any brand manager or company with expectations of building a strong brand must create a viable and attractive online strategy.

In addition to the use of the Internet as a brand-building vector by traditional brands, we have recently witnessed the gradual demise of traditional advertising and other media, as the Internet has given consumers more power in the brand-building process. The growth of the digital world has hit traditional brand building with a tsunami-like force, and brands can now be built with enormous speed. Companies such as Google, YouTube, MySpace, and Facebook have all developed into hugely powerful and valuable brands in just a short time, fulfilling the wish by today's consumers to be involved with brands that look after their needs while helping them to express themselves and build their own personal brands. The success of these brands endorses the fact that it is *consumers* who build brands; companies merely give them the opportunities to do so.

The impact of the digital world will be discussed at length in Chapter 7.

Change from Managing Brand Performance to Managing Brand Value and Equity

Companies have now become much more concerned with the total value of their brands, not just with profitability. The valuation of brands is by no means an exact science, but the sale of brands for prices far in excess of their asset valuation has meant that brand building has become a business in its own right. For the brand manager, this means that several measures of performance have to be taken into account simultaneously, as brand equity measurement can include a whole host of variables, including brand awareness, brand loyalty, perceived quality, price, market share and cash-flow premiums, internationality, support, protection, and many others.

Brand valuation has come into play over the last two decades as a technique for justifying, and measuring returns on, brand investment. Brand management has now become the management of profitable strategic assets (brands) that can often be worth multiples of the net assets of the business, and so the performance of brand managers is now more closely evaluated on this basis.

Change from Financial Accountability to Social Responsibility

While those people responsible are very much judged on the financial performance of the brands under their charge, they also have to balance this with a commitment to social responsibility. Many companies are now tying their brands to the needs of communities, and helping to solve societal problems. Examples are HP, with its community programs, and General Electric (GE), with its environmental initiatives. Brand management isn't just about creating profit at all costs, as Naomi Klein would have us believe; it is about encouraging people to do better, and helping them to enjoy a better quality of life.

Neither is it about capitalizing on events that are problematic to other people. The terrible events of September 11, 2001 gave some companies the opportunity to make money out of the tragedy and human suffering. But other companies acted in a more socially responsible manner. As Professor Stephen A. Greyser said, "Some of the immediate donations of goods and services presumably were driven by a clear philanthropic motivation." Hallmark Cards Inc., which saw sales of greetings cards rise rapidly, was meticulous in its brand management by subjecting all cards to a special test so as not to offend. In fact, the company's first action was to search for cards among current offerings that might be offensive. Avoiding offense was more important than boosting card sales, and Hallmark withdrew nine cards from distribution. Its second action was to create cards that fitted the changing mood of the nation. Hallmark delivered new, patriotic cards in six weeks as opposed to the 12–15 months normally required for new product development. Dan Sifter, general manager of Hallmark's seasonal card unit, said: "It's a question of finding the right balance between what consumers want to say to each other—finding warmth—and striking the right patriotic note without being jingoistic."

American Greetings took a similar stance. Within 24 hours of the attacks on New York and Washington, it posted four patriotic electronic greetings on its website (*www.americangreetings.com*), which offers e-cards free of charge. Visitors to the sites sent 350,000 of these greetings during the first week after the attacks.

Brand management is all about building relationships with consumers, not about taking advantage of those relationships. Companies such as Enron that behave in an unsatisfactory way are likely to proceed to bankruptcy or to face legal action, or both. An abundance of such cases revealing poor accountability, transparency, and corporate governance in the last few years has led to an increase in corporate social responsibility (CSR) activity; in fact, CSR is now an important part of brand management. A good CSR strategy has become a necessity for brands wishing to build and maintain trust and loyalty.

All in all, the above changes mean that brand management is a much more dynamic and complex function than it has ever been. The challenge now for many companies is to develop the right blend of skills and experience in their managers, whose focus must be clearly on the consumer, the source of brand equity and value.

So, Who Owns and Builds Brands?

The movement toward a focus on the relationship between the brand and consumers has forced managers to answer the question of who actually owns and builds brands. Until recently, many companies believed that it is *they* who build brands. The correct answer to this question, now acknowledged by leading brand companies, is that it is the *consumer* who owns and builds brands. The enlightened companies have remembered that brands exist only in the minds of consumers, and without the psychological commitment from consumers, they are merely companies, products, and services, and will remain so.

This undisputed fact is the rationale for replacing corporate visions with brand visions, and for allowing the brand to dictate business strategy. The fact that it is consumers who own and build brands doesn't mean that brand management has nothing to do with the brand-building process. On the contrary, brand management is the catalyst that helps consumers to recognize and build relationships with brands. Brands are relationships, and brand managers have to nurture the relationships between brands and consumers. This means, of course, that brand managers have to understand the consumer even better than before, and gain real insight into how consumers' minds work. This only comes from outside-in thinking, as opposed to inside-out thinking—a topic that is explored in the next chapter.

Building a Brand Strategy

Brand Management Begins With Brand Strategy

Incoming chief operating officer of Nissan, Carlos Ghosn, said: "One of the biggest surprises is that Nissan didn't care about its brand. There is nobody really responsible for the strategy of the brand" (quoted in *Business Week*, October 1999). To my mind, this is one of the most common mistakes made by companies that want to have a strong brand, but that don't make the grade: *they don't have a brand strategy*. Without a brand strategy, brand management becomes very difficult, if not impossible. Strategy gives focus and direction to brand management, and provides the platform that enables brand managers to gain consistency in all their brand-related activities.

But we all know that strategy starts with the business. And for too long, companies have refined the art of inside-out thinking—researching and developing products they think the market will want. The truth is that the most brilliant strategies come from deep consumer insight—really getting inside the minds of the consumers that you hope will build your brand (that is, outside-in thinking). It is this continual search for outside-in thinking that can lead to unusual but real insights into how people perceive things, and what "hot buttons" will switch them on to your brand.

If we use consumer insight, the business of the brand might be different from the business of the business; so, before we consider the key elements of brands, let's think about the *business of brands*. It's quite easy—all you have to do is ask yourself one important question: "What business is my brand in?" Consider the following examples.

What Business is Your Brand In?

Charles Revson, of Revlon Cosmetics, when asked what business Revlon was in, famously replied: "We are not in the business of selling cosmetics; we are in the business of selling hope." He clearly saw that to think of his business as just cosmetics would lead to non-differentiation. By saying this, he was expressing the business of the brand. Cosmetics manufacturing/selling is clearly what the business *does*, but the brand also *gives hope* to those who want to be more attractive and beautiful, perhaps like the Revlon Girl of the Year. This real consumer insight led to a great positioning and, ultimately, global success.

Whiskey is another such "commodity," but when Johnny Walker Black Label was researched by watching consumers drink it, the brand changed its business strategy. Videos of people drinking with others on different occasions led to a paradigm shift in thinking. After an 18-month boardroom "discussion," it was decided that the company was in the business not of manufacturing and selling high-quality liquor, but of marketing fashion accessories. The consumer insight was seeing people "wear" their drinks as they would a watch, bracelet, or other fashion accessory. Nike isn't in the business of marketing sports shoes and accessories; the brand says it wants to help athletes and ordinary people get the best out of themselves. Nike stands for winning, an attribute strongly supported by endeavor and empowerment.

I was once engaged in discussions with a CEO who had also had a paradigm shift in thinking. His company makes products that "make things shine," such as car polish, shoe-care products, and so on. He has now decided that his brand is in the "feelings" business, because the end-result of using his brands is that consumers feel good about themselves and their image. This paradigm shift in thinking has impacted greatly on the company and is taking it into previously unsought areas.

Perhaps one of the best examples of looking at the brand as a business is that of Hallmark Inc., detailed in the following case study.

CASE STUDY 2: HALLMARK INC.

The Business of the Hallmark Brand—A Paradigm Shift in Thinking

If you were to ask people what business they think Hallmark is in, most of them would likely say that the company is in the business of manufacturing and selling greetings cards—and indeed, Hallmark is famous for that type of product. But this isn't what the Hallmark brand business is all about. The Hallmark brand is focused clearly on the business of enriching people's lives. In a powerful brand vision statement, it says it wants "to be the very best at helping people express themselves, celebrate, strengthen relationships, and enrich their lives." Taking this view of its business has led Hallmark Inc. into a tremendous array of business opportunities that have proved to be highly successful and profitable.

The company, which has existed for nearly a century, has around 5,000 stores that generated consolidated revenues of US$4.4 billion in 2007. Hallmark Entertainment is now the leading producer/distributor of mini-series, TV movies, and home videos, and the *Hallmark Hall of Fame* has won more Emmy awards than any other series. The company is also involved in cable TV, real estate, and the retailing of other relationship-building products such as Crayola Crayons, Silly Putty, party plates, gifts, wrappings, and more.

The whole of the Hallmark brand and business is built around emotion, and it genuinely cares for its customers. The Hallmark beliefs and values statement starts by saying, "Our products and services must enrich people's lives." Such statements to employees and the public at large are not just the foundation for good brands; they are a powerful driver of human emotion and behavior. Hallmark manages to build emotion into every touchpoint with the consumer, and it generates brand loyalty in return. Another example can be found in Hallmark's strong corporate social responsibility program, which emphasizes its commitment to building relationships and enriching people's lives. The program involves, among other initiatives, employee volunteerism to assist community projects, philanthropic contributions to various programs that will improve the lives of the underprivileged, and helping people to connect with their loved ones who are far away.

By expressing its business in a brand-related way based on enriching lives, Hallmark has found the key to becoming one of the world's top privately owned brands.

REFERENCE

http://corporate.hallmark.com/Company/Hallmarks-Beliefs-And-Values

The Role of Consumer Insight

Hallmark and the other examples referred to above indicate that brands are now driving business strategy, but *only* when they reach deeply into the psychological world of consumer insight. The really "hot buttons" that consumer insights unveil are emotional, not rational, and lead to excellent brand performance.

It is the brand manager's responsibility to work with brand strategy consultancies and other agencies to discover these insights, which are sometimes far from obvious. However, as it is consumers that create brand power, brand managers must discover the underlying motives that exist in their minds that will trigger favorable attitudes and compulsive desires toward their brands.

Living With the Consumer

In the never-ending search for consumer insights that may give a paradigm shift in thinking for brands and businesses, some companies are now hiring research crews to live for a few days with "prototype" consumers, in order to learn how they think and behave in their everyday lives. (Bedroom and bathroom scenes are usually, but not always, excluded!) Traditional research—both quantitative and qualitative—has the drawback of relying on what consumers *say*, which is sometimes different from what they actually *do* in real life. What brand management has to do is find out how to press the "hot buttons" that "turn on" consumers, and this means gaining a full understanding of what motivates them in real-life situations.

Companies trying to create consumer brands are waking up to the fact that the place to start understanding consumer behavior is in the home—where people's real lives are lived in the context of wide-ranging emotions, the sometimes-conflicting demands of different relationships, and relaxed, rather than ideal, personal standards—as opposed to the office or a research room. For example, when Procter & Gamble filmed housewives going about their daily routines, the company noticed that mothers were usually multitasking. One mother was seen feeding her baby while preparing a meal and snatching glances at the television. In natural scenarios such as this, companies can see what programs and advertisements attract homemakers, and what products they use or could use. A bank in the United States has undertaken similar research to discover the process by which families at various stages of their life cycle discuss and make major financial decisions. Unilever has sent staff out into rural villages in underdeveloped areas to live with the villagers and learn more about their way of life, in order to help with brand relationships and product development (see Case Study 3).

CASE STUDY 3: UNILEVER MALAYSIA

Romancing the Consumer

One of Unilever's "Path to Growth" strategic agendas is "reconnecting with the consumer," with the aim of:

- focusing everyone in the company on the consumer;
- turning knowledge gained about the consumer into creative insight; and
- anticipating and responding to consumer change.

According to Unilever, the only way to achieve this is by:

- deepening its knowledge of consumers' habits and attitudes;
- having a culture of "getting close" to the consumer; and
- having the skills to tap insights into the consumer and to turn them into business opportunities.

Unilever has this strategic thrust as a global initiative, but this case shows how it has been done in this operating company in Malaysia.

Preparations for its "Romancing the Consumer" program involved the following:

- Managers of Unilever Malaysia visited 50 homes and held face-to-face interviews bi-monthly to gain consumer insights.
- Twenty staff brought 120 consumers to the factory quarterly for face-to-face understanding dialogue.
- All staff were given cross-category training so that not only could inter-brand communications be enhanced, but also staff could answer questions about any brands asked of them by consumers.
- A specific project—Project Rambo—was devised. The whole company was closed for one day, and every employee—old and young, from the tea lady to the chairman—went out to do merchandising of products in shops to ensure that the visibility of Unilever products at retail customers' premises was first class, and to get retail feedback.

Project Rambo saw high energy and a high commitment by Unilever Malaysia's entire workforce to work with trade partners to enhance product displays to better attract shoppers' attention. The experience even inspired Unilever's employees to tidy up merchandising in stores where they usually shop!

The Rural Marketing Program was another initiative aligned with reconnecting with the consumer, but primarily with those in the rural market. The idea of this program when it was conceived was to raise the awareness of Unilever products in the rural areas of the country by having rural-relevant activities, and at the same time putting products on sale. The program was also aimed at providing Unilever Malaysia with the opportunity to engage rural consumers with Unilever brands and people. The first event—held in October 2000—was a tremendous success, and similar events followed over subsequent years in different parts of the country.

Additional activities included marketing staff staying in villagers' homes for two days to gain a detailed insight into the usage and buying patterns of household, personal care, and food products. All such events were planned well in advance and started with a meeting with the head of the village and his committee. The team was briefed on the objectives of the event and the type of activities to be organized. These often included traditional games to enable participation by all age groups. The local villagers took charge of these activities, and Unilever staff organized prizes and appearances by special guests. Each of the events attracted between 3,000 and 6,500 people.

The company's "Romancing the Consumer" program proved successful in developing a culture of gaining consumer insights and using them to drive its business.

Moen Inc., a maker of plumbing equipment, actually videotaped American women in the shower (naturally, with their permission), and discovered that they tended to hold on to the shower unit heating control with one hand while shaving their legs with the other! This safety risk, which hadn't previously been apparent, led Moen to redesign its shower unit to prevent accidental burns.

Research of this kind underlines that brand managers must do their homework country by country, as cultural nuances determine consumer behavior. For instance, in the United States and in Mediterranean countries the kitchen is the central part of a family's home life, where they congregate and talk about their day; whereas in China, say, the kitchen is usually a small area designated just for cooking, and the family gather in the hall or living room to spend time together.

Intel employs anthropologists and ethnographers—people who study human behavior and culture—to gain insights into what consumers really want, and why they like to buy. The insights gained from studying "the minutiae of daily life" help in making technology much more friendly and fun for consumers. Again, this involves making visits to people's homes, and accompanying them on shopping trips and other excursions away from the home. Intel, like many other companies, has come to see that creating products, and then trying to persuade consumers to buy them, isn't enough; if companies really want to understand what makes consumers tick, they must look closely at their behaviors. For instance, the design of products such as the Sound Morpher and the QX3 Computer Microscope for children took into account the behavior of eight- to 14-year-olds, who tend to be a bit rough with the things they use and are very hands-on. The QX3, for instance, although functioning when connected to a personal computer, was designed to be detachable from its stand so that children can share the experience with their friends.

In Asia, where Intel found that people are less individualistic and tend to share a lot more than do people in the West, the company is developing devices that will facilitate the sharing of technology. As Intel moves into healthcare and other markets with its products, it is employing more scientists, doctors, and healthcare workers in order to understand more about real customer needs.

Consumer insight is the gateway to understanding people's rational and emotional behaviors, and there is no doubt that brand strategies that are built on emotion and the realism of everyday life have a better chance of success than those that are not so based.

In Chapter 6 you will read about how Procter & Gamble uses its consumer insights and understanding in different markets to localize its communications for global brands such as Pampers and Always, and successfully appeals to the cultural norms that drive people's innermost emotions and aspirations. Meanwhile, in the following section, you will see how powerful the world of emotion can be in building and managing strong brands.

Building a Brand Strategy

The Rational and Emotional Sides of Brand Strategy

We must never forget that brand promises are often made in the world of commercial reality—in terms of exceptional quality, service, and, nowadays, innovation. However, this isn't where the source of success for brands lies. These elements are merely the price a company has to pay to get into the branding game, and the branding game is a mind game. As parity becomes the norm, and brands match each other feature by feature and attribute by attribute, it is becoming harder to create a brand strategy through rational means. So, while consumers screen the rational elements of quality and other compelling product attributes as part of the buying process, the real decision to buy is taken at an emotional level.

A brief excursion into modern science tells us why this is so. The notion that the rational, conscious part of the brain dominates the non-rational parts has now been disproved. MRI scanning has revealed that people's decision making is mostly quick and emotional, is often done subconsciously, and is much more intuitive than was previously thought. It is now an undisputed fact that emotion drives reason, and not the other way around. Our feelings happen with great rapidity and precede conscious thought. The emotional part of the brain is considerably larger than the rational part and outpaces it in terms of intensity, sending 10 times as many signals to the rational brain as opposed to the reverse. What's more, recall and memory have been proven to be a result of emotional experiences.

The following questions and statements provide a simple example of how this takes place. The *rational* thoughts tend to be analytical, but it is the emotional statements that drive the purchase decision.

Rational	Emotional
Do I need it?	I want it!
What does it do?	It looks cool!
What does it cost?	I'm going to get it!
How does it compare to . . .?	I only want this one!

Neuro-science makes it clear that brand managers need to employ emotional brand strategies, as the endgame for any brand strategy is trust and loyalty, which are emotions and not rational thoughts.

Given the increasing scientific evidence of the power of emotion in people's decisions and actions, we can categorically state that without emotional brand strategies it is impossible to build great brands! If we look at the powerful brands around the world, we see that they elicit thoughts like those listed above in the right column. Great brands build tremendous emotional capital with their strategies.

Characteristics of Power Brands—Emotional Capital

Brand managers are increasingly turning to the emotional side of strategy in order to win and keep customers. Power brands develop emotional capital, because they:

- Are very personal—people choose brands for very personal reasons, whether they be self-expression, a sense of belonging, or other reasons.
- Evoke emotion—brands sometimes unleash unstoppable emotion, arousing passion and unquestionable excitement.
- Live and evolve—they are like people in that they live, grow, evolve, and mature. But luckily, if they are well managed, they have no life cycle and can live forever.
- Communicate—strong brands listen, receive feedback, change their behavior as they learn, and speak differently to different people, depending on the situation, just as people do. They believe in dialogue, not monologue.
- Develop immense trust—people trust the brands they choose, and often resist all substitutes.
- Engender loyalty and friendship—trust paves the way for long-lasting relationships, and brands can be friends for life.
- Give great experiences—like great people, great brands are nice to be with, good to have around, and are consistent in what they give to their friends.

Given these facts about the emotional capital that brands develop, we need to understand that brands are relationships. The head of Starbucks,

Howard Schultz, once said in a note to his employees: "I want to emphasize that the key to our success lies in our values, our culture and the relationships we have with our partners and customers. When we're at our best, we create emotional experiences for people that really enhance their lives." If this is true for all top brands—and I have no doubt about that—what is the process of establishing an emotional relationship with consumers? How do the top brands build such relationships?

The Emotional Brand Relationship Process

In order to build an emotional brand strategy there are certain steps brand managers have to take, like the steps of a ladder, as shown in Figure 2.1. Let's think of it as a relationship between two people, as opposed to a brand and consumers. One person sees another across a room at a particular function, and wants to meet them. Following this awareness, an opportunity to meet may arise, and although the conversation is short, it leads to the decision as to whether or not the interest is sufficient to carry the relationship further. Further meetings reinforce this mutual respect, and the two people become friends. If the friendship

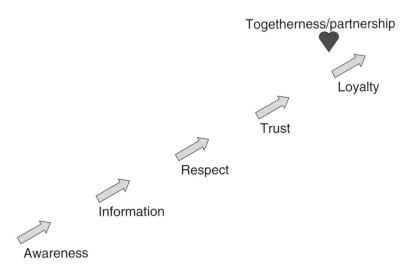

Figure 2.1 The emotional brand relationship process

blossoms, it generates trust and loyalty between them, and it is highly likely that they will become friends for life or have a lasting relationship.

The brand–consumer relationship grows in a very similar way. Awareness comes first, followed by involvement and purchase—a few meetings—which can lead to the friendship and trust levels, which in turn lead to brand loyalty and lifetime customer relationships. The power brands get to and past the friendship and trust levels. Brands such as Starbucks understand that doing so isn't merely an option. If it *didn't* become friends with its customers, and develop that sense of comfort, familiarity, and dependability, then it would never have reached power brand status. Companies that don't get to the critical friendship level often get stuck at the awareness stage.

Big spending on awareness follows many brand launches, but the subsequent management of the brand may not take it up the ladder. Lots of awareness may build a level of "infatuation," but as we all know, true friendship and love go much further than the initial excitement. Building friendship takes a long time and has to be earned through consistency and dependability; without these qualities, there is no trust. Great brands develop such emotional relationships, but some brands sometimes forget what it takes, and consequently fail. For example, at one stage in its history, Lastminute.com received 84 percent brand awareness ratings but only a 17 percent trust rating. Some brand managers spend millions on awareness—which is an essential step to achieve—but then neglect the emotional side of the brand–consumer relationship, which is necessary for real long-term success. The emotional part of any brand strategy is derived from what the brand stands for, as explained earlier in this chapter, and the personality of the brand that is used to build attraction, trust, and loyalty.

Brand Personality, Attitude, and Trust

Building Brand Charisma

Probably one of the most successful ways to build an emotional brand strategy is to create a personality for your brand. The people in the real world who stand out from the crowd always seem to have some kind of "charisma." They have a personality and attitude that others respect and are sometimes in awe of. They have a presence that almost commands people to follow without asking, and others always want to be around them. They aren't necessarily extroverted or introverted, but people feel good when they are around. Great brands are like great people in this respect, and the role of the brand manager is to manage the brand–consumer relationship by building a powerful and irresistible brand personality.

Like human relationships, whether they turn out right or wrong isn't usually a function of logic and rationality; rather, it is a result of emotional hits and misses. Given this reality, it seems strange that in many cases brand management continues to focus on the non-emotional side of the relationship, promoting features, attributes, price discounts, and so on, which have little impact on the growth of the brand–customer relationship. Such activities might bring in short-term sales increases, but they are open to imitation and won't attract and retain customers by developing an emotional relationship with them. In fact, they may well discourage this and "cheapen" the brand in the eyes of consumers.

Relationships thrive on emotions; they survive or perish, depending on the emotional fit between people. Brands have therefore to reflect personalities that people like, and this means having an emotional basis or edge to them. Indeed, the best brands have personalities carefully crafted to suit them and their target audiences. People have a universal longing to be liked, given attention, and to be loved. But brand management often ignores this. Research clearly shows that companies lose 68 percent of their customers because they feel neglected or aren't given attention. (For details of this research and similar findings, see the book *Romancing the Customer*, by myself and Martin Trott, John Wiley & Sons, 2001.) This makes the emotional dimension of the brand–consumer relationship very important, and it is the personality and attitude of the brand that attracts and keeps people loyal to it. Case Study 4 shows how an established brand took itself to a higher level in the light of more competition, by creating an appropriate personality based on transforming rational attributes into emotional ones.

CASE STUDY 4: LAND ROVER

Turning Rational Attributes into an Emotional Brand Personality

The attraction of a strong personality is irresistible, and clever brand managers build personality into their companies, products, services, countries, and places. Land Rover agrees that the brand (or marque) gives products an identity, as well as authenticity and authority. But it also agrees that the rational traits and attributes that products have aren't powerful enough discriminators in the consumer's decision to buy.

Land Rover took the rational attributes determined by research and turned them into emotional personality characteristics, emphasizing that brands have to appeal to the heart as well as the head.

The rational attributes held by Land Rover were:

- 4 × 4 engineering and capability;
- heritage;
- robust; and
- individualistic.

Land Rover decided that these attributes weren't enough, and that more muscular emotional values had to be articulated and introduced into everything Land Rover did. This was especially important as competitors could copy the rational attributes through engineering, quality, reliability, specifications, performance, and styling. So, the following emotional values were created, based on the rational attributes.

- *Individualism*—as opposed to the quirkiness of "individualistic."
- *Authenticity*—as opposed to "heritage" with its museum-like, musty connotation.
- *Guts and determination*—as opposed to "robust."
- *Supremacy and leadership*—as opposed to "4 × 4 engineering and capability."

Land Rover then added the characteristics that its target audience could relate to, namely:

- the excitement of adventure; and
- the love of freedom.

These characteristics were felt to be much more powerful and expressive of the Land Rover marque, and differentiated Land Rover's products from the rest of the crowd.

Another of the world's most famous brands, on the other hand (still extremely valuable, despite legal problems), has built its identity on just two personality characteristics, though they, too, are emotionally based. The brand is Marlboro, and the characteristics are *strength* and *independence*. The projection of these characteristics has made the brand world-class, with the Marlboro cowboy (strong and independent), Marlboro country (wide open plains and imposing mountains), packaging (strong red and white colors), and appropriate sponsorships (such as with Ferrari for Formula 1 in 2007, and Ducati for MotoGP in 2009) all symbolizing these two personality traits.

Nike is a similar brand that has risen to fame through its "Just Do It" attitude, symbolizing the urge to get the best out of oneself, to push beyond one's limits, to win—a truly heroic brand. Brands such as these manage not just to develop a personality that the target audience likes; they also have an "attitude" toward life that attracts people, as can be seen in Case Study 5.

CASE STUDY 5: ABSOLUT VODKA

A Brand Built on a Powerful Personality

BACKGROUND

Absolut is a brand that dates back more than a century. When the product was introduced to the US market in 1979, it initially received a cold reception. In a crowded market with established competitors, no one expected Absolut to succeed in dominating the category. Nevertheless, it subsequently did and became a world-renowned brand.

Prior to 2007, the growing popularity of higher-priced vodka brands such as Grey Goose, Belvedere, Chopin, and others saw Absolut Vodka decline to midshelf status, which produced a substantial drop in sales. However, a new marketing campaign, "In an Absolut World," launched in May 2007, has seen a revival in popularity of the brand.

In 2008, the Swedish government, which owned the brand, sold it to Pernod Ricard for US$8.3 billion, far in excess of the value its investors had predicted.

ABSOLUT'S BRAND PERSONALITY

Absolut's success can be attributed to the skillful management of the brand. It is a brand that invokes a strong emotional connection with its target customers through its distinctive and appealing personality, made up mainly of wit and humor. It is Absolut's wit, rather than its taste, that accounts for the brand's success. Former company president Goran Lundqvist described it thus: "Absolut is a personality. We like certain people, but some people are just more fun and interesting."

Absolut's brand personality projects wit, intellect, optimism, and boldness. Through its current "In an Absolut World" campaign, it has created and projected vision statements that appeal to society in general. Some examples of advertisements from the campaign include the following:

- "In an Absolut World, currency should be replaced with hugs of kindness."
- "In An Absolut World, all of our conflicts would be resolved in peaceful and fun exchanges."
- "In an Absolut World, everything is wheelchair accessible."
- "In An Absolut World, the moon wouldn't just light up the night."

In addition to conveying the brand's personality through the traditional print and broadcast media, Absolut uses the Web and new media such as Facebook. Its website invites visitors to the site to share their visions of how things might be "in an Absolut World" and to comment on others' visions. This initiative provides a platform for stimulating the imaginations of its online community. "Our consumers are intelligent, and we hope they have a gut reaction that sparks conversations and challenges them to think about their vision of an Absolut World," says Tim Murphy, senior brand director. Similarly, Absolut has used Facebook to extend its advertisements that communicate its personality traits.

Through all these cleverly executed communications, and with its famous bottle packaging, Absolut has developed a highly differentiated personality, and one with a consistent attitude to life that people like.

REFERENCES

www.absolutad.com/absolut_about/history/story/
www.intelligentnaivety.com/2009/06/05/visions-in-an-absolut-
    world/
www.marketwatch.com/story/pernod-ricard-execs-tout-
    defend-absolut-acquisition
www.nytimes.com/2008/04/01/business/worldbusiness/01iht-
    vodka.4.11588217.html

Brand Attitude

Brand attitude is a complexity of things, but for the consumer it is based largely on what the brand stands for, and in particular, how the brand personality is communicated. Brand attitude is a product of brand communications—how the brand talks to the consumer. It is contained in the visuals and the copy of advertisements, for example. If a brand has a personality constructed around the words "warm," "friendly," and "approachable" and communicates this well, it will be perceived as having a "caring" attitude. The words "knowledgeable," "trustworthy," and "professional," when brought to life through communications, suggest a more businesslike attitude.

The key to the way in which the brand should be communicated is often found in matching the attitude and personality of the brand to that of the consumer, so the importance of understanding what makes a target audience tick shouldn't be underestimated. If that understanding isn't there, then the attitude of the brand may turn off the emotional relationship process. It may either "invite" or "alienate" consumers. So, for example, if a brand's character exudes confidence, it may make some consumers feel inferior and others smart. An ambitious or sophisticated brand attitude can invite those with ambition, but turn off those who think they will never be able to climb to those heights. A fun brand might make some people feel shy and others really good about themselves. A reliable brand could make someone feel either secure or bored, and a tough brand might attract the active but turn off gentle people, and so on. Attitude is a two-way street, and brand managers have to manage these inner thoughts and self-directed feelings of consumers.

Flexing the Brand Values

Some brands cleverly mix the rational and emotional characteristics of their brand's personality, so that they can flex the brand character to suit the audience they are addressing. By having several brand personality characteristics, they can emphasize different aspects of their character to different target audiences. So where, for example, a telecommunications company brand has a set of characteristics such as

- friendly,
- innovative,
- trustworthy,
- understanding, and
- contemporary,

it can put across all these characteristics to each of the two main target audiences, but emphasize "friendly," "contemporary," and "trustworthy" a little more than the others for the residential consumer, and emphasize "innovative" and "understanding" more to the business community. In brand communications, the attitude of the brand personality would thus appear more emotional to the residential audience—because they are more attracted by an emotional attitude, and more rational to the business audience—because this is their attitude toward decision making. The brand–consumer relationship will still be based on emotional strategy, but the degree of emotion exhibited is controlled according to the needs of the consumer group with whom the brand is trying to build a relationship, and is represented by the attitude of the brand when communicated. (Further illustrations and examples of how to build brand personality can be found in my book *Branding in Asia,* John Wiley & Sons, 2001.)

So, brands often mirror consumers' thoughts, feelings, attitudes, behaviors, lifestyles, and personality. Several successful brands have achieved global status because of brand management's ability to relate to and keep in touch with consumer emotions, mirroring their minds. Brand managers must be specialists in "coaching"; bringing out the best of the relationship between all the players—the brand and consumers. And there is no better way to do this than by managing attitudes, feelings, and emotions. Brand management is in the reflections business—anticipating what consumers want to see reflected back at them through the brand mirror.

Brand Trust

An essential part of any brand management strategy must be the establishment of trust in the brand. This is really the key to reaching the long-term emotional relationship with consumers that makes brands famous. Many writers say that trust is derived from the quality of the brand experience that the branded product or service provides. Trust in the corporate brand also derives from this. While it is true that meticulous attention must be paid to quality, reliability, and, these days, innovation, there is much more to it than that. Trust is a very emotional issue, and not particularly a rational one. If consumers own and build brands, as I have stated, then there is more that can be done to catalyze this process, in addition to the development of personality and attitude as described above.

Adding Romance and Sensuality

If we look at some of the brands that really have captured the emotions and spirit of people, we see that they also build in a degree of romance and sensuality. Some do this on the service side, but others manage to do it on the design side. Apple's iPod and iMac are good examples of the creation of an emotional connection with consumers via design. People want to hold them, touch them, and choose from among the attractive colors such as hot pink, purple, blue, orange, or green. (Steve Jobs once said that forthcoming products from Apple "will be so gorgeous you will want to lick them.") Sensuality enhances the "wanting to own"' process, by touching the mind of the consumer in a highly emotional way.

Montblanc was the first company to achieve this emotional sensuality with its writing instruments. Such design features built into brands trigger passionate responses in the subconscious mind. And this is where emotions outweigh rational thoughts, making brand decisions easier. Most people don't know what an iMac can do, yet many still want one, and they may not realize that other brands have the same attributes of a good writing instrument as a Montblanc pen. The fact that a BMW bike can outperform a Harley-Davidson with ease might never enter the mind of a Harley buyer. Emotions trigger the mind 3,000 times faster than rational thoughts, so brand managers must give thought to owning the dimensions of passion, sensuality, "coolness," nostalgia, mystery, and spirit.

While good design is a must-have for consumer brands, it cannot be sporadic. Indeed, design has now become a part of the innovation process, and innovation now takes place at an increased pace. Case Study 6 demonstrates how Apple weaves a wonderfully complex web of innovation, personality, attitude, emotion, and design in order to gain total attraction, trust, and loyalty from its customers. It also shows how fragile that trust can be.

CASE STUDY 6: APPLE

Creating Appeal, Desire, and Trust

Consider this: masses marching mindlessly in unison toward yet another video broadcast, proclaiming new ideologies and self-congratulatory messages—an obviously dramatic visual presentation of George Orwell's classic novel *1984*, which envisions totalitarian states using technological advances to keep their party members and masses under careful observation and control. Against this backdrop of total dominance and numbing control, a single woman rushes forward and swings a sledgehammer, literally and symbolically destroying the broadcast and its ideological messages. The copy—"On Jan 24, Apple Computer will introduce Macintosh, and you will see why 1984 won't be like '1984'"—appears before fading off to Apple's distinctive logo.

This groundbreaking advertisement, shown only once during Super Bowl XVIII in 1984, along with the subsequent "Think Different" campaign, really amplified to the world Apple's emotional attitude and message: that Apple thinks differently.

In fact, the company's original vision statement—"Man is the creator of change in this world. As such he should be above systems and structures, and not subordinate to them"—still resonates today with Apple's core emotional attitude of "thinking differently."

Today, Apple's products continue to exemplify this vision of "thinking differently," with line innovations including the Mac, iPod, and iPhone crossing the three vast domains of computing, music, and telecommunications. And these products ensure a dedicated following among Apple fans. There is even an online community of hardcore Apple fans dedicated to all things Apple at www.cultofmac.com.

The continued relevance of the brand's emotion, and its intricate design thinking, inspire deep brand trust among its fans and account for its success today.

DESIGN

Not a lot is known about Apple's design process, but interviews with Jonathan Ive, senior vice president of design at Apple and the celebrated creator of such iconic products as the iPod, iMac, and MacBook, offer a glimpse of the company's design principles.

In an interview with the Design Museum in Britain, Ive described the defining qualities of Apple's products as ease and simplicity of use. Describing the new MacBook, he said: "I do not know how we could make something any more essential, any simpler than the new MacBook."

He has also spoken about caring beyond the functional imperative; acknowledging that products have significance beyond traditional views of function. For example, commenting on the iMac's handle, he notes that "while the primary function is obviously associated with making the product easy to move, a compelling part of its function is the immediate reference it makes with the user by unambiguously referencing the hand. That reference represents, at some level, an understanding beyond the iMac's core function. Seeing an object with a handle, you instantly understand aspects of its physical nature—I can touch it, move it, and it's not too precious." A perfect delivery of "thinking differently," indeed, amidst the ever-increasing array of me-too products in the marketplace.

And it's not just the products; Apple's retail store is an experience in itself and has often been described as the "Nordstrom of Technology." Enter Apple's retail store and you will realize how the entire retail concept ties in and is coherent with Apple's brand vision and its products. The brand touch-points in the store have all been carefully designed; for instance, "specialists" provide assistance in knowing the product, and "geniuses" provide hands-on technical support and repair at the Genius Bar, while the "concierge" is the guide to the store who will point you in the right direction. Personalized help aside, the store layout is also very well thought out; it is visually spare, preferring to focus on a selection of essential messages instead of cluttering the customer's field of vision. Products are also placed in context of use; for instance, iPhoto software is set up beside a digital camera.

It is this remarkable and rigorous consistency of Apple's brand promise across the products, ambassadors, and retail stores that has further brought Apple's brand to life.

TRUST

Mac users are by far one of the most passionate brand communities around. For some, the reason for their affinity with Apple is the brand's message of being the antithesis of Microsoft—the uniting desire to root for the underdog and the "cool" alternative to the dominant other. For others, the reason is Apple's commitment to great design that is functionally superior and aesthetically pleasing, in both its hardware and software.

And this affinity runs deep—far beyond a transactional relationship with Apple. This intense love and passion for Apple is the reason why, in July 2008, fans in Japan queued for two days before the launch in that country of the new iPhone, undiscouraged by rain or freezing temperatures. Hiroyuki Sano, a 24-year-old graduate student who was first in line after traveling 225 miles to Tokyo, commented: "I told my professor I was going to go buy an iPhone and he gave me permission. He is an Apple lover too, and he sent me off cheerfully."

This brand trust had been tested when the price of the iPhone was slashed by US$200 (from US$599) barely two months after the launch of the product in the United States, making it more accessible to the American public. "We want to make iPhone even more affordable for even more people this holiday season... We want to put iPhones in a lot of stockings this holiday season," said Steve Jobs. Not surprisingly, early adopters who were passionate about Apple products and motivated to differentiate themselves from the rest of society by paying a hefty sum for the product at launch felt betrayed, and a slew of disapproving emails followed.

Steve Jobs issued an apology and announced that it would offer $100 worth of store credit to those who paid the initial US$599 price. "We want to do the right thing for our valued iPhone customers," Jobs wrote in an email to purchasers of the product. "We apologise for disappointing some of you, and we are doing our best to live up to your high expectations of Apple."

Apple learned a valuable lesson about the deep value of brand trust, and about the passionate relationship that exists between the brand and its fans.

REFERENCES

www.designmuseum.org/design/jonathan-ive
www.reuters.com/article/technologyNews/idUSSYD257438
   20080709?feedType=RSS&feedName=technologyNews
www.apple.com/retail/
http://asia.cnet.com/reviews/mobilephones/
   0,39050603,62032012,00.htm
http://money.cnn.com/2007/09/06/technology/iphone_price/
   index.htm

Speed, Agility, and Innovation

If a company wants to develop a great brand in today's world, then it will need to develop the attributes of speed, agility, and innovation. These attributes used to be a "nice to have" set of characteristics, and companies could utilize them as they preferred. However, the situation today is different. Consumers are demanding new products, and they want them with increasing frequency; this is forcing companies to use these characteristics constantly. Speed, agility, and innovation are now a part of everyday corporate life. However, if firms can respond to these demands, they can generate huge success. The case studies on Zara and Samsung below illustrate how two brands have made innovation and speed a part of their business process, and how this has provided them with a competitive advantage.

CASE STUDY 7: ZARA

For Fast Fashion Fans

Zara is a prime example of speed, agility, and innovation in retailing and it has become a global brand though demonstrating its prowess in these three areas.

Owned by the Inditex Group from Spain, Zara opened its first store in 1975, and had more than 15,000 by December 2008.

Zara produces around 11,000 products each year, far more than most fashion retailers, and to accomplish this it has developed the ability to drastically shorten the product life cycle. Indeed, from the design stage to being in store can take as little as four to five weeks. If the design is just a modification, it may take only three weeks. No one design stays in the stores for more than four weeks, and if the first week's sales are not up to scratch the item is withdrawn and production stopped.

This has an interesting and positive impact on the consumer. First, it means that Zara shoppers have a constant source of new, fresh products to choose from. Second, customers know that any item they buy will be more "exclusive" than those from other stores, as their items will only be on sale for a month. The benefit for the company is that Zara customers tend to visit stores around 17 times a year, as opposed to the fashion retailing average of three of four times. (These are figures for Zara in Spain.) The frequent turnover encourages them to buy, as they know the products will only be available for a short time.

The time limitation for fashion clothes is the speed of design, with traditional fashion houses tending to have few designers who take up to six months to produce new designs and thus only have two or three collections per year. Zara has a large team of designers, which enables the company to react quickly to new trends and consumer demands. Zara's founder, Amancio Ortega, calls this business model "instant fashions."

The speed required is augmented by a computerized inventory system that links the factories producing Zara's large number of products to the retail outlets. This system significantly reduces the need to hold large inventories.

All in all, it's a win-win situation for Zara and its customers.

CASE STUDY 8: SAMSUNG

Speed, Innovation, and More Choice for Customers

Samsung is another famous brand that has gained ground because of its speed, innovation, and agility, focusing on getting innovative technologies to market quickly and providing consumers with more choice.

SPEED

The strategy of speed, which Samsung has developed to a fine art, allows the company to take advantage of decreasing product life cycles. In some product categories, they have been reduced to a number of weeks. This tremendous life-cycle compression is likely to be a permanent feature of the consumer electronics marketplace, where, paradoxically, the sheer ubiquity of mass-customized products has led to commoditization. They are now regarded by Samsung (and consumers) as perishable goods!

With this in mind, Samsung has moved away from the lower-volume, higher-priced products to much higher volumes of products and more line extensions offered to consumers at lower cost. Another piece of smart thinking is that Samsung now plays in both business-to-business and business-to-consumer markets, producing not just the end-user products but also their components. This has given the company the diversity, massive scale, and cost leadership that generates acceptable margins in commodity markets. One of the clear benefits to consumers, apart from lower pricing, is more choice.

Additionally, in order to enhance innovation, speed, and agility, Samsung has reduced its involvement in research and development work, which is both costly and slow, and instead uses technologies invented by others quickly, focusing on getting its products to market at least as fast as, if not more rapidly than, its competitors.

CHOICE

In commodity markets, Samsung has also realized that more is better. Consumers want choice. They want customized products to reflect their lifestyles and personalities. While some competitors haven't got to grips with such market trends, Samsung has used its cost and diversity advantages to produce more products in the categories in which it operates. For example, while Nokia launches around 20 new models a year, Samsung produces around 100. This allows its brand to cater for the very fragmented market that now exists in consumer electronics, where individuality is demanded at low prices and where the number of segments is rapidly increasing.

Mass customization is the name of the game, and Samsung has been the best at reinventing itself as a way to deal with this through the route of huge design improvements. In order to drive innovation throughout the company, many policies have been changed:

- Designers with new product ideas can now go direct to top management.
- Young designers can even challenge their superiors if they believe a change is needed. (This goes against the national Confucian culture, which stresses order.)
- Engineers have to find out how to accommodate technology into new designs, instead of the reverse.
- Designers are seconded to work at fashion and design houses.
- Consumer insight is the norm, and Samsung studies how consumers actually use products. The idea is to move on from just concentrating on the look and feel of its products to improve their usability. The company has a "usability laboratory" in Seoul.
- Samsung now has design centers in London, Los Angeles, San Francisco, Shanghai, and Tokyo.

In order to become a global brand, Samsung has reinvented itself. The company has transformed from a copier to a leader in innovative technology and design, taking advantage of the other giants, such as Sony, who appear to have taken their eye off the design ball.

Summary

For brand managers in the 21st century, there are many complex tasks to undertake, but achieving brand loyalty and lifetime relationships with consumers are the true goals, because only when these are achieved will the brand last and grow in value. Brands are at their most powerful when they determine business direction, and when they bind themselves to consumers through emotional associations.

The power of emotion has been present since life began—it is the great motivator and the prime driver of the human spirit. Although rational attributes may attract, emotional attributes sell.

In building powerful brands, emotional associations are greatly enhanced through good design, and design coupled with innovation can add a competitive edge to a company's business and brand strategy.

In the next chapter, I will discuss positioning and many of the strategies available to brand managers. An emotional positioning strategy is one of them, and you will see how this can, and should, be linked with other strategies chosen. While reading the next chapter, keep in mind that all great brand positions stem from a well thought-through brand vision, often based on consumer insight.

Positioning and Brand Management

How Does Positioning Fit into Brand Management?

Positioning is vital to brand management because it takes the basic tangible aspects of the product and actually builds the intangibles in the form of an image in people's minds. It focuses on the chosen target audience(s) and influences their thoughts about the brand in relation to other brands. Through the strategies described in this chapter, positioning seeks the best way of convincing people that a particular brand is both different from and better than any other brand.

This chapter explains the critical role played by the positioning process in helping to make the strategic leap from being perceived as an ordinary brand to being seen as a leader, with all the rewards this brings. Strong, or even world-class, branding is impossible without powerful positioning.

The Positioning Process

If *personality* is the main part of brand identity, *positioning* is the other pillar of a brand's strategic platform. It is partly to do with how the core brand values are projected to the outside world. Someone can have a great personality, or a company can create a unique personality for itself or its products, but unless people see it and perceive it as such, it will have little effect. Conversely, positioning can be much more successful if it is personified, because personality is a differentiator in itself. However, as will be seen below, even personality isn't enough to completely differentiate a branded business.

Avoiding the Perception Gap

All brand managers aspire to build a great image for their brand(s). Brand image, however, may not turn out to be the same as the identity and personality we want the brand to be perceived as having, because image is subject to perception—the way in which people think about something, or even imagine it to be. So, if we project the identity wrongly, or not strongly enough, the people whom we want to acknowledge our identity might view it as something entirely different. They might not see us as honest, or might think our packaging looks cheap. Image can be based on fact or fiction, depending on how people perceive things. The difference between identity and image is what is often called the *perception gap*, which must be avoided at all costs.

To avoid the perception gap between identity and image, we must ensure that what is offered is what is acknowledged—that the target audience sees and relates to our brand personality/identity, and this will depend on their perceptions.

Positioning is also about creating a perception of *difference*, and brand managers use a variety of strategies to convince and persuade people that they are both different from and better than the brands of the opposition. The main goal of positioning is to create a perceptual space in people's minds that your brand owns, and that differentiates it from others.

Positioning is more than just differentiating a brand on personality. In positioning a brand, the brand's actual performance can be introduced, as well as its personality. This brings into play competitive business dynamics, as well as brand attributes and values. The idea is to portray a brand's strategic competitive advantage, and positively influence the perceptions of the target audience(s) so that the brand stands out from the crowd. Here are some of the most effective positioning strategies.

Thirteen Power-Positioning Strategies

There are 13 strategies that can be used, either individually or in a combination, to establish a powerful position. The fundamentals of these strategies are described below, together with some of their advantages and disadvantages that need to be given consideration.

1. Features and Attributes

This is probably the most obvious strategy and is traditionally the most frequently used in many industries. With this strategy the focus is on those brand attributes that can be used to endorse the perception that here is something that is different, or better, or both.

The motor vehicle industry is a typical user of this strategy, and most car manufacturers either do this now or have had to do this in order to stay in the forefront of people's minds. Volvo is one of the best examples, having for many years positioned its vehicles as being the safest on the road. Service companies can also use this strategy, an example being the Ritz-Carlton hotel group advertising its uncompromisingly high service-quality standards. It gets its staff to think in this way by saying to them, "We are ladies and gentlemen serving ladies and gentlemen."

ADVANTAGES   With this strategy there is the potential to own it for a long time, as with Volvo, or it might last only for a short period of time, as in the case of laser jet printers, or 3M with nasal dilatory strips. In either case, it can result in the creation of a rapid market share, particularly if your product is first into the market with a new or distinctive feature or attribute.

DISADVANTAGES   Features and attributes can be copied sooner or later (with increasing speed as technology advances), and this will erode market-share gains. Competitors may produce enhancements that cause your offer to be obsolete, and repositioning might consequently be difficult. Technological change is militating against this strategy by increasing the speed with which products can be copied, and by reducing product life cycles.

2. Benefits

This strategy takes features and attributes to the next stage by describing what benefit(s) the customer will receive as a result—for instance, a toothpaste containing fluoride (a feature) helps fight decay (a benefit).

The benefits positioning strategy really answers the question consumers have in their minds regarding "What's in it for me?" The safety feature of a car means protection. The introduction of airbags in cars as an additional feature might mean more expense, but in the consumer's mind the benefits of a life-saving attribute outweigh the cost.

ADVANTAGES This strategy helps give a company and its products more appeal by allowing people to see clearly what the brand attributes actually mean. Like features, benefit positioning can establish short-term competitive advantage, and can lead to market leadership and quick gains. It is a reasonably flexible strategy, and can be extended in a clinical, logical way (aimed at the left brain) or in a more emotional way (aimed at the right brain).

EXAMPLE

Feature	Rational Appeal	Emotional Appeal
Safety	Protection	Keeps your loved ones safe

DISADVANTAGES As with the features strategy, the benefit positioning strategy can be somewhat short-lived, and what is a benefit and competitive advantage today may be part of tomorrow's basic product. It is based around the concept of a USP (unique selling proposition) that is vulnerable these days to easy replication, further enhancements, and technological innovations. I can buy a personal computer today with a huge processing speed, currently the state of the art, only to find six months later that there is a new industry standard for that product category.

3. Problem–Solution

This is another widely used, and often highly effective, strategy. It is based on the premise that consumers don't necessarily want to buy a product or deal with a company strictly for that purpose. What they really want is a *solution to a problem* they have that can be provided by the product or company. Here are some examples.

People often regard some banking products as a necessary evil. It is highly unlikely that they will wake up one morning gleefully shouting, "What a great day for an overdraft!" It's more likely that they will lie awake at night worrying about how they are going to solve an immediate financial problem to which an overdraft might be the solution.

Oracle and many other companies use this strategy. (See my book, with K.C. Lee, *Hi-Tech Hi-Touch Branding*, John Wiley & Sons, 2000, for other examples of technology companies using this positioning strategy.)

ADVANTAGES   This strategy is clearly appropriate for industries such as financial services, IT, and communications, but it is also more widely applicable. Because problems always have an emotional consequence or impact on the consumer, it is a useful strategy because emotion can be built into this positioning, often being accomplished by suggesting an emotional benefit attached to the solution.

EXAMPLE: LIFE INSURANCE

Problem: What happens to my family if something happens to me?

Solution: Life insurance

Emotional benefit: Peace of mind; my family will be looked after if a disaster occurs.

DISADVANTAGES   Other competitors can also solve the same problems consumers have, perhaps even improving on the solution. In technology-led industries, this strategy is now becoming so overused that other means of differentiation are essential.

The big crunch can come if you claim the solution approach but don't deliver—for example, with warranties that don't perform. Also, to maintain brand credibility with this strategy (particularly in technology-driven industries), new product development is vital because life-cycle compression means the rapidity of new product innovations makes today's problems disappear fast. The pace of change also creates different problems for consumers. You have to stay on top of the game at all times.

4. Competition

Every company must always be aware of the competition—what it is doing and what it intends to do. Depending on competitor strategies, it may be necessary to change your position—a reactive strategy. On the other hand, it is possible to be proactive and change your position and thus disadvantage the competition. One of the biggest business wars, which has been ongoing for years now, is between Internet software and hardware suppliers. In a full-page advertisement in the *Far Eastern Economic Review* of July 19, 2001, Oracle claimed that it ran SAP four times faster than IBM. Using a large chart to emphasize the point, Oracle also claimed: "that's why SAP customers choose Oracle over IBM 10 to 1. Interesting." In a similar vein, HP and Oracle ran a co-branding campaign in 2009. The front-page advertisement in the *Wall Street Journal* of June 19–21 had the headline, "Runs Oracle 10x Faster," followed by: "The World's Fastest Database Machine. Hardware by HP. Software by Oracle."

A simple, neat, but aggressively to-the-point advertisement was this print ad run by Durex some years ago: "To all those who use our competitors' products: Happy Father's Day." The Durex logo was placed in the bottom right-hand corner of the page. You can't get much more direct than that.

ADVANTAGES   Competitive strategies tend to be more effective when used for positioning companies rather than products. Corporations tend to have more unique characteristics in the form of personality, culture, size, and visual identity that people can more readily associate with, and an image that can help keep a company one step ahead when managed well. However, with products there is often less to work with in terms of differentiators, especially in today's increasingly cluttered markets. Notwithstanding this, if a positioning strategy is based on facts or statistics it is possible to own a position, as long as consumers believe the figures!

DISADVANTAGES   Competitive positioning can invite retaliation, and in some countries this is prevented by legislation. It can lead to a lot of wasteful expenditure and embarrassing public incidents, as in the case of ambush marketing. The message here is that you had better be sure your product or company has something to offer to your target audience that others cannot match.

5. Corporate Credentials or Identity

Some companies rely on the strength of their corporate name to endorse products, positioning them by the house-brand reputation. This can be very powerful, as demonstrated by companies such as Sony, IBM, and Nestlé. The sheer power and ubiquity of the parent brand name can make life very difficult for would-be competitors trying to establish their own position.

ADVANTAGES   The power of the corporate name can help strengthen or make a strong position for even an average product. A well-known name can cross different markets and, in some cases, create global product positions, as in the case of Sony moving into the entertainment industry from consumer electronics.

DISADVANTAGES   If the company goes through a bad time, so does the product, and the position can lose its credibility. A badly managed corporate image will make life very difficult for products positioned around the strength of the parent's name and reputation. It can also work the other way round, as was the case with Firestone tires, which became a major cause of anguish for parent company Bridgestone and caused huge problems for the end-user, Ford.

6. Usage Occasion, Time, and Application

This strategy can be an effective differentiator, but it is appropriate for products and services, rather than companies and larger institutions. The strategy gains its value from the fact that people not only use products in different ways, but may do so on different occasions and at different times. For instance, some people eat Oreo cookies for a between-meals snack (time usage). A nutritious chocolate drink is used by some people before going to sleep (time usage), and by others as a food supplement at various times of day (application). Champagne is usually enjoyed only at celebrations (occasion usage).

ADVANTAGES   Products and services can gain a market position that is more easily defendable, and the strategy is as flexible as the capability of the product's possibilities for different usage situations.

DISADVANTAGES   Products with more effective usage may usurp the position, and as consumer behavior changes over time, the time or nature of usage might also change.

7. Target User

The target user positioning strategy is a very good example of focus in marketing. Companies that know their target audiences well can be effective in positioning a generic product to many customer groups, as is the case with Nike, which has trainer footwear dedicated to each sports group.

ADVANTAGES   This strategy is good for getting into, and defending, niche markets, and for building strong customer relationships. It is clearly a winner for developing a product range where a wide range of customer groups exist for a generic product, but where slightly differing needs or applications allow a wide low-cost product range. In 2008, Nike had revenues of around US$18 billion, and produced one in every two trainers sold in the United States.

DISADVANTAGES   The strategy relies on accurate segmentation and, therefore, research. Companies that know the market structure and dynamics, but don't understand customers' real needs and wants, may well come unstuck. The strategy can be limiting, and user profiles will change over time. Nike, for instance, found it relatively easy to go from trainers to sports apparel, but less easy to move into leisure apparel for older people.

8. Aspiration

Aspirational positioning can be applied in many forms, but the two most common ones are concerned with:

- status and prestige (related to wealth achievement); and
- self-improvement (related to non-monetary achievement).

In both cases the strategy relies on self-expression, and as most individuals have a need to express themselves in one way or another, associating themselves with companies or brands that facilitate this is helpful.

With respect to status and prestige, Rolex and Rolls-Royce are power brands that people use to make a statement about their financial achievements in life, among other things. On the self-improvement side, Adidas's "Impossible is Nothing" platform taps into the sports lifestyle and sporting achievement.

ADVANTAGES   Everyone has aspirations, and they are always emotionally linked. By appealing to these universal feelings, brands can quickly become global players. When combined with other strategies, this one can be immensely powerful.

DISADVANTAGES   Not everyone sees himself or herself as a winner, and thus this strategy can be a turn-off for under-achievers. It is essential, therefore, to know your target audience.

9. Causes and Ethics

This positioning strategy is also linked to emotion, and focuses on people's belief hierarchies and their need to belong. Avon, Benetton, and other companies target customer groups whom they believe will subscribe to a certain philosophy or who want to relate to a specific group or movement. Avon targets women and supports women's causes; for instance, it once conducted a survey of 30,000 women in 43 countries to discover what they feel are their greatest challenges, what is needed for personal happiness, and what things are most important in their lives. Shell is focusing on the environment and conservation of the world's resources. This strategy is becoming more widely used and important, as it relates to freedom of thought and speech, environmental responsibility, democracy, the liberation of women, and other social trends. It is also a positioning strategy that is extending its use and appeal through the concept of ethical branding, a good example of which is Innocent Drinks, discussed in Case Study 9.

CASE STUDY 9: INNOCENT DRINKS

Ethics and Social Responsibility Can Mix with Fun

Innocent Drinks, a UK-based company best known for its smoothies and quirky brand messaging, is actively involved in several cause-related marketing initiatives. It says very clearly on its delightful, refreshing website: "We want Innocent to become a global, natural, ethical food and drinks company, always remaining commercially successful and socially aware."

Each year, Innocent donates 10 percent of the company's profits to charity. The majority of this is channeled to the Innocent Foundation, which aims to improve the lives of the rural communities dependent on sustainable agriculture in those countries where Innocent sources its fruits. In September 2007, Innocent became the first company in the world to launch a bottle made from 100 percent recycled plastic. Other sustainable characteristics in Innocent's packaging include using the least possible amount of material per pack, using materials with a low carbon footprint, and using materials for which there is a widely available sustainable waste management option.

Innocent's ingredients are also sourced in a responsible manner. Buying priority is given to farms that look after the interests of both the environment and the workers. For example, all of Innocent's bananas are Rainforest Alliance certified. Innocent also aims to be a resource-efficient business by paying close attention to its carbon and water footprints, and actively seeks to lower both in its business activities.

Although Innocent sold a 20 percent stake in its business to Coca-Cola in 2009, it says it will not change its ethical positioning. Co-founder Richard Reed said in an article in *Guardian* of April 6, 2009: "Every promise that Innocent has made, about making only natural healthy products, pioneering the use of better, socially and environmentally aware ingredients, packaging and production techniques, donating money to charity and having a point of view on the world will remain. We'll just get to do them even more." Do have a look at its website, as this is a brand that enjoys having some fun, too. From its corporate headquarters, named "Fruity Towers," to an area on the website for bored people, Innocent proves that being an ethical and socially aware brand doesn't mean that you have to be serious all the time.

REFERENCE

www.innocentdrinks.co.uk/us/ethics

ADVANTAGES   Companies can own a strong position through this strategy. It can be very powerful when linked to other strategies concerning applications, target users, and emotion.

DISADVANTAGES   Causes can go in and out of fashion, and while being welcomed by some, others might be offended; thus, proper targeting is vital. Additionally, while a cause is in vogue, the "bandwagon" effect often occurs, as is the case now with literally hundreds of companies giving us steadfast promises that they will do everything they can to protect the environment. If you embark on this strategy with your brand, you are also committed to the long-term and to a high marketing budget in order to prove to the cause audience that you really mean what you say.

10. Value

Value is often related to what people pay, but this strategy isn't to do with price. There are two main elements of value positioning:

- *Price/quality*—that is, value for money, a positioning used by Virgin and Carrefour.
- *Emotional value*—that is, the associations people have when they own, for example, a Mini car. BMW has successfully brought back these memories and emotions with an enhanced new Mini car, fighting on the nostalgia platform with Volkswagen's Beetle.

ADVANTAGES This is a good strategy when it combines the two elements, and can also be used tactically via promotions. The key is to concentrate on *value*, not *price*.

DISADVANTAGES It tends to be commodity-oriented when it concentrates on price, and not suitable for those building a power brand and looking for high premiums.

11. Emotion

As a positioning strategy this can exist on its own, but it is often used as an overlay position, adding value and strength to other strategies, as previously mentioned. It is highly important because, as research shows time and time again, emotion sells. Häagen-Dazs ice cream is a case in point, and the brand's success has been phenomenal. It broke into a market dominated by giants such as Nestlé and others, and sold its products at prices up to 40 percent higher than its competitors. The key to its success was the creation of a unique positioning around the concept of sheer luxury and the enjoyment of the moment. Some of the advertisements for the product portrayed this with romantic and sexual imagery, or by using fantasy.

ADVANTAGES Emotional positioning strategies move people to want things. Emotion creates desire, and can be very powerful indeed. Positioning without emotion tends to be less persuasive and to lack motivation.

DISADVANTAGES As a strategy on its own, it might not sway the minds of the "cold fish"—the more calculating, careful-planning, thrifty types of people. For those who are very price-sensitive the cost will be the decisive factor, overpowering the emotional feelings.

12. Personality

As mentioned in the previous chapter, brand building based on personality creation can be extremely effective, being frequently used by companies to build world-class brands. But people won't respond to a personality they see as being either not relevant or not likable.

Personality characteristics such as the following have proven to be extremely attractive to most people:

- caring;
- modern;
- innovative;
- warm;
- independent
- strong;
- honest;
- experienced;
- genuine;
- sophisticated;
- successful;
- inspiring;
- energetic;
- trustworthy;
- reliable;
- approachable; and
- fun-loving.

ADVANTAGES   People are very responsive to this strategy, and, when combined with others, it can produce high market share, loyalty, and profitability. It is the only way really to gain and sustain a strategic competitive advantage.

DISADVANTAGES   The strategy relies on a very clear understanding of the target audience, and a great deal of investment, to ensure that the customer experiences a consistent personality on all occasions. Building a corporate personality, for instance, demands that the entire culture of the organization be changed so that all staff live that personality in their everyday work.

13. Claiming Number One

This is an enviable position to have, as it generates perceptions of leadership. In the hi-tech field it can work wonders for the brand and provide a perception of difference, even though product service and quality may be similar between major players. This is essentially what has happened to Amazon.com, which remains the brand leader in its field, even though other companies offer similar products and services. Accenture (previously Arthur Andersen), the consulting firm, was the first company to position itself as a technology specialist, and has remained number one in this category ever since.

ADVANTAGES   Your brand is widely perceived as the market leader, and if you can maintain constant innovation you could own this position.

DISADVANTAGES   The obvious concern here is keeping ahead of the pack when innovation is happening all the time. You will need to invest considerably in research and development

Gaining Power from Combining Strategies

The power positioning strategies discussed above can be combined in various ways as companies and people wish. A well-known example of this is the sports shoe and apparel manufacturer Nike, one of the world's most admired brands.

CASE STUDY 10: NIKE

Multi-Positioning Strategies

Nike, one of the world's best-loved brands, elegantly employs a combination positioning strategy, allowing its brand to be differentiated across its multi-product lines, sub-brands, and business interests by drawing on the best benefits of each relevant positioning strategy. These positioning strategies include features and attributes, benefits, cause-related/ethical marketing, emotion, personality, and aspiration.

FEATURES AND ATTRIBUTES

Nike has taken the marketing of features and attributes to a higher level with the introduction of NIKEiD across both its online and retail channels. NIKEiD gives consumers the power to design, personalize, and customize the features and attributes (such as choice of colors, sole, inner lining, etc.) of selected Nike performance and sport culture footwear, apparel, and equipment. It is the beginning of a consumer-driven, Nike-supported community whose members share ideas, concepts, and a passion for NIKEiD. Each shoe designed will have the name of the creation, the designer's name, their country of origin, and the date it was designed. According to Nike, the NIKEiD business has more than tripled since 2004, with more than three million unique visitors visiting the NIKEiD website every month.

This positioning strategy also allows Nike to reach out to new users (see "Target user" positioning strategy, above) who may be seeking customized designs as a way to express themselves and differentiate themselves from the mass majority.

BENEFITS

Nike Free (into its fourth version in 2009) is a good first example. Promising the benefits of barefoot running while wearing a shoe, it allows the foot muscles to gain strength by providing less constriction. Various features of the shoes are adapted to provide this end benefit. For example, the lacing system has been redesigned to be on the side of the shoe in order to reduce pressure over the top ridge of the shoe, while distinctive grooves on the outsole mimic the natural movement of the foot. Models offering different degrees of "barefoot running" and shoe support are also available to ensure consumers get the right fit.

Another recent example of Nike's positioning by benefit is the development of Flywire (much like the theory of a suspension bridge), which allows fibers to support the shoe at key points instead of using whole layers, which increases weight. With Flywire, shoes can be made extremely light, yet not compromising support, a benefit especially relevant for sports such as athletics, basketball, and football (soccer).

Cause-Related/Ethical Marketing

Since 1993, when Nike introduced its footwear recycling program (Reuse-A-Shoe), sustainability has been a key area of development for the brand. This initiative was timely, given consumers' growing expectations for brands to embrace a greater sense of environmental consciousness.

Nike Considered Design, which combines sustainability principles with innovations in sport, is a natural extension of Nike's sustainability initiatives. The goal is to create performance innovation products that minimize environmental impact by reducing waste throughout the design and development process, the usage of environmentally preferred materials, and the elimination of toxins. Nike has also developed a Considered Index, which measures the predicted environmental footprint of a product prior to commercialization. Only products scoring significantly more than the corporate average are designated as "Considered."

The latest collection of Nike Considered Design, for spring 2009, includes all of Nike's six key categories: basketball, running, football (soccer), women's training, men's training, and sportswear. Pegasus, Nike's best-selling shoe, celebrating its 25th anniversary, is the first pinnacle running shoe to be a Nike Considered Design.

Emotion

Nike embraces the emotional aspects of its brand very well and this positioning strategy is frequently used in an overlay position, adding value and strength to the other strategies employed, particularly personality and aspiration. The ads for the brand frequently show a range of emotions, often revolving around the various expressions of winning, courage, and the call to "Just Do It." For example, the "Courage" campaign that debuted in 2008 celebrates the 20-year anniversary of the "Just Do It" campaign by presenting an inspirational collage of some of sport's most-loved athletes in their finest moments. Thirty-plus athletes from 17 different countries are featured, including Michael Jordan seen kissing his National Basketball Association trophy and Lance Armstrong, who overcame cancer to win the Tour de France.

"The TV ad celebrates quite frankly what we felt is one of the most inspirational brand statements of all time—Just do it," said Joaquin Hidalgo, Nike's vice president of global brand marketing. "It's at the core of an athlete's persona whether they are a professional or amateur. It's a call to arms to do better, to get to the next level."

PERSONALITY

Nike has become well known over the years for using celebrity athletes to endorse its brand. Some of these famous names include Michael Jordan, Kobe Bryant, Tiger Woods, Roger Federer, Liu Xiang, and Maria Sharapova. They are more than Nike spokespersons; they add credibility, and their popularity, personality, and influence within their respective domains augments Nike's brand personality.

These personalities speak to consumers emotionally and seek to inspire consumers to be like them, to excel in their sporting achievements, to "Just Do It" in their Nikes. As a further benefit, they give added credibility to the products—for instance, if Michael Jordan can play an entire season with a pair of Nikes, surely the weekend enthusiast can trust their durability.

ASPIRATION

Nike's mission statement is to bring inspiration and innovation to every athlete (if you have a body, you are an athlete) in the world. And they have delivered on both inspiration and innovation exceedingly well. Product innovation aside, Nike has religiously and consistently communicated the inspirational aspects of the brand, best summed up by their trademark swoosh and the tagline "Just Do It," through brand activation events and campaigns.

The recent Nike + Human Race is a wonderful example of inspiration delivered. Held on August 31, 2008, the world's biggest-ever one-day running event offered around one million runners across the globe the chance to compete together. The 10km event was staged in 25 cities, including Los Angeles, New York, London, Madrid, Paris, Istanbul, Melbourne, Shanghai, São Paulo, and Vancouver. There is a possibility that the race may become an annual event.

"The Nike + Human Race is about inspiring and connecting a million runners worldwide," said Trevor Edwards, Nike's vice president for brand and category management. "We are offering runners new ways to compete and race, courses through legendary landmarks, each ending with a headlining musical act. It's an unprecedented way for us to bring an entirely new running experience to consumers around the world."

REFERENCES

www.nikebiz.com/media/pr/2007/10/4_nikeid_nyc.html
www.nikerunning.com.sg/siteshell/index.html#/nikefree/
http://news.cnet.com/8301-17938_105-9998061-1.html
www.nikebiz.com/responsibility/
www.adweek.com/aw/content_display/creative/news/
    e3i50336777802bc299c1d9ae542bbbce8d
www.nikebiz.com/media/pr/2008/05/01_HumanRace.html

Capturing Hearts and Minds

Whatever strategies are used, the key to positioning is capturing people's hearts and minds, by appealing to both the rational and emotional aspects of their psychological make-up. Astute brand managers are those who understand this and know how to combine strategies that satisfy the emotional and rational needs of consumers.

Summary: Choosing a Positioning Strategy

Whatever strategy or combination of strategies you eventually choose, there are certain points you need to remember:

- The position must be salient or important to the target audience you are trying to reach and influence. It is no good communicating messages to them that are of no interest, as they will either ignore them or forget them quickly.
- The position must be based on real strengths. Making claims that cannot be substantiated can cause enormous loss of credibility.
- The position has to reflect some form of competitive advantage. The whole point of positioning is to inform and persuade people that you are different from and better than the competition, so whatever that point of difference is, it must be clearly expressed.
- Finally, the position must be capable of being communicated simply, so that everyone gets the real message, and of motivating the audience. The aim of positioning is to provide a call to action to the target audience, and communications must be created carefully.

Repositioning

As mentioned at the very beginning of this chapter, most positioning is *repositioning*. Unless you have a new company or product that no one has heard of, you will already have an image in the marketplace; consequently, you will need to reposition if you want to change it. In most situations, therefore, it is very important to understand what your image is and whether it actually matches the identity you are trying to portray.

Eight Reasons for Repositioning

There are eight main reasons why companies attempt to reposition themselves or their products. They are where there is a:

- poor or tarnished (or outdated or inconsistent) image;
- fuzzy or blurred image;
- change in the target audience or in their needs and wants;
- change in strategic direction;

- new or revitalized corporate personality/identity;
- change in competitor positioning or new competitors;
- momentous event; or
- rediscovery of lost values.

1. Poor, Tarnished, Outdated, or Inconsistent Image

For whatever reason, the image you have may not be all that is desired. The automobile brand Rover had a clear problem here, and even when taken over by BMW, with millions of dollars spent on the brand, it never regained its former glory. BMW was forced to admit failure and sell the brand for a token sum to a Chinese manufacturer, which has also failed to resurrect the brand.

2. Fuzzy, Blurred Image

Sometimes the perception people have of your company or product isn't clear. It's not that it is poor; it may be that people don't think strongly about it one way or the other—they are indifferent, if you like. This is usually caused by unclear positioning and/or lack of brand communications support.

3. Change in the Target Audience or in Their Needs and Wants

If the marketing focus changes, then repositioning is a must. Theoretically, this might prove difficult to do, depending on how close the new focus is to the previous one. So, for instance, if Coca-Cola decided to target the over-sixties age group, repositioning would not only be necessary, but would also be a major challenge in convincing those people that the product isn't a drink made for the younger set. When considering extending the marketing of your company or product to new market segments, it is imperative that a reality check be carried out through market research to see whether or not a new position could be a reality, or whether the task would be too large and costly, perhaps even damaging the perceptions held by existing customer groups. If Coke tried to access the over-sixties segment with the major advertising that would be necessary, how might young people respond?

Another case in point is British horseracing. In an effort to stop the decline of interest in the sport, a branding project was initiated in 2008. The problem that activated this was that the main customer base for horseracing was aging and declining, and younger people didn't share the same interest. In addition to this, other sports were capturing people's attention and wallets. British horseracing therefore has the task of broadening its appeal in order to penetrate new target markets.

According to a report published in *Guardian* on May 12, 2009, research by a branding agency revealed that: "Roughly 10% of the British population goes to the races at least once a year. Roughly a third of these attend on a regular basis, while the other two-thirds are once-a-year race goers. The aim of the rebranding project is to convert irregular race goers into more regular ones, while also reaching out to at least some of the remaining 90% for whom the sport is effectively invisible. In particular, there is a concern that unless at least a proportion of the internet generation is recruited to racing to some degree, the sport's popularity and prosperity will inevitably decline. The 18–30 age group, and young women in particular, is seen as a key target group, along with over-55s."

4. A Change in Strategic Direction

As mentioned, one type of directional change is when there is a need to move from one category to another. This situation usually arises when the category a product is in becomes too crowded, and symptoms of high competitive pressure, such as the erosion of sales and margins, occur. Categories exist in consumer minds and shouldn't be defined by a company. They depend on how people organize information about the things they see, be it by name, usage, attribute, or other descriptors. Successful category repositioning depends on possession of the attributes necessary for acceptance by consumers in the new category, and this should be tested out prior to relaunch as slight product modifications or enhancements and repackaging may prove to be necessary. Care should be taken to ensure correct definition of perceived categories. IBM has successfully repositioned itself away from being perceived as a seller of computer hardware to being seen as a solutions-based information technology company.

5. New or Revitalized Corporate Personality/Identity

This is the corporate equivalent of plastic surgery. Some companies find it worthwhile to change their identity completely—not just with a new logo, but possibly also with a name change, a new structure, and a new personality—in order to overcome problems of the past or to take advantage of new opportunities. The name change of Lucky Goldstar to "LG" is one example of a company that has attempted quite successfully to move up-market with its image and to target more profitable customer groups.

CASE STUDY 11: LG ELECTRONICS (LG)

"Life's Good"

LG was founded in 1947 as Korea's first chemical company. It also became the nation's first electronics company when it entered the home electronics market on October 1, 1958 under the name "GoldStar Co.," with radios being the first product. In 1995 the company changed its name to LG Electronics, by which time it was making refrigerators, batteries, elevators, cosmetics, plastics, and other products in conjunction with the LG Group's chemicals division. However, it suffered from image problems; in particular, it was associated with poor quality.

Some other Korean companies that had enjoyed little brand success in the late 1980s and early 1990s also turned themselves around in the late 1990s. Samsung is one example. LG, however, found it necessary to change its name in order to escape from the poor image associated with the name "GoldStar." It officially made the change in 1995, and set about establishing a new brand identity that suited its globalization objectives. It is now seen as a major player in the global consumer electronics market, with LG Electronics the star of the new show.

THE NEW BRAND IDENTITY

The new brand identity was encapsulated in the words "Delightfully Smart," an overarching umbrella for everything the LG brand stands for. LG says it is "dedicated to making life Delightfully Smart."

Further explanation of the "Delightfully Smart" brand identity stems from the spirit that is captured by LG, and described by the company as follows:

> LG is delightful (consumer-oriented) because LG is founded with delight by those who encounter LG products. For people who are inspired by the latest digital technologies, advanced designs and stylings, and innovative yet practical functions, choosing LG is a form of self-expression, and self-satisfaction, an amazing comfort in knowing you made the perfect decision.

> LG is smart (product-oriented) because its products are smart and developed fundamentally to provide smart solutions for your everyday problems. "Smart" is the expression of the means and the way that our products are innovated. LG products enhance your life with their intelligent features, intuitive functionality, and exceptional performance.

As well as the change in brand identity and the name change that accompanied it, LG also changed its logo, and underlined all these changes with a new tagline.

THE NAME, LOGO, AND TAGLINE CHANGES

Naming

"LG" originally stood for "Lucky GoldStar." LG Electronics was known as GoldStar Electronics in Korea and used the GoldStar brand on its products everywhere. The company changed its name from "GoldStar" to "LG" because, in part, it was felt it had a more modern feel. LG says:

> As LG is not an acronym, there is no full name for LG. On renaming the Group, we considered "LG" to be the most appropriate for a new group name that could integrate different images of two mainstreams of the Group's businesses, the chemicals led by "Lucky" and the electronics and telecommunications led by Goldstar, while including various brand images of other business fields.

Logo

The logo also changed. The company says that "L" and "G" represent the world, future, youth, humanity, and technology, while the symbol colored in red represents friendliness and gives a strong impression of LG's commitment to the best.

The Tagline and Brand Promise

A new tagline, "Life's Good," was also created to express LG's new brand promise, which is discussed later in this case. The "Life's Good" promise reflects LG's belief that life is enriched and enhanced by products that are ingeniously designed and expertly built. It expresses LG's will to provide solutions for an enriched, good life by continuously developing innovative and "delightfully smart" products.

ADDING EMOTIONAL APPEAL THROUGH BRAND COMMUNICATIONS

The philosophy of the brand's positioning is that it provides people with products that help them feel that "Life's Good." It is clear from the brand communications that LG is trying to establish an emotional connection with consumers, something that has eluded it in the past, but which is essential to its future success. It is always used in communications to highlight the brand's breakthrough technologies and latest products. For example, an advertisement in *Forbes* magazine of January 10, 2005, highlighted the LG 3G phone. The copy reads:

7am–10am: Last minute client meeting in Beijing to discuss major structural change. 11am–4pm: Intense meeting with engineers to defy the laws of physics. 7pm–11pm: Motivational meeting with contractors to pull off the impossible. (11.10pm: Angry voice message from fiancée in Los Angeles complaining that you forgot to call.) (11.15pm: Call to fiancée to show her you never stopped thinking about her for a second.)

The LG 3G Phone enables you to see and talk to someone in real time. When you need to most.

It's just one way LG makes life good. To see more ways, visit www.lge.com.

The brand promise contained in the tagline 'Life's Good" is always contained in advertisements such as this one, but is also physically delivered in real ways, principally through product innovation and user-friendliness.

Thinking Global, Acting Local

Market sensitivity is one thing that the brand hasn't forgotten in its rapid rise to global power and reach. It tailors its products for different markets, and so manages to achieve mass customization, a feat that has defied some other companies.

For example, LG has introduced what is called a "Mecca phone" for the Islamic market, predominantly in the Middle East. Called officially the F7100 Qiblah phone, the product features included a prayer time alarm, a direction indicator, and a built-in compass. Muslims say their prayers, while facing Mecca, five times a day. This GSM phone helps them do so, wherever they are, in whatever terrain, and across 500 cities. In India, where much of the population eats less meat and more vegetables, LG came out with a refrigerator that has a smaller freezer and a larger crisper for keeping vegetables fresh. Both of these examples of good consumer insight and consequent product adaptation have been very successful.

LG calls this "customization"; it represents the company's ability to listen to the needs and wants of various consumer segments. The research and development demands are thus very high, and LG spends over 4 percent of its annual sales budget on this "field management" activity.

LG isn't thrifty when it comes to marketing spend and is certainly willing to invest in brand building. In the United States, LG has long been regarded as a cheap, follower brand, copying products from other companies. In order to portray itself as a premium brand in the US, LG now spends more than US$100 million a year. The strategy seems to be working, as its phone sales are rapidly rising, with customers such as Sprint and Verizon. LG has acquired a local US subsidiary, Zenith, to take care of the low end of the market, so that it can keep its own premium brand name and not dilute it, yet still access the high-volume, lower-value mass market.

PRODUCT INNOVATION

The R&D effort backs up this promise to make life good with innovative products. As examples, in addition to the "Mecca phone" described above, LG was a pioneer in the introduction of 3G phones.

On the white goods front, there are refrigerators that include Internet displays that enable users to be online while also preparing a meal in the kitchen. The company was the first to bring to market the world's largest (71-inch) plasma television, and the largest (55-inch) all-in-one LCD television, which can receive digital signals via a set-top box. At the huge Consumer Electronics show held in Las Vegas in January 2009, LG won 14 innovation awards.

There are many other examples of innovative leadership, where LG has excelled. This is not ad hoc product enhancement, but an extremely focused part of LG's brand strategy, the aim of which is to capitalize on convergence and enable LG brand owners to do many things at one time, so that *life is good*.

Making the Complex Simple and User-Friendly through Product Identity

One of the keys to the brand's success in making life good is simplicity. LG focuses not just on the visual identity of its products, but also on the user interface. In building what it calls "Product Identity," LG always ensures that its products are:

- *user-friendly*—comfortable fit, intuitive and efficient, safe;
- *solid*—accurate with fine details, confident and firm, fine finishing;
- *expressive*—advanced, attractive, with originality; and
- *reflecting lifestyles*—needs, value, with vision.

But technology is nothing without skillful brand marketing. LG has improved in this respect, particularly in getting close to the consumer, as mentioned above, but there are many more improvements that need to be made. With this in mind, LG knows it has to gain more global awareness. Importantly, it has to differentiate itself strongly from the competition, which is fierce.

Brand Positioning and Segmentation

"Life's Good" is a broad enough and interesting value proposition, capable of multi-segment appeal; but the devil is in the detail. A massive brand promise such as this has to be capable of execution in all markets.

One of the questions that LG must be debating now is how to target the youth with all its fickleness, by understanding and appealing to its values, and yet still target other demographic segments with product ranges that don't interest the youth. The "Life's Good" brand promise is capable of this, but a comprehensive communications strategy is needed to pull everything together.

Brand Personality

At present, LG appears to be trying to base its brand-building effort on leadership in product features and benefits, but this can never be sustainable, as other big brands such as Sony have discovered. Being state-of-the-art is necessary in technology branding, but what LG seems to be missing at the moment is emotion in its branding. Until now, there has been a lot of concentration on product, perhaps at the expense of brand personality development. A strong corporate brand personality would help add the much-needed emotional dimension to the "Life's Good" proposition and enable LG to be flexible and appealing in addressing all markets. Its home rival has the same challenge of little emotional connection with consumers, but is still ahead on the numbers side.

UPWARDLY MOBILE

LG now has its sights set on the luxury market, and a move into the prestige categories, with co-branded mobile phone products with companies such as Prada. (See the Prada Phone by LG at www. pradaphonebylg.com.) Looking at its progress so far, LG is a brand on the move and seems destined and determined to be a major global Asian brand.

A further example of this kind of repositioning is TAG Heuer, the well-known professional sports watch brand, which launched several expensive global advertising campaigns using sports personalities in an effort to move away from its former cold, mechanical, technically efficient image to one that is perceived as warmer and more human. The basic position of mental attitude overcoming adversity and being in control of oneself is still present; however, the company says: "Through the association of the brand with these key players in sports, who have succeeded through sheer physical and mental effort, we hope to make a comeback to a more humane face." The brand itself was also given a new personality, and the strategy worked. TAG Heuer's success has been so great, it has now been taken over by the LVMH Group (see Case Study 17 in Chapter 4).

6. Change in Competitor Positioning

Sometimes the competition moves its positioning closer to yours, and you may feel it is best to move away and reposition. BMW, in the United States, had to do this when Lexus encroached upon its position and started to erode its customer base.

Another example is Bentley. Although owned and produced by the same companies for many decades, Bentley cars were perceived as a cheaper version of Rolls-Royce cars. This was thought to be a position that endangered the sales of both vehicles, but particularly of Bentley. The repositioning of Bentley cars, through the creation of a sportier image supported by product development with high-performance engines, moved it away from the "poor relation" perception into a powerful position as one of the world's most luxurious sports vehicles. For example, the affectionately named "Baby Bentley" has been bought in large quantities by English Premier League players, and this has started somewhat of a craze for the car among celebrities and "wannabees." Overall, sales have soared, making it a highly successful example of repositioning.

7. Momentous Event

Occasionally, a momentous event might occur that demands repositioning. A momentous event could be a sudden, unexpected crisis. The media usually seize on such crises as opportunities to highlight the failings of a brand. For instance, when Coca-Cola endured another ignominious public revelation in March 2004, the UK *Guardian* newspaper wrote of it on March 20 as follows:

> First, Coca-Cola's new brand of "pure" bottled water, Dasani, was revealed earlier this month to be tap water taken from the mains. Then it emerged that what the firm described as its "highly sophisticated purification process", based on Nasa spacecraft technology, was in fact reverse osmosis used in many modest domestic water purification units.
>
> Yesterday, just when executives in charge of a £7m marketing push for the product must have felt it could get no worse, it did

precisely that. The entire UK supply of Dasani was pulled off the shelves because it has been contaminated with bromate, a cancer-causing chemical.

The article went on to say: "Coca-Cola said it was voluntarily withdrawing all Dasani 'to ensure that only products of the highest quality are provided to our consumers'." Consumers might not have found much consolation in that statement.

This rather problematic situation led the company to embark immediately on major corporate social responsibility campaigns and activities concerned with water scarcity and other global water issues, in which it is still involved today.

Another example of a momentous event was the public relations disaster resulting from the British Airport Authority's delay in opening its new Terminal 5 at Heathrow Airport. As the media were quick to point out, "The chaotic scenes as the new Terminal 5 at Heathrow opened yesterday were a classic example of a British public relations cock-up. Instead of being met with a high-tech, hassle-free travel experience, passengers were faced with overcrowding, delays, cancellations, ill-trained staff and baggage chaos" (www.telegraph.co.uk, March 28, 2008).

The lessons for brand managers are clear: first, don't advertise what you can't deliver; second, don't make claims that aren't true; and third, never compromise on quality. (Public relations and crisis management will be dealt with more thoroughly in Chapter 6.)

8. Rediscovery of Lost Values

Sometimes when a brand has reached a point where consumers are almost taking it for granted and sales are stagnant or worsening, instead of trying to create an entirely new position, it might be worthwhile looking at successful strategies from the past, or evoking nostalgia for past values. Kellogg's once ran a campaign for its Corn Flakes product with the tagline, "Try Them Again For The First Time." Such a strategy, based on brand heritage, can be very successful, especially when competitors are relatively new and the target audience is open to the emotional value of nostalgia. Consumers can easily answer in their minds why that company or product is different and better.

Repositioning and Change—
The New Paradigm

Ten to 20 years ago repositioning was a fairly unusual event, driven mainly by the factors described above, but today it is becoming more frequent as companies seek to keep up with the pace of change and innovation. As constant innovation becomes mandatory for success, so repositioning follows in an equally mandatory manner. Repositioning of brands is now the norm rather than the exception, taking place on a much more frequent basis. This means that brand managers have to take a different view of how they sustain and improve their market leadership and/or ambitions.

Here are some factors to consider in repositioning your brand in the world of change:

- Accept that repositioning is an essential part of brand development.
- Ensure you don't alter the personality of your product/service/ company, as this will place your brand in the "schizophrenic" category.
- Gather market intelligence on what the changing needs of your customers are, and the competitive response.
- Remember that you are dealing with the management of perceptions, and this means that you must budget for it. Repositioning means cash outflow in image and product communications to change perceptions and make people *think* you are still, or are now, different and better. The more entrenched the perceptions, the more you will have to spend.
- Bear in mind that all the products/services you have in the pipeline have to be changed according to your new positioning; if this is difficult, then your repositioning may encounter problems. In the case of motor vehicles, for instance, this can take up to seven years, as products are in the pipeline that will slow down major repositioning.
- Get buy-in from everyone who can make an impact on the brand in your company, or the repositioning effort won't work.

- Remember the basics: in order to reposition, you either have to add more value to the brand proposition or change the target audience.

Should Positioning be Revolutionary or Evolutionary?

Revolutionary positioning is a term that tends to be applied to a situation where you are starting from square one, say, with a new product, company, or personal goal. In such a situation there is no current image, and a position has to be created for the first time. In other words, once you are nowhere, you have to go somewhere. In this case, positioning has to be revolutionary. You have to choose a powerful position amid all the established competitors, and make an impact.

Evolutionary positioning, on the other hand, is about developing your image gradually. Here the issue is that once you are somewhere, you have to decide where to go next and not be left behind. This is a repositioning problem and it can be extremely dangerous. The danger lies in suddenly stepping completely away from the position you have been occupying, and to which consumers, particularly existing customers, are accustomed, without alienating them and losing your unique identity.

In most cases, brand managers have the dilemma of balancing the two approaches. For example, Giorgio Armani, in an interview with CNN, described his biggest problem as keeping his classic design stylish while at the same time adopting fashionable change. He saw it as a true dichotomy. On the one hand, the existing customer base expects to see his classic style; on the other, fashion is moving faster due to technological advances and media hype. Armani said that the media are now less sensitive to individual style and more attuned to what mass designers are producing. So, if the latest mass-designed fashions include the color red, everyone (Armani included) is expected to deliver something in red. If not, he said, he would be left out of media support for that season. The dilemma for designers such as Armani, therefore, is how to remain true to his distinctive style—that is *positioning*—and yet incorporate the latest trends. His answer is: evolutionary change, not revolutionary change. He has to position his products to satisfy the conflict of identity versus modernity. He must remain constant to his customers and meet their expectations both of classic style and contemporary fashion.

Positioning for Equality

Time passes quickly, and people's wants, needs, and aspirations change over time. Sometimes you just have to accept the fact that you are falling (or already are) behind the pack, and have to catch up. You have to convince people that you are "with it," not out of touch with the latest trends are up-to-date, contemporary, and can match what others offer. This means positioning for equality—showing people that you aren't disadvantaged.

Quite often this type of positioning is concerned with the more basic competitive elements of features and benefits, and keeping up with the needs and wants of the people you are trying to retain or acquire as customers. It is also mostly confined to positioning against the competition in specific categories, such as personal computers. With this category the life cycles have shortened so much that when customers start to use their left brain and analyze and justify which particular brand's features and benefits will both do the job and give value for money, the next range of upgraded models has already made the choice obsolete. Positioning here, then, is aimed at giving your customers the message that you have the necessary elements to be a legitimate competitor in that specific area of interest. So, as a computer manufacturer or retailer, you have to have models with the latest chips, hard disk sizes, memory capabilities, speed, and so on.

Positioning for Superiority

Everyone likes to be superior, the best, everyone's choice, but this position is difficult to create and maintain. It goes far beyond equality positioning by seeking to create inequality, a differential advantage, and an image of being a cut above the rest, an undisputed leader. Some companies, including several of the world's leading brands, have already done this. Others have it firmly placed on their boardroom agenda.

Positioning for superiority is only achievable once the target audience acknowledges equality. In other words, you have to demonstrate that you are at least as good as the competition with whatever it is you are offering, and only then can you persuade people that you really have something extra or special to give.

Companies that gain a superior position can be said to have achieved a sustainable competitive advantage (SCA), being the most preferred choice in their field of competition.

The Need for Positioning Statements

Unless you are in total control of all aspects of creating your image through communications, which is most unlikely, there needs to be a communications brief for people to follow. This is one of the main reasons for having written positioning statements. If positioning statements aren't in writing, there is a real danger that the ideas might be misinterpreted, the strategy warped, and the key messages not expressed clearly. The result could well be confusion in the minds of the audience. Positioning statements are essential if you are to keep messages clear and develop a consistent image and position.

What are Positioning Statements?

Positioning statements are internal documents, not meant for public consumption. They summarize strategy, and act as a guide for strategic marketing and brand management. They state specifically and briefly what you want people to think about you, your product or company, or country. They not only spell out the desired image you wish to have, but are also a good test for strategy, as they quickly tell you whether the perceptions you wish people to hold are believable, credible, and achievable. Positioning statements aren't easy to write, and often need several attempts. It is best to write them with inputs and agreement from other people. In companies, for instance, a corporate positioning statement would need to be considered by as many senior managers as possible to gain consensus agreement and buy-in, and to ensure execution. Product managers would also need to seek other opinions and endorsements.

Before writing a positioning statement, it is vital that there is a complete understanding of the following areas:

- *Your brand*: This seems obvious, but you have to be very clear about what you can really offer that will attract the people you are trying to influence. With products, this will mean looking closely at all the features and attributes, and the benefits that people will derive from them. All the time you should be looking for factors that will help differentiate what *you* have to offer from what the competition is offering. The same goes for services. What service standards can you present that will give you the opportunity to suggest a competitive advantage? Companies themselves often have distinguishing characteristics, such as global stature, track record, personality, and other unique features that can be highlighted and used as differentiators.
- *The target audience(s) you want to influence*: Knowing what people need and want is critical, and there is a difference between the two. I might *need* some food to eat, but what I *want* is a curry. More than that, I might want a *vegetarian* curry because that kind of food fits in with my belief structure. It becomes important, therefore, to understand people's intangible requirements as well as their more tangible ones. Unless there is precision in customer understanding, the messages we send may be irrelevant and lose us credibility.
- *The competitors you are up against (competitive set)*: No strategy is complete without a thorough understanding of the competition, whether you are a football manager, marketing manager, entertainer, managing director, or prime minister. Some of the questions to ask might include:
  - Which competitors do customers consider?
  - What positioning strategies are the competitors using, and why?
  - What key messages are they sending?
  - What appears to be their competitive advantage and the key points of difference?
  - Why do customers buy from them?
  - What image do they currently have?
  - What differences do customers see between them and us?

- What competitor would they switch to if they moved from us? One of the major problems that can arise here is deciding just who the competition is. This issue is particularly relevant for fast-moving consumer goods, where the definition of categories becomes extremely important, but it does need to be considered in any positioning situation. For instance, if we were to ask whether or not Elton John is in the category of "rock music entertainers," we would almost certainly answer "yes"; however, if we were to ask whether he is competing with The Rolling Stones, we would probably say "no." Definition of the product category is therefore a critical first stage in competitor analysis, and is vital to the positioning effort.
- *Why you are different from and better than the competition*: Analysis of the above areas will allow you to make some accurate judgments as to what position to choose and which positioning strategy you need to employ in order to influence the perceptions of the target audience(s).
- *The desired perception you would like people to have of you*: Always set a goal in terms of how you want to be seen by people. When you are writing down this goal, try to do it using the language of the customer or the persons you are trying to influence. If you put yourself in their shoes, there is a greater likelihood that you will understand how they think and be successful in managing their perceptions, and you will find it easier to track whether you have achieved the intended image. When you write your positioning statement, certain things contained in it may be aspirational in nature and some factual. This doesn't matter, as these statements are for internal purposes only. However, the aspirational or desired consumer perceptions must be worked on hard in order to deliver on the promise. Communicating parts of the positioning may have to be delayed, therefore, until the brand can actually do what it says it can.

Some of the above analysis might entail commissioned research if you don't have the internal resources to carry it out, and it may take some time, but your communicated position will be much more focused and accurate as a result. Once you are ready to write the positioning statement, try to be as concise as possible.

How to Write and Use A Positioning Statement

There are many ways of writing positioning statements, but they should all contain certain elements. From past experience I have found the following template to be the most practical.

A POSITIONING STATEMENT TEMPLATE

BRAND X

is better than

COMPETITIVE SET

(The main competitors your brand is competing against in your category, industry, etc.)

for

TARGET MARKET

(The customer group or groups you are aiming for, stated, if possible, in terms of their needs and wants. For a master brand this would be broad, but for each customer segment it would be more clearly defined.)

because it

STRATEGIC COMPETITIVE ADVANTAGE

(The SPECIFIC advantage(s) your brand has, compared to others, in meeting those needs.)

with the result that

KEY PROPOSITION

(The real emotional—wherever possible—and rational benefits to be experienced by your target audience, derived mainly from the SCA.)

The Brand Personality (Character)

This is the personality your brand has, as discussed in earlier chapters. This can be stated separately at the end; or more usefully, the words that describe the personality can be used in the text of the positioning statement itself.

If you work methodically through this statement, you will achieve answers to the main questions of:

- Why are you better?
- Why are you different?

These two questions are of the utmost importance to consumers, who want to know why they should buy your brand in preference to others on offer. Only if these questions are answered truthfully and adequately will you be able to persuade customers that you should be their preferred choice. Great care must therefore be taken to ensure that the content of positioning statements is credible, believable, deliverable, and relevant to the wants and needs of the audience whose perceptions you are trying to influence.

Example: A Positioning Statement for an Airline

In this particular example, you will see the master brand personality for an Asian airline, which will differentiate it from other international carriers. You will also see how this can then be transferred down into positioning statements for each target audience. It is important in positioning statements to go into detail for segments, because their needs and wants are different, and so your total proposition will be different. However, the segment positioning statements take direction from the master brand statement to ensure consistency, while also ensuring relevance.

This is a real case in which all major segments of the market are addressed. The main things consumers look for when choosing to travel with airlines are safety, convenience, and a great brand experience via service, whether pre-flight, in-flight, or post-flight. You will find this reflected in the statements. You will also notice that the brand's strategic competitive advantage is carried throughout the different statements.

MASTER BRAND POSITIONING STATEMENT

AIRLINE BRAND X

is better than

Other international carriers

for

All users of airline services

because it

Employs state-of–the-art systems and technology, with global presence, complemented by the naturalness, warmth, and traditions of service of a national personality that represents the very best of *all* of Asia

with the result that

Every customer can have complete confidence in the understanding of their personal needs and wants and the natural, genuine willingness of Airline X people to care.

ECONOMY CLASS

POSITIONING STATEMENT

Airline Brand X

is better than

Every other international carrier

for

Those seeking a comfortable, safe, convenient journey that offers new standards in air travel with a fascinating cultural dimension

because it

Employs state-of-the-art systems and technology, complemented by the naturalness, warmth, and traditions of service of a national personality that represents the very best of *all* of Asia

With the Result That

Their voyage becomes a unique experience and a lasting memory.

SUPER ECONOMY CLASS

POSITIONING STATEMENT

AIRLINE BRAND X

is better than

Every other international carrier

for

Those seeking the space, comfort, and privacy of a new,
upgraded standard of air travel, along with the
experience of a fascinating
cultural dimension

because it

Offers all these benefits at a much lower cost than
conventional Business Class travel, with all the
naturalness, warmth, and traditions of service of a
national personality that represents the very best
of *all* of Asia

With the Result That

They arrive fresh and less stressed, having experienced
the air journey of a lifetime.

BUSINESS CLASS

POSITIONING STATEMENT

AIRLINE BRAND X

is better than

Every other international carrier

for

Business Class travelers seeking a vastly enhanced
experience of pure enjoyment

Because It

Offers all the Business Class space, luxury, and special
features expected of a sophisticated global airline, made
truly special by the naturalness, warmth, and service traditions
of a national personality that represents the very
best of *all* of Asia

With the Result That

They arrive happier, more refreshed, and more relaxed,
having enjoyed a superior form of delivery of all the privileges
and attention they deserve.

FIRST CLASS

POSITIONING STATEMENT

AIRLINE BRAND X

is better than

Every other international carrier

for

Those seeking absolute luxury, convenience, privacy, and individual recognition

because it

Offers unique First Class privileges and, in the naturalness, warmth, and service of their attendants, an incomparable experience of Asia

with the result that

Their flight becomes "a journey" in indulgence—given color and excitement by the fascinating traditions and combined personalities of the world's most exotic continent.

When you have positioned the company in this way, these statements must then be applied rigorously to product, service, staff, communications, etc. This part of brand management will be covered in later chapters.

Development of Taglines

Taglines are phrases that normally appear consistently after the brand name, supporting its personality and positioning. They are never used in isolation, always being prefaced by some form of communication. They cannot (and, indeed, don't have to) say everything. Rather, they have to be broad—able to lock down several messages, the thrust of which may change over time. They should, however, impart a sense of direction and provide the penultimate "full stop"—representing the final impression and, ideally, call to action, conveyed to the viewer, listener, or reader. Once created, they can be very successful in connecting the brand with the minds of target audiences, and in cementing the emotional association. Taglines need to firmly present "difference", claim superiority, effectively cover personality, service, and technical sophistication if necessary, cope with change, and be equally relevant to local and foreign markets. Most of all, they have to convey a sense of promise, excitement, and experience. All in just three or four words!

With respect to the positioning statements for the airline given above, here is one of several taglines suggested: "Your World of Difference." Does this tagline pass the test? Here is the justification:

- This line powerfully highlights the promise of difference, reinforcing the personality-based positioning and related, differentiating product development.
- It attracts interest and a desire to know more.
- It communicates what the airline's developmental process is all about—a quest to be different and better—both to consumers and their own staff.
- It implies superiority.
- It is broad, able to encompass and lend power to a host of messages. No specific promise is inherent.
- It becomes a most effective "full stop" for any and all specific messages conveyed in communications, reminding consumers that the benefits featured are not available elsewhere.
- "World" communicates globality, coverage, size (and, therefore, sophistication), yet in a way that supports the personality position.
- "World" communicates the feeling of a "cocoon," removed from the chaos and inconvenience that can accompany the air travel experience.
- Given the context in communications, a "World of Difference" becomes a reference to the country's cultural diversity, representative of the very best of all Asia.

- "Your" puts the emphasis on the customer. It encourages a sense of relationship. It conveys the impression that the airline puts the customer first.
- The line has a "softness" in tune with the brand personality traits.
- It is tight, simple, with ease of recall.
- It is confidently in tune with the strategy of outflanking and enveloping key competitors.
- It is safe. Should a radical change in market circumstances require a shift from the position, this statement will still apply to what has become an essential process of differentiation.

The following case concerns the Chinese company Haier. Haier has bravely created a niche position for itself in the United States and avoided the country-of-origin quality perceptions that might have arisen. However, positioning itself in a mature and sophisticated market was no easy task for an unknown foreign company.

CASE STUDY 12: HAIER

Positioning an Asian Brand in a Sophisticated Western Market: Those Who Dare Wins?

As a great deal of my time is spent within Asia, I often advise would-be global brand players from Asia to get to the number one position in their home market, then dominate their region, then go global if need be. The rationale behind this is simply that few global brands have ever become global without first being number one in their home market. Second, while researching foreign global markets, the common-sense approach suggests that you then go for number one in your region. This second step is tough enough, as Asia represents around half the world's population, but the task is a little easier for Asian companies as opposed to Western ones, as the understanding of cultures isn't a big problem. Finally, when you have size, volume, an established name, and experience, go for the global market if you feel you can support it and can make it into the top two or three.

Fast Track

China's top white goods manufacturer, Haier, has taken the fast track, in contrast to the normal progression suggested above. CEO Zhang Ruimin took a non-driven state enterprise making poor-quality goods, made quality the imperative, and turned it into a company that is now the world's fourth-largest white goods manufacturer, churning out 43 million products annually that span across 15,100 varieties of appliances. Haier is ranked number one in the China market and generated US$17.8 billion in worldwide sales revenue in 2008. In that year, it sold 12 million refrigerators, becoming the world number one in this category. It has won numerous accolades; among others, it is the only Chinese brand to be in the Top 100 global brand rankings for three consecutive years. So popular is the Haier brand in China that people pay a premium for it, according to Carrefour, which is located in Qingdao. In fact, its washing machine costs more than a similar US Whirlpool-brand model. But can this brand perception be carried to overseas markets?

Zhang has recently cut straight to his ultimate goal of being a top-five maker of white goods in the United States by taking Western companies such as GE and Whirlpool head-on, despite his brand still not being a household name in Asia. However, the quality dimension first had to be addressed, as no brand can survive without first-class quality, with which Asian companies traditionally haven't been associated. Zhang has always realized the importance of quality. Such is his passion that, as a senior manager in the 1980s, he once gathered his staff together and smashed a selection of defective refrigerator products with a sledgehammer to get across his point of view on the vital importance of quality.

Country-of-Origin Issues

One of the most critical problems facing Asian brands in recent years is the perception of "cheap and poor quality." This perception has persisted for many decades, and has proved difficult to shift. It took 30 years for the Japanese brands to shift a similar perception, but Chinese goods are still in the "poor quality" category, which is why Haier has chosen just this issue on which to fight its battles. And the chief executive really has taken the fight to the commercial "enemy"—the US—where quality begins at home.

THE STRATEGY

The strategy for Haier wasn't to build at low cost and export to the US products that would be seen as "made in China." The company realized that while the Nikes of this world—because of the power of their brand names—could market products made in Asia, the Haier brand name would suffer from the home country labeling.

Instead, a strategy was used to reverse the conditions of manufacture so that Haier was made in the US. The company bought land enough for several factories in Camden, South Carolina, and spent US$30 million on its first refrigerator plant. This was an important part of "managing perceptions"—what brand management is all about—and establishing a secure base for the future, albeit at an increased cost of production. Staffed mainly by local people, Haier now uses the label "Made in the USA."

Haier claims to have helped grow the market in certain categories. Since its entry into the US, Haier has established itself as the top-selling brand for compact refrigerators and home wine coolers; while being ranked number three in freezers. In fact, Haier has been instrumental in growing the compact refrigerator market by 50 percent a year after the brand's entry into the US. Haier is also sensitive to the needs of different markets, and it is keen to give consumers aesthetic value. The introduction of the wine cooler in the US is a good example of this understanding, with its sophisticated smoked-glass door, curvaceous lines, soft lighting, and chrome racks. It is very much an up-market product, selling for about US$400, and has been featured on the cover of the International Wine Accessories catalogue. This innovation was also brought to the market quickly, with less than a year from product conception and design to retail availability.

Haier has recognized that the price-commodity trap is waiting, and is trying hard to avoid competing on price and promotions, through a focus on quality, design, innovation, and giving consumers what they really want. One of the key initiatives that Haier has taken to improve its image is by demonstrating its concern for the environment. Using innovation and technology, it has started to introduce eco-friendly appliances that help project the image of a company that cares for the environment, as well as its customers' concerns. For example, in 2008, Haier, with GE, developed environmentally friendly washing machines that have the latest energy-saving technology, low noise emission, and more user-friendly features.

PARTNERSHIPS AND STRUCTURE

Haier America Trading has been looking for strategic partnerships that will give its brand both recognition and credibility, and has managed to get Wal-Mart, among others, to carry some of its products, mainly small refrigerators and freezers. Haier adds value to its retailers by providing logistical assistance, inventory management, and stress-free customer service.

Speed to market and product innovation are essential items for Zhang, who claims, "In this information age, whoever is the fastest to meet customer demands wins. I work with whoever can give me the information and technology to meet consumer needs." For this reason, Haier has teamed up with renowned brand names such as Ericsson, with the intention of using Ericsson's Bluetooth wireless technology in its products. Such alliances are giving Haier access to a valuable R&D base that it currently doesn't have. As far as innovation goes, Haier has about 400 new products hitting the market each year. Some of these products are positioned at the frontiers of technology, such as the company's recently launched LCD HDTVs and iPod-enabled TVs that can play video, audio, and graphic files from iPod devices via the built-in iPod dock. As of June 2008, Haier had already accumulated 8,333 patented technology certificates under its name, and its dual-drive washing machine technology was included in the IEC standard proposal. This demonstrates that Haier has acquired world-class innovation capabilities in product R&D. All these developments are consistent with Zhang's vision of making innovation a key driver in his business model.

Haier's failure/success rate isn't known, and one wonders if the company can keep up with this rate of change. Zhang's response is: "Wherever we go, the strategy is always to break in with one product, then introduce more and more along the way. The strategy has worked in every market." Zhang says that Haier uses niche marketing and can produce a run of around 30,000 units of one product before moving on to the next. Some of them are clearly *very* niche—for example, a washing machine featuring a virtual fish tank! Currently the company is in 56 categories of products and is practicing mass customization.

Haier has learned from the mistakes of others in managing its brand. Typically, Japanese companies operating in the US have a wholly owned subsidiary headed by headquarters' executives. Zhang has a different philosophy: he is smart enough to recognize that his staff are still many years behind their counterparts in developed countries, and he actively encourages the joining together of foreign experts and his managers. In the US, Haier America Trading is a joint venture between Haier, which has the majority shareholding, and a small group of US investors. The Haier parent company is involved only in corporate and brand strategy; while the US stakeholders, who understand the market, run the operations. They are given a great deal of autonomy, and this enables both speed and flexibility in decision making. According to Michael Jemal, president and CEO of Haier America Trading, it is "the opportunity of a lifetime to launch a brand, to build a brand, to create a market."

BRAND CULTURE

Lexus, the company and brand created by Toyota to break into the luxury car market in the United States, sent its Japanese managers to the United States well ahead of start-up time in order to gain a better understanding of the market and US consumer behavior, by staying with American families. It then placed these executives in charge of operations. Haier, however, has again taken a different route. The top managers are American.

The brand culture is important to Haier, and prospective employees must successfully complete a 40-hour initiation program before they are appointed. The program emphasizes teamwork, safety, and the importance of quality. On the factory floor, memorabilia from the Haier heritage are displayed, including a photograph of the sledgehammer incident. Employees can earn a trip to China to help them appreciate the values of the company and to experience Chinese culture, which for some is a once-in-a-lifetime experience. Thus, Haier attempts to blend the best of East and West in its employee relations.

The Future

With 20.6 percent growth in 2008, Haier is going from strength to strength. The company is currently a recognized leader in nine products in terms of domestic market share, and is the third player in terms of three products in the world market. Haier employs more than 50,000 people around the world across its 64 trading companies (19 overseas), 29 manufacturing plants (24 overseas), eight design centers (five overseas), and 16 industrial parks (four overseas); with its products found across 160 countries. It currently has 30 percent of the small-refrigerator market in the US. The Haier brand is on TV sets, home theater systems, air-conditioners, DVD players, and mobile phones, in addition to a restaurant chain and Haier Brothers Cartoons. Zhang admits that Haier is learning much from the power brands, such as Nike and Dell, and instead of manufacturing most of its output, will seek more outsourcing opportunities.

Haier wants to be a global brand, like the Asian brands Toyota and Sony. In terms of makers of kitchen appliances it is already number six, behind Whirlpool, Electrolux, GE, Bosch-Siemens Hausgerate, and Samsung Electronics. This focus will help Zhang's brand to reach its goal, but the temptation of brand extensions could lead Haier to try to do too much too soon. For instance, an extension into pharmaceuticals hasn't been successful. There is no doubt, however, that if it can survive in the US and not dilute its brand equity too much, by trying to be all things to all people, then a global brand will emerge. The passion is there.

This is just one Chinese company. More entrepreneurs like Zhang, with ambition, passion, and flair, and controlling huge companies such as Haier, will emerge from this tremendous country. And China's entry as a member of the World Trade Organization in 2001 will almost certainly mean the end of the domination of global branding by Western companies in some basic goods categories over the next few years.

I would like to conclude this chapter by emphasizing that good positioning brings about differentiation and brand strength. When a brand occupies a distinctive position in consumers' minds, it is difficult for competitors to gain the advantage. The more salient that position is to consumers, the stronger the brand will be. Good positions are built by really understanding what turns consumers on—the consumer insight I mentioned in Chapter 2. When brand managers achieve strong positions, there is always the temptation to try and extend the brand into other categories and markets. The issues involved here are considered in Chapter 5. The next chapter also deals with the selection of brand architecture, which can impact positioning and brand strength.

Brand
Architecture

Brand architecture is an extremely complex subject, where few rules apply, but no book on brand management would be complete without some discussion of it. This chapter summarizes the basic choices and arguments for different types of brand architecture.

Levels of Branding

Several levels of branding can be identified:

- product branding;
- line branding;
- range branding;
- corporate branding with product descriptors;
- shared branding; and
- endorsed branding.

Each level represents different degrees of differentiation and origin. I will briefly explain the differences between them below, and discuss the main advantages and disadvantages of each.

Product Branding

This is where a brand name and exclusive position are allocated to one product. Companies adopting this approach give complete autonomy to every brand, and each brand stands or falls on its own merits. There is no apparent connection between the brand and other brands. (For instance, Procter & Gamble has used this approach extensively with products such as Ariel and Dash in the household detergent market;

while Novotel, Regency Park, and Ibis are product brands of the Accor Group aimed at different target audiences.)

ADVANTAGES

- They can occupy precise positions and be aimed at precise target audiences.
- As a result, the multiple brands can occupy the whole category.
- They allow for risk, as failure doesn't damage the parent.
- Retail shelf space may be easier to get, as the brand stands on its own.
- One brand name per product helps customers perceive difference.

DISADVANTAGES

- They are costly, as each requires its own advertising and promotion (A&P) budget.
- There is little room for extension, which is only achieved by product renewal and innovation. (For instance, Tide has had over 70 changes to product, design, and other aspects of the brand.)

Line Branding

Line brands offer one basic product under one name, but also offer complementary products, as is the case with Vidal Sassoon shampoos, rinses, hair salons, and so on. Dove not only has soap, but also now has facial wipes, body washes, anti-aging cleansers, deodorants, and more.

ADVANTAGES

- The brand can be extended to some extent.
- Complementary extensions can reinforce and strengthen the brand image.
- Marketing costs can be shared across products.

DISADVANTAGES

- Lines are limited to the discrete positioning.
- Other extensions are difficult.

Range Branding

Range brands have a unique brand positioning but many products under the brand name—examples include Bird's Eye frozen foods and competitor Schweppes soft drinks, which have dozens of products under the range names.

ADVANTAGES

- Focuses on one brand name.
- Can be a source of heavy brand value.
- Synergy of communications across all products.

DISADVANTAGES

- Excessive extension can dilute brand success, and sub-brands or lines may have to be brought in to liven up the brand (as was the case with Lean Cuisine) and develop personality.
- Expenses start to mount up, as various lines under a range need different packaging, and so on.

Corporate Branding with Product Descriptors

This is where one single brand name, the company name, covers all products, as with Canon cameras, facsimile machines, and printers. The products don't have names, but tend to have other descriptors, either functional (Canon MX 7600 printer) or alpha-numeric (Mercedes S320).

ADVANTAGES

- There are economies of scale across communications platforms.
- Every product contributes to overall brand awareness, equity, and value.
- It becomes easier to enter new markets.
- Multiple extensions are possible, but only with good new products.
- Horizontal extensions are easier than vertical ones.

DISADVANTAGES

- A poor corporate brand image hinders new brand introductions and existing brand success.
- Extensions are easier, but are not always accepted by the public.
- The more categories the brand goes into, the weaker the overall image may become.

Shared Branding

This strategy is another corporate-linked approach, except that the products are named (for instance, Calvin Klein's MAN and Microsoft Windows). The product and parent brand share the spotlight, but the corporate brand name is usually shown in front of the product brand. In this way, there is full leverage of both brands.

ADVANTAGES

- Parental support adds trust and confidence.
- The product can ride on parental core values and image.
- Less expensive to launch than the above brand strategies.
- Products add to parental brand value.

DISADVANTAGES

- Restrained by the core brand of the parent, and what it is known for.
- Allows for less freedom than the endorsement strategy (see below).
- Failure can damage reputation across the major corporate activity and devalue the corporate brand.

Endorsed Branding

Here the difference from shared branding is the fact that the parent brand takes only an endorsement role—for instance, Band Aid (where the parent company name Johnson & Johnson appears only in a lower corner of the packaging).

ADVANTAGES

- More freedom to extend into many categories.
- Parent acts as a guarantee of quality and legitimacy.
- Products add to parental value.
- Failure doesn't transfer across many categories.
- Least expensive way of giving branding support.

DISADVANTAGES

- Bad corporate reputation and performance can affect the product brand.

The above options represent a continuum from which a company can choose its architecture. However, there is a trend nowadays to favor the corporate end of the spectrum.

The Company As the Brand

There is a definite trend toward the company being involved in the branding process, whether through shared and endorsement branding, or by other means. Even the master of product branding, Procter & Gamble, now has a worldwide strategy to leverage the corporate brand name by attaching it to some of its product brands as a source reference.

To sum up, there are several reasons for the company brand name to appear in one form or another:

- For every product, you get a double message underlining the product and the company.
- The core values of the company wrap around the product, resulting in consumer confidence.
- There is less confusion for consumers, as they know the source of the product.

- There are more possibilities for brand extensions.
- There are many synergies and cost savings in A&P.
- The financial value of the company brand is enhanced, corporate brands being strategic business assets in their own right.
- Corporate branding increases overall image power and reputation.
- And as the late Akio Morita, founder of Sony, said: "I have always believed that the company name is the life of an enterprise. It carries responsibility and guarantees the quality of the product."

Portfolio Management and Sub-Brands

As discussed above, the decision as to whether to have different brands requiring different branding strategies varies by company, and there are no hard-and-fast rules about what to do. The main reason for holding many brands is that no one brand can cover every market, or even every sector of a single market. Some companies attempt to do this by using saturation strategies, such as Seiko with its global range of over 2,000 watches under the Seiko, Lorus, and Pulsar brands. Others, such as Mars, hold only a few "power" brands that are advertised strongly and produced efficiently in volume. Some companies adopt corporate and product brand strategies. For example, Cadbury uses the corporate brand for chocolate bars and product branding for sweets. Toyota, a brand that is well established in most price sectors of the car market, found that the parental image wouldn't transfer to the luxury car segment, and so it had to create a stand-alone brand, Lexus. This was a good move that is in danger of backfiring, so to speak, as the Lexus brand moves down into lower price ranges and opens up the dual possibilities of cannibalization of Toyota brands and a dilution of the Lexus brand. In the first quarter of 2009, Lexus no longer occupied top position in the luxury car segment in the US.

What must be clearly established, whatever is contained in the multi-brand portfolio, is that there is no overlap between brand territories, as this can result in consumer confusion and sub-optimization of sales. Finally, it isn't unusual to find a company with many brands promoting some to the detriment of others. It is vital that annual brand audits are undertaken, and financial valuations of each brand carried out if possible, to determine which brands are doing well and which are flagging, and why. Shell values each of its brands every year, and then uses this information in deciding how to allocate market resources to the various brands.

Sub-brands are often confused with product brands, and tend to be used in industries dealing with fashion, trend-related categories, and fast-moving consumer goods, where different positions are required for different offerings and a single brand cannot cover them all. Versace presents itself under the main brand for its mature customer base, with Versus for the younger segment. Armani does the same with Emporio Armani.

Sub-brands don't tend to be used when the main corporate brand can cover all products or services, as is the case with heavy machinery, consumer durables, and computers.

Case Study 13 illustrates how a fast-growing brand in a niche market pays attention to building corporate brand value through a consistent naming architecture across its product and sub-brand portfolio.

CASE STUDY 13: RAFFLES INTERNATIONAL

Master Branding Endorsement

In 1996, there was one hotel in the Raffles Group—the famous Raffles Hotel in Singapore. In 2001 there were 38 hotels under Raffles management. The Raffles International brand started in 1989, built around a famous product associated with top-quality service. The word "International" was introduced to add vision to the brand, and now the brand name stands for the promise of product and service excellence. Since then, Raffles has acquired other famous brand names, such as Brown's Hotel in London and Hotel Vier Jahreszeiten in Germany. Many other property acquisitions followed, including the Swissotel chain. The aim was to have the scale of 12,000 rooms by the end of 2003.

But despite this rapid niche area growth, there was always a conscious effort to build a consistent and meaningful brand architecture. The focus of the business of the Raffles brand is lifestyle, not property. The Raffles International master brand developed a two-tier strategy: the Raffles-branded hotels and resorts targeted affluent leisure and business travelers; while the Swissotel and Merchant Court hotels aimed to give quality and comfort to the modern business traveler. The challenge for Raffles management was how to keep the brand equity of all the famous brand names in the portfolio, and yet build up the equity of the Raffles International master brand. The link was accomplished by keeping the "Raffles International" name in taglines on all hotel corporate identity and communications materials. For example, for the prestigious brand hotel Brown's, the endorsement was "Brown's Hotel, a Raffles International Hotel," while for the Swissotel and Merchant Court hotels each name was signed off with the tagline, "Managed by Raffles International." On September 30, 2005, Raffles International announced a change in its ownership from Raffles Holdings Limited to Colony Capital, LLC. This change followed the successful completion of the sale by Raffles Holdings of its hotel business to Colony Capital, LLC for an enterprise value of S$1.72 billion. The successful Raffles branding brought huge financial rewards.

Linking Visual Identity with Architecture

Top brands are good at linking their brand architecture well with the brand's visual identity. A case in point is Intel, which uses a shared branding approach. Intel is the corporate master brand, and there are three branded platforms, with all products fitting into one of these platforms. With every product, the parent name "Intel" precedes the product name, and the logo is consistently used on packaging along with the corporate colors. An example of this is shown in Figure 4.1 in simplified form.

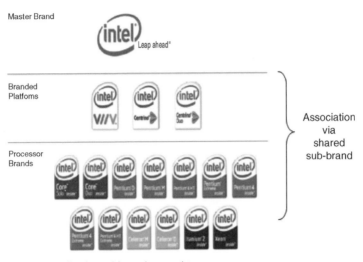

Figure 4.1   Intel's shared branding architecture

The issue of concern is not with Intel's visual architecture—it looks very good, and is very consistent with respect to how the shared branding approach is applied. The issue is that, although neatly lined up, consumers have difficulty in understanding the differences between products (not all of which are shown in the figure). For instance, according to Intel's website, the Core family at present includes: Core Solo, Core 2 Solo, Core Duo, Core 2 Duo, Core 2 Quad, Core 2 Extreme, Core i7, and Core i Extreme Edition. Pentium was supposed to have been phased out but still appears to be in the line-up. From a brand management standpoint, there is a lack of clear explanation in the product promotional material.

While consumers are trying to get to grips with what all these product brand names mean to them, Intel has just announced that it will again be changing its branding line-up. Centrino won't remain as a "platform," where it stood for technologies that included a microprocessor, a separate product category called a chip set, and chips that manage wireless networking. It will remain only as representing wireless networking technology. The brand name "Core" will be the flagship brand. But brand extensions such as Core 2 Duo will also go. Instead, three performance grades will be branded as i3, i5, and i7. Pentium and Celeron will remain. Now, how about that for simplicity?

These changes are supposed to help us, the consumer. Intel spokesperson, Bill Calder, is quoted in the *Wall Street Journal* of June 18, 2009 as saying: "The . . . fact is, we have a complex structure with too many platform brands, product names, and we've made things confusing for consumers and IT buyers in the process." Right!

Co-Branding Opportunities

This topic could just as easily have been addressed in either of the two following chapters, but I will deal with it here, as it can play an important role in, and potentially do damage to, attempts to increase the value of a brand name. Co-branding, sometimes called cross-platform marketing, is increasingly popular as firms look for new ways to reach their target audiences. Credit cards are good examples of co-branding, linking up with all sorts of businesses. The main reason for co-branding is to reach more of the consumers you want who are currently customers of someone else. Another reason is that co-branding enables marketing costs to be shared—an important consideration when a major campaign can cost in excess of US$100 million. An example here is Formula 1 teaming up with SingTel to promote its inaugural night race in Singapore. In this instance, Formula 1 was able to leverage SingTel's marketing efforts in respect of its various services to promote its race in Singapore. In a similar vein, SingTel was able to garner massive exposure through co-branded marketing events and programs with Formula 1. Of course, the third major factor in considering co-branding as a business opportunity is to give more benefits to your own customer base and so enhance brand loyalty.

There are many opportunities for co-branding in every industry. For example, ANA and Intercontinental Hotel Group (IHG), two large organizations in the hotel and leisure industry, formed a joint venture in April 2007. Through this arrangement, all ANA hotels across Japan will be co-branded with the IHG group of hotels and be renamed to one of the following: ANA Intercontinental, ANA Crowne Plaza, or ANA Holiday Inn. "The pace of our co-branding effort means that we are serious about making our hotels the preferred choice among guests, corporate clients and event planners across Japan. Our key focus now is on gaining even deeper insight into the needs and expectations of our customers in order to further enhance our product and service offerings," said Chris Moloney, chief executive officer, IHG ANA Hotels Group of Japan (www.asiatraveltips.com/news07/203-JapanHotels.html).

Another significant co-branding exercise was the huge commitment by Coca-Cola to the 2001 Harry Potter movie, *Harry Potter and the Philosopher's Stone* (*Sorcerer's Stone* in the United States). Coca-Cola poured US$150 million into the movie, in return for which it received exclusive global marketing partner status. This allowed the beverage company to do what it had wanted to do for a long time, which was to reach out to its young target audience without alienating parents. What is more, it gave Coca-Cola better and faster brand communications coverage than traditional advertising. For the movie-maker Warner Brothers, there was a huge funding boost that took care of its advertising budget worries.

Coca-Cola is currently sponsoring the hugely successful television show *American Idol,* whose judges are all seen by the show's millions of viewers drinking from large cups of the famous drink.

When considering a co-branding opportunity, it is important to evaluate it carefully before making a commitment, as certain things must be in place for success to be achieved. Unless your customers are going to receive (and will be *aware* that they will receive) real benefits from the exercise, don't bother. Second, ensure that the target audiences of the partners have similar types of demographic and psychographic profiles. Third, ensure that the partners have brand values similar to those of your brand; otherwise, there will be significant strategy problems and working together will be problematic. Finally, make sure that the brand partner you have chosen doesn't eclipse your own brand name. If you get it right, co-branding is a good way of extending the reach of your brand portfolio without product extensions and new product launches.

Orphan Brands—Brand Trafficking

Orphan brands are branded products that have been neglected by their parents, and either left to die or sold off to new parents. Usually, they haven't made the grade within major brand company portfolios, and as a result of their mediocre performance aren't given the star treatment.

Global brand holding companies such as Unilever and Procter & Gamble try to sell these orphans in order to regain some of their investment cost. The brands themselves are often in the ruthless "kill or be killed" category of fast-moving consumer goods. Other companies with lesser portfolios buy them in the belief that, given more attention and nourishment, they will produce good returns on investment. They also buy these brands because they already exist, have their own identities, have proved to be reasonably accepted by the public, and don't come with the high costs of market launches. But this strategy hasn't always proved to be a successful one for the new "parents."

For example, in 1996 Aurora Foods Inc. (now known as Pinnacle Foods Corporation after a merger in 2003), which was then part of a private investor group, Dartford Partnership, bought a number of brands from Unilever, including Mrs. Butterworth's (a brand of syrup), for a little over US$114 million, citing a significant growth potential that hadn't been realized due to a lack of corporate support and marketing resources from Unilever in recent years. Unilever had made the decision to cut its brand portfolio from 1,600 to 400 brands in order to reduce costs, and to increase its focus on power brands that the company felt were really going to go places. Mrs. Butterworth's was clearly not a power brand in Unilever terminology, with annual sales registering zero growth prior to being acquired. Aurora purchased another "orphan" brand, Duncan Hines, from Procter & Gamble in 1997. Duncan Hines then generated less than US$400 million in sales, as compared to Procter & Gamble's overall annual sales revenue of US$35.3 billion. After acquiring Mrs. Butterworth's and Duncan Hines, Aurora started to develop them with innovative offering, packaging, and marketing efforts. For instance, in a recent product development effort, Duncan Hines introduced frozen, ready-to-bake mixes that offer a fuss-free and convenient approach to home baking. Today, Duncan Hines has the top-selling cake mix in the US; while Mrs. Butterworth's is growing at a relatively fast rate, recording double-digit growth in 2007.

The "buy an orphan" strategy has theoretical promise, but in practice new parents—in this case, Aurora—underestimated the power of the retailers in determining sales through shelf space support, which they often reserve for power brand owners. Also underestimated was the power of the grocery store chains to give preferential shelf space to their own private-label brands.

So, while many retail "orphan" brands are attractive, unless they receive substantial support they are unlikely to perform. And whether they can ever get to be top performers is questionable if the corporate branding giants have already cast them aside.

Hybrid Branding

Hybrid brands are brands born out of the intercourse between two or more companies or brands. The rationale is similar to that of co-branding, but there is one extra ingredient here, and that is that the companies often are similar in what they produce, but they combine their experience in the hope of creating a winning brand that they might not be able to create on their own. It is a little like a merger, but where a newly formed brand is the focus. An example is Virgin Atlantic joining up with Singapore Telecom's mobile company, Singtel Mobile, to form Virgin Mobile for the Asian market. Singtel had a good knowledge of Asia but not a really acceptable regional brand name, while Virgin had the brand name but little knowledge of mobile telephony and Asian markets. Potentially, it was an ideal marriage, which in 2001 was consummated by a grand launch, profiled and reinforced by somewhat fun, cheeky, and very different marketing activities in line with Virgin's brand values. Sadly, it wasn't a successful marriage and the brand was withdrawn from the market.

Another example, discussed in Case Study 14, is that of Sony and Ericsson. This hybrid brand has also been unsuccessful, due to poor brand management.

CASE STUDY 14: SONY AND ERICSSON

A Winning Partnership?

In September 2001, Sony Corporation and Telefon AB L.M. Ericsson launched a 50:50-owned new mobile telephone brand and logo called Sony Ericsson Mobile Communications. For Ericsson, one sensed at the time an air of desperation, as the brand's market share had dropped consistently over the previous few years to under 10 percent—left, like Motorola, in the wake of the Nokia revolution. Ericsson was literally banking on this new venture to pull it out of the financial problems it faced—namely, debt, a lack of profitability, and little consumer confidence in its brand, given a flagging market scenario.

For Sony, whose ambitions reached (as they still do) well beyond consumer electronics into infotainment, the proposition was expected to be a boost to its existing business in a market where it lacked expertise and needed to grow its relatively small market share in mobile telecommunications.

The "big idea" was that Sony Ericsson would provide the technology capability and Sony the market understanding. The new president of Sony Ericsson, Katsumi Ihara, claimed the new hybrid brand made perfect sense. "We are still complementary. Ericsson is strong in wireless, and we are a little weak in that respect. But we know the consumer."

The author's opinion of this "wedding" was, and still is, that there are several obstacles to overcome before both suitors would gel, namely:

- the "logo = brand" mentality;
- spending on the product versus spending on brand;
- the volatile market;
- the fickle consumer;
- the incumbent giant; and
- what's the big difference?

Let's have a quick look at each of these.

1. *Logo = Brand:* Sony Ericsson created a new logo that looked like a green throat lozenge, and was to be seen moving in an animated phone screen as well as appearing on ads. On handset screens the logo would react "with emotion," according to company spokesman Mats Georgson. "It will behave like it's alive," he said. "It can morph and jump around—it's liquid identity or 'another me.' We want something that can constantly evolve and surprise you." To me, this is a creative overruling strategy. Logos are only valuable as memory recall devices and are usually constantly applied. This sounded like a gimmick that could backfire. Too much attention and money was given to the logo production. Logos aren't brands and aren't prime differentiators.

2. *Spending on product versus spending on brand:* Asian companies are famous for not investing in brands, which is one of the prime reasons why there are few global brands coming from that region. Japanese companies are typical of this and don't manage their brands as effectively as they might. Hence, we saw Sony Ericsson president Katsumi Ihara saying a big investment in this new brand wasn't required because the name on the logo speaks for itself. "It doesn't make sense to spend a lot of money," he said. "People will already know what it is. Instead of spending a lot of money on the brand, it makes more business sense to spend on the product." This is dangerous thinking, as new brands aren't successful without strong promotional support.

3. *The volatile market:* With the launch of a new brand you have only one chance to get it right, and this brand was launched in a volatile market, which remains volatile and highly competitive. The mobile phone market has experienced a slowdown due to the global economic crisis that set in during the fourth quarter of 2008. IDC

(a global technology consulting firm) has reported that the global market for mobile phones has since experienced a decline of 12.8 percent in shipment volume. With strong competition, Sony Ericsson is now in fourth position in the global rankings. With Nokia, Samsung, and LG leading the pack with their attractive brand appeal coupled with innovative technology and features, Sony Ericsson has to contend both with the competition and the global economic crisis.

4. *The incumbent giant:* Nokia rules the market with a share in excess of 39.1 percent as at the end of 2008. Sony Ericsson's share of 8.4 percent has never really made an impact on its own. Neither Ericsson nor Sony has created the emotional associations that consumers love, and which breed brand loyalty, and I see nothing to suggest that things are going to be different with the new venture. Indeed, brand spend isn't a high priority, as we have seen above, and this is how emotional associations are largely created. Neither Ericsson nor Sony is an expert at branding, unlike their giant rival.

5. *The fickle consumer:* Consumers of mobile phones are already product and brand savvy. Sony Ericsson will have to do a lot of persuading to get customers to switch from brands with which they are already familiar—and, to some extent, happy. With minimum brand spend, this is unlikely to be achieved unless the product itself is spectacularly different. It is unlikely that this will ever be the case, as Sony Ericsson is still a follower in new product development and innovation. Moreover, consumers are now more knowledgeable about corporate affairs, and neither of the two partners has been pushing out great results recently; just the opposite, in fact. Consumers are risk adverse.

6. *What's the big difference?:* Mobile phones are commodities, being more or less the same in terms of size, weight, battery life, features, and so on. Nokia is far ahead of the

rest of the market because of its superior branding and design. Only strong brands can command a differentiated offering that appeals emotionally to their followers. This was illustrated by Apple, which, although it had no track record in producing mobile phones, was able immediately to carve out a segment of the mobile phone market with its iPhone because of its massive emotional brand appeal among Apple brand loyalists. The question for Sony Ericsson is: Given the absence of powerful branding, why is its product different and better? Logo differentiation won't be a sufficient reason for success.

Merger and Acquisition Issues

Naming and Consumer Confusion

Mergers and acquisitions (M&As) can sometimes create problems for brands. For instance, if the names of the brands aren't retained, or if the names are joined, as was the case with ExxonMobil and DaimlerChysler, then there is the issue of how to explain this to consumers. ExxonMobil explained its name change to consumers soon after the merger of the two companies in 1999. An advertisement that it ran in the press read:

> We're as brand loyal as you are.
>
> Loyalty is a two-way street. So along the street, road or motorway we aren't about to confuse our customers. Yes, we've merged. But our brands Esso, Mobil and Exxon will still be there. What will change is the company behind them. ExxonMobil is a new name for technology, efficiency and service. Helping our old names treat you better than ever.

The ad, which included a website address, showed the two company logos, with the sign of ExxonMobil. Here was a company that cared about its customers and their emotional associations with their brands. It took the trouble to reassure them, and at the same time promise them a better experience.

By contrast, DaimlerChrysler, which also was formed in 1999 following a merger, took two years to explain its position to consumers. In the *Asian Wall Street Journal* of October 9, 2001 and in *Fortune* magazine of October 15, the company produced what I consider an appallingly uncreative advertisement, the copy for which showed on the left-hand page a telephone operator saying: "Good morning. Welcome to Mercedes-Benz-Jeep®-Dodgesmart-FreightlinerSterlingSetra. How can I help you?" This was followed by a headline on the right-hand page: "Just call us DaimlerChrysler." This, in turn, was followed by:

> We don't really need to introduce our brands anymore. They have all made history through their own achievements, and their names are known the world over. Of course, the fact that they all work under one roof means we will always have a wealth of experience and innovative ideas to draw on. Something that will help us stay miles ahead of the competition in the future. Find out more at www.daimlerchrysler.com.

The sign-off was the name "DaimlerChrysler" with the tagline, "Answers For Questions To Come."

I am tempted to say, "Words fail me." Now, I don't know what the DaimlerChrysler brand personality is, or even whether it has one, but any company that advertises will create a personality in consumers' minds, whether by default or not. This ad sends out awful messages about the DaimlerChrysler personality from the tone and manner of the copy. And I have no clue as to what the tagline meant. Take a look at the example of copy analysis for Malaysia Airlines given in Chapter 6 (Case Study 26), and then analyze this example.

When agencies present brand managers with advertising copy, it should be checked against the brand personality to determine whether it is "on strategy" or not.

Brand Names and Equity

As can be seen from the above efforts, some companies believe that there is considerable brand equity in established and famous brand names, and remove them at their peril. Others seem not to care. For example, when Rhone-Poulec and Hoechst merged, they removed both brand names and created a totally new and meaningless name, Aventis. Huge amounts of money have had to be spent to raise brand awareness, but still the brand equity has been lost, and consumers lack clarity about the brand's heritage and what it stands for.

New names, like new logos, have suddenly become a "must have" for some companies, who sometimes will pay large sums for nonsensical or irrelevant names. Importantly, the main purpose of branding—differentiation—appears to be forgotten, as many names are very similar. The end-result is that the consumer is mystified, confused, often irritated, and totally clueless about the message the name is supposed to contain.

In an extraordinary move, in 2001 Acer spun off its parts and accessories business to create a company called Benq, with a stated intent to spend US$30 million in advertising to promote the name and concept. The name meant something to Acer—it is a compression of "Bringing Enjoyment and Quality to Life." The chairman and co-founder of the Acer Group, Stan Shih, said: "We are changing the brand name for the future."

Apparently, market research studies among consumers, including focus groups, revealed that people thought the name strange but unique, with some pronouncing it as "Ben-Q" and others "Beng." President K.Y. Lee said at the time, "More importantly, strange name notwithstanding, they said they will remember it."

But memory is one thing and emotional association is another. In this case, Benq never seemed to be fully understood by the public, and hasn't proved to be successful, although its name was only one of its problems. It is most unusual for well-known and accepted brand names to throw away brand equity and value that has been painstakingly built over time, and although I have bought from Acer in the past I'm not so sure I would like to buy from Benq!

The British Post Office Group received a public relations caning when it changed its name to Consignia. Consumers were affronted, offended, and bewildered. One reader of the *Daily Telegraph* wrote: "I hope the new name will be consignia'd to the dustbin."

By the way, are you driving an Acura, Asuna, Altima, Cortina, Integra, Elantra, Sonata, Sentra, or Maxima? Whatever happened to meaningful differentiation?

Dave Barry, in the *International Herald Tribune* of April 7–8, 2001, summed up the situation as follows:

But my question is: Why do companies keep changing their names? And why do they always change them to names that don't MEAN anything? We consumers like names that reflect what the company does. We know, for example, that International Business Machines makes business machines, and Ford makes Fords, and Sara Lee makes us fat. But we don't know, from the name "Verizon," what Verizon does. As far as I can tell, Verizon consists of some big telephone companies that joined together. So why couldn't they call themselves "An Even Bigger Telephone Company"?

And what in the world is "Accenture"? This is a company that buys a LOT of ads, the overall message of which seems to be: "Accenture—A Company That Buys A Lot Of Ads." I checked the Accenture Internet site, and here's what it says about its name: "Accenture is a coined word that connotes putting an accent or emphasis on the future"...

This brings me to my idea for how you can make big money. You start by inventing a new, modern-sounding company name, such as "Paradil" or "Gerbadigm," which are coined words that connote a combination of "paradigm" and "Gerbil." Then you print official-looking invoice forms for this company, and you send out a mass-mailing of bills for, let's say $20.38 apiece, to several million randomly selected people. You enclose an announcement with a perky corporate marketing statement that is clearly a lie, and thus appears to be totally realistic, such as: "We've changed our name to serve you better!"

Barry's article has a terrifying element of truth in it. To summarize, names should be:

- short;
- memorable;
- meaningful;
- relevant; and
- different.

The following case study illustrates how one company, Marriott, absorbed another and found itself with architectural and positioning problems; while Case Study 16 provides an example of two companies— Carrefour and Ahold—that have adopted the two extreme positions of the brand architecture continuum in their M&A activities.

CASE STUDY 15: MARRIOTT INTERNATIONAL INC.

Acquisitions and the Problem of Brand Fit

In some industries it is difficult to grow the brand and the business via normal means, such as extensions. This is typified by the service industries, such as hospitality, where the process takes too long to accomplish, and/or the capital cost of doing so is enormous. Instead, mergers and acquisitions are often the route through, providing fast vehicles for business development and returns on investment. Sometimes the brands fit and sometimes they don't. The latter case can prove difficult for brand management, as was the case with hotel chain Marriott International Inc. when it acquired 114 Renaissance-branded hotels for US$947 million in 1997. The Renaissance collection was an eclectic one, comprising both large and small hotels; as a result, the brand was somewhat confusing to consumers and franchisees, as well as to Marriott.

BRAND SCHIZOPHRENIA

After the takeover, Marriott's operational expertise increased Renaissance's profits significantly, but brand problems still lurked menacingly beneath the surface. Property design was inconsistent and service levels differed tremendously, with the result that travelers were never sure what to expect when they made a booking and arrived at their destination Renaissance hotel. In brand terms, the real issue was that Renaissance had no clear and consistent identity—it was a schizophrenic brand. Marriott realized that the long-term future lay in producing a solution to this problem, and that the market confusion caused by this inconsistency didn't augur well for long-term growth, where brand consistency is key to brand power and shareholder value.

Whereas some companies would have been satisfied with short-term gains to the bottom line, Marriott saw the writing on the wall. Other problems also started to appear. For example, Renaissance hotels were found to be cannibalizing Marriott sales, and so repositioning of Renaissance became the focus for brand development. The dilemma was given visibility by Jurgen Giesbert, senior vice president of Marriott responsible for the Renaissance brand, who stated: "When we bought Renaissance, nobody knew what to do with them, whereas Marriott is a clearly defined brand. Everybody knows what it is."

WHEN IN DOUBT, GIVE BRAND MANAGEMENT A SHOUT

Clearly, this wasn't a straightforward strategic brand challenge, but Marriott took several interesting steps. First, it recruited a brand manager from Nike—one of the world's leading power corporate brands; second, it brought in a designer from Beverley Hills who specialized in unique, independent hotels. This was a potentially good combination of branding skills, partnering someone who understood and was used to the discipline of focused corporate brand management, with a specialist who understood the product design elements and markets that Renaissance had grown up in. Then another good decision was made, which was to do some homework. For two years, principally qualitative focus group research was carried out to provide a thorough understanding of the moods and feelings of the desired market segments. In other words, there was a deliberate attempt to gain consumer insight.

UNIQUE BOUTIQUE?

The end-result of this process was a repositioning of the Renaissance brand into a more focused "boutique" collection of hotels, with an interesting positioning summed up in the phrase, "Give Me A Surprise." Bill Marriott, chairman of Marriott International Inc., revealed that the research clarified that 30 percent of the total market for hotel accommodation was attracted to the element of surprise in the brand experience. This significant proportion of the market consisted of people who didn't want the boring certainty and sterility of a predictable "sameness" in whatever hotel they checked into. So, the paradox of branding had become apparent to the company: consistency is key, but there are always sections of the market that want to be different and experience difference. Marriott had found a niche for Renaissance that would, if managed properly, cater for the needs of a different segment of the market, stop cannibalization between brands, and at a single stroke, eliminate confusion and create a new and forceful brand identity. But attention now had to switch to the competition.

PRODUCT DEVELOPMENT AND COMPETITION: OUT OF THE FRYING PAN INTO THE FIRE?

This switch of brand positioning took the Renaissance brand into a new category of competition, where it now has to fight the likes of the Starwood brand and Ian Schrager's designer hotels. Renovation was undertaken at numerous key properties, and Renaissance changed its brand identity and image. This hotel chain, renowned and acclaimed for consistency in product predictability and service quality, incorporated the repositioning of an acquired brand that was the very antithesis of its traditional way of brand management—namely, the development of a brand that was based around planned inconsistency.

The big question for every brand manager is: What would you do if you were given an acquired brand? How do you decide whether your policy is conformity or autonomy?

CASE STUDY 16: CARREFOUR SA (FRANCE) VERSUS AHOLD NV (HOLLAND)

Mergers and Acquisitions—Global versus Product Naming

"To change or not to change? That is the question." (Apologies to William Shakespeare.)

They sound like two football teams, but Carrefour and Ahold are, in fact, the two largest supermarket chains globally after Wal-mart Stores Inc. Interestingly, they have traveled down different branding routes in terms of naming strategy/architecture in the course of their rapid development over the last few years.

Carrefour is trying to build a global brand by acquiring other chains and changing their names to its own. For instance, in 2007, it bought Artima (in Romania) and Atacadao (in Brazil) for 55 million Euros and 1.5 billion Euros, respectively. In France, the French retailer has decided to rebrand all the Champion stores to the Carrefour banner. This is following similar projects in Spain, Argentina, Poland, Brazil, and Turkey. The initiative forms part of Carrefour's multi-format, single-brand strategy.

Carrefour is tactful in the rebranding exercise. Since 2007, it has been testing its rebranding plans in 13 Champion stores that were transferred to the Carrefour banner as part of the trial. The feedback is positive: customers have been satisfied with the wider product range and modern layout, and as a result, they have placed their confidence in the Carrefour brand. This satisfaction has led to an increase in store visits.

Ahold has done the opposite. Rather than converting its newly acquired stores to the Ahold format, which holds little resonance with customers outside Europe, the company has kept the local names and management in place—for instance, Giant, Stop & Shop, Peapod and Martin's in the US, Albert Hejin, Etos, and Gall & Gall in the Netherlands, Albert and Hypernova in the Czech Republic and Slovakia, and ICA in Sweden and Norway. Ahold's CEO, John Rishton, says: "At Ahold, our global strategic focus continues to be the transformation of all our banners into powerful consumer brands."

Ahold is a taskmaster at retail management, and is concerned with improving performance behind the scenes. The changes are at the back end, where ordering and shipping benefit from Ahold's global network, helping to lower costs.

Carrefour says it caters to local preferences by tailoring its food products to local tastes in 95 percent of cases. For instance, in China, most of the products sold in Carrefour stores are procured from China, and the store managers are empowered to run the stores according to the local requirements. "Our stores offer local products that local people want," explains a spokesperson for Carrefour. "In China, we are Chinese. In Malaysia, we are Malaysian." Food analysts say that food retailing doesn't behave like other categories, as most shopping for groceries is done close to home. If this is true, they say a trusted single brand will be difficult to realize. Mmmm—food for thought!

REFERENCES

www.carrefour.com
www.ahold.com
www.annualreport2008.ahold.com/documents/pdf/ar_summary_2008.pdf
www.gerbertechnology.com/case_study/Carrefour.pdf
www.progressivegrocer.com/progressivegrocer/content_display/supermar-
　　ket-industry-news/e3ia50cdcb373435f1baf0909c9fa243f79

The Brand Collectors

The Fascination with Luxury Brands

The ultimate pleasure for any brand manager must be having charge of a luxury brand, with all its concomitant global glamor, prestige, and fame. This isn't to say, however, that competition isn't fierce, but it is surprising that ordinary products such as pens (sorry, writing instruments) can be priced on the same level as rock stars' and football players' salaries. Of course, it's back-to-basics branding techniques and the management of perceptions, but the returns are huge. One would think that, in times such as the current global economic downturn, luxury brands would experience poor results, but this doesn't appear to be the case, as will be illustrated below.

"Watch" This Space: Opportunities to Cross-Brand

Typical of a luxury goods category that seems to have an endless range is watches (sorry, timepieces). Everyone appears to be extending their brands into the timepiece category. Calvin Klein has moved into wrist-watches that tie in with the overall Calvin Klein clothes look. Emporio Armani has done the same thing, and Versace has a whole collection of different watch brands. There is an endless stream of others, including DKNY, Adidas, Bally, Benetton, Carven, Chanel, Christian Lacroix, Hugo Boss, Lacoste, Karl Lagerfeld, Lanvin, Nina Ricci, Pierre Cardin, Timber-land, Yves Saint-Laurent, and more. The market has exploded, and it is estimated that in the US alone in 2008 over US$9.5 billion-worth of these fashion accessories were sold, and that the market is still growing quickly. Fashion-branded watches come in all shapes, sizes, and prices, but there is little doubt that consumers love them, because they love their brands.

If you aren't into fashion but prefer technology, don't despair. Breitling, Seiko, Nike, Casio, and other manufacturers are producing hi-tech timepieces, in some cases capable of downloading MP3 format files from the Internet or direct from CDs via a home computer. There are watches that monitor heart rates, store electricity, receive emails, measure speed and distance for athletes, and send out distress signals. Many companies are finding that extending their brands via this method keeps the sales tills ringing and brand awareness high.

The Dream Sellers

But let's move on to real luxury products. The very smart companies are those that have a business strategy of creating and buying luxury brands. These are the brands that cause hearts to flutter, create insatiable desire, and sell more as the price rises. They are the stuff of dreams. They are truly emotional brands and are held by few companies. The two biggest holding companies of these luxury brands are LVMH Group and Richemont. Both of these groups give their brands relative autonomy in brand management, because most of them are power brands in their own right. The corporate branding face is rarely seen, and the brands stand alone. Both of the companies have been referred to as "The House of Brands," as opposed to the brand house.

Richemont (Compagnie Financière Richemont AG) is a "Swiss luxury goods group with a view to the long-term development of successful international brands," according to its website. In addition to its luxury goods business, Richemont holds investments in the tobacco, financial services, wine and spirits, and gold and diamond mining industries. Being Swiss, it is predictably very low key in talking about its own identity. It leaves the talking to its brands, which include Vacheron Constantin, Purdey, Baume & Mercier, Jaeger-LeCoultre, Lange & Sohne, Cartier, Officine Panerai, IWC, Piaget, Lancel, Alfred Dunhill, Van Cleef & Arpels, Montblanc, Montegrappa, Chloe, Alaia, Shanghai Tang, and Roger Dubuis.

In the year to March 31, 2009, Richemont racked up sales of 5.4 billion Euros, but it is well behind its more high-profile competitor, whose profile and ways of managing luxury brands are described in Case Study 17.

CASE STUDY 17: MÖET HENNESSY LOUIS VUITTON GROUP (LVMH)

The House of Luxury Brands

LVMH's revenue for 2008 was 17.2 billion Euros. LVMH is a retail network of more than 2,300 stores in France and around the world, with 77,000 employees. It describes itself as "a young group, an ongoing expansion." Its brand portfolio boasts around 50 percent of the world's most powerful brand names across various categories, as shown below. One of these brands, Christian Dior, is itself one of the indirect holders of LVMH.

- *Watches/jewelry*: TAG Heuer, Zenith, Hublot, Dior Watches, FRED, Chaumet, De Beers.
- *Fashion*: Louis Vuitton, Loewe, Celine, Berluti, Kenzo, Givenchy, Marc Jacobs, Fendi, StefanoBi, Emilio Pucci, Thomas Pink, Donna Karan, eLUXURY.
- *Wines/spirits*: Möet & Chandon, Dom Perignon, Veuve Clicquot, Krug, Mercier, Ruinart, Chateau d'Yquem, Hennessy, The Glenmorangie Company, Belvedere, Chopin, Domaine Chandon California, Bodegas Chandon, Domaine

Chandon Australia, Cloudy Bay, Cape Mentelle, Netwon, Terrazas de los Andes, Cheval des Andes, 10 Cane, Wenjun.
- *Perfumes/cosmetics:* Parfums Christian Dior, Guerlain, Parfums Givenchy, Kenzo Parfums, Benefit Cosmetics, Fresh, Make Up For Ever, Acqua di Parma, Perfumes Loewe.
- *Selective retailing:* DFS, Miami Cruiseline Services, Sephora, sephora.com, Le Bon Marche, Samaritaine.
- *Other businesses:* Les Echos, Série Limitée, LesEchos.fr, Enjeux-Les Echos, Investir, Investir Magazine, Investir.fr, Capital Finance, Radio Classique, Connaissance des Arts, CLASSICA, Les Editions Aléa, La Fugue, La Salon des Entrepreneurs, Les Echos Conférences, Les Echos Formations, Les Echos Editions, Les Echos Institut, Eurostaf, SID Presse, TPE-PME.com.

THE LVMH VISION

In LVMH's case, at least, we know that this isn't merely random buying of brands. Chairman Bernard Arnault says, "LVMH's vision is to represent around the world the most refined qualities of Western 'Art de Vivre.' LVMH must continue to be synonymous with both elegance and creativity. Our products, and the cultural values they embody, blend tradition and innovation, and kindle dream and fantasy."

THE LVMH VALUES

There are five priorities that reflect the fundamental values shared by all group stakeholders, as published by LVMH Group on its website. These are:

Be creative and innovate

Group companies are determined to nurture and grow their creative resources. Their long-term success is rooted in a combination of artistic creativity and technological innovation: they have always been and will always be creators.

Their ability to attract the best creative talents, to empower them to create leading-edge designs, is the lifeblood of the Group.

The same goes for technological innovation. The success of the companies' new products—particularly in cosmetics—rests squarely with research and development teams. This dual value—creativity/innovation—is a priority for all companies. It is the foundation of their continued success.

Aim for product excellence

Group companies pay the closest attention to every detail and ensure the utter perfection in their products. They symbolize the nobility and perfection of traditional craftsmanship. Each and every one of the objects their customers buy and use exemplifies our brands' tradition of impeccable quality. Never should Group companies disappoint, but rather continue to surprise their customers with the quality, endurance, and finish of their products. They will never compromise when it comes to product quality.

Their search for excellence goes well beyond the simple quality of their products: it encompasses the layout and location of the stores, the display of the items they offer, their ability to make their customers feel welcome as soon as they enter our stores. . . All around them, their clients see nothing but quality.

Bolster the image of our brands with passionate determination

Group brands enjoy exceptional reputation. This would not amount to much, and could not be sustained, if it was not backed by the creative superiority and extreme quality of their products. However, without this aura, this extra dimension that somewhat defies logic, this force of expression that transcends reality, the sublime that is the stuff of our dreams, Dior would not be Dior, Louis Vuitton would not be Louis Vuitton, Möet would not be Möet. . .The power of the companies' brands is part of LVMH's heritage. It took years and even decades to build their image. They are an asset that is both priceless and irreplaceable.

Therefore, Group companies exercise stringent control over every minute detail of their brands' image. In each of the elements of their communications with the public (announcements, speeches, messages, etc.), it is the brand that speaks. Each message must do right by the brand. In this area as well, there is absolutely no room for compromise.

Act as entrepreneurs

The Group's organizational structure is decentralized, which fosters efficiency, productivity, and creativity.

This type of organization is highly motivating and dynamic. It encourages individual initiative and offers real responsibilities—sometimes early in one's career. It requires high entrepreneurial executive teams in each company.

This entrepreneurial spirit requires a healthy dose of common sense from managers, as well as hard work, pragmatism, efficiency, and the ability to motivate people in the pursuit of ambitious goals. One needs to share and enjoy this entrepreneurial spirit to—one day—manage a subsidiary or company of the LVMH Group.

Strive to be the best in all we do

Last but not least is our ambition to be the best. In each company, executive teams strive to constantly improve, never be complacent, always try to broaden our skills, improve the quality of our work, and come up with new ideas.

The Group encourages this spirit, this thirst for progress, among all its associates.

As an expression of what a real brand champion thinks and feels, I think we need look no further than the above statement. But let's have a closer look at how LVMH manages its brands.

In an interview in the *Harvard Business Review* of October 2001, Arnault describes the characteristics of what he calls "star brands":

- timeless;
- modern;
- fast-growing; and
- highly profitable.

And there are fewer than 10 of these star brands in the luxury market. The reason for the paucity of numbers is that it is extremely difficult to balance all four of these characteristics at once. For instance, fast growth and high profitability have some tension between them, as do timelessness and modernity.

Timelessness takes years to develop, but Arnault says that the perception of this characteristic can be generated by fanatical, uncompromising quality. Innovation drives modernity, which is harder to achieve as "you must know the past and invent the future at the same time." Much of his design teams' time is spent on this, as star brands have to be current, fashionable, edgy, sexy, and modern—fulfilling a fantasy. Constant brand reinvention is a key. Growth is a function of consumer desire, and depends to some extent on advertising to create that desire, but Arnault won't let his marketing people near advertising; it remains with his design teams, who, in his opinion, can better project the desired image.

The biggest mistake any company can make is to delegate advertising to the marketing department. For example, the advertising for the Dior brand personality (very sexy, modern, very feminine, and energetic) is often created by the Dior design team and John Galliano himself. Profitability for each brand comes later, of course, after all the innovation, advertising, and other expensive processes have been pumped in.

Product quality and training of staff feature highly at the "front end" of the star brand-building process, according to Arnault. For example, each model of Louis Vuitton suitcase is "put in a torture machine, where it is opened and closed five times per minute for three weeks. And that is not all—it is thrown, shaken, and crushed." That is how Arnault's company makes an heirloom. "A single purse can have up to 1,000 manufacturing tasks, and nearly every task is done by hand. People who work in the factories are trained for many months before they are even allowed to touch a product." Planning and discipline are paramount in the production process.

As for brand management, Arnault says many brands have the star potential, but are poorly managed. Brand management with luxury goods takes time, because all four elements have to be aligned, and that you cannot hurry. The up-side is that once you get there and manage the brand well, the returns are spectacular.

Summary

Brand architecture is possibly the most difficult area of brand management, in that there are simply no rules, and endless opportunities to try out many variations. Some variations work, while similar ones don't. Corporate branding in one form or another is the trend, but sometimes product branding is necessary. Careful thought must be given to all decisions in this area, and specialist advice may be necessary.

Those companies who continue to believe that spending millions on new logos and names is going to change their brand, its experience and relationship with the consumer, and its profitability, are sorely mistaken. Nothing changes unless the customer *experiences* change, so if you are looking for an image change, look at changing the brand experience first. If you have to create a new logo, do it in an evolutionary way, rather than a revolutionary way. If you have to create a new logo, or a new name, choose a local design house that will do a good job for a fraction of the price. Don't be taken in by the giant agencies.

Getting brand architecture right isn't easy. The next chapter looks at some more tough decisions brand managers need to make, regardless of how well their brands are doing.

Three Great Dilemmas:

Brand Stretch, Brand Revitalization, and Brand Deletion

Brand managers will face three great dilemmas at some stage in their careers, and all are concerned with the life of the brand. While brands, if well managed, may live forever, there are situations that occur through both success and neglect that test the skill of a good brand manager. The three great dilemmas are: (1) whether to stretch a brand name into other areas—either inside or outside its existing category—when it is doing well; (2) what to do when a brand has been neglected and needs revitalizing, and whether this can be achieved; and (3) whether to kill or delete a brand if the future holds no prospects. None of these decisions is easy, and I will examine cases of each type of decision in this chapter.

The Great Temptation: Stretching the Brand

One critical question that all brand managers have to face at some stage is whether or not they should stretch or extend their brand, to which the answer is: it all depends. At its most basic level, extending or stretching a brand involves producing variants of the same brand in the same category. At another level, there is the issue of stretching a brand so that it breaks into other categories, but still sits in the same industry. Finally, there is the question of whether or not a brand can be stretched so far that it can move into totally different industries. The temptation is great to stretch a successful brand, and there are no rules to guide the brand manager here; at the end of the day, the *consumer* will decide, as it is consumers who own and build the brands. The limiting factor really is the brand promise and personality, and whether or not the consumer makes an emotional connection.

There are, of course, some brand extensions that just wouldn't work, and it is possible to look at various examples, and to make some judgments as to when brand extensions are possible. However, first I will clarify some of the basic reasons for brand extensions, as well as some terminology.

Reasons for Brand Extensions

There appear to be three basic reasons for extending brands.

1. Natural Causes

One of the main reasons for brand extensions is what I call "natural causes." This is where a brand may produce a product that is very close to its original offering, but which satisfies the desires of a different, or even the same, audience without significantly cannibalizing existing sales. These extensions are a "natural" development as brand managers uncover and exploit more of the needs and wants of the consumers that exist in their category. Such was the case with the famous After Eight Mints. The Classic Dark Assortment has been complemented by the White Mint Assortment, while other extensions added by the brand include After Eight Straws, After Eight Orange, and Mint Ice Cream Bar. These kinds of brand extensions not only make sense, but are almost mandatory if companies are to grow and keep competitors at bay in the category.

2. Market Growth Reductions

Companies may try to widen their brand portfolio if their existing market(s) show signs of slower growth. For example, Intel—the world's number one semiconductor manufacturer—has countered the slowdown in the growth of its processor unit due to decreasing sales of personal computers, by building devices that connect to, and increase the value of, home computers, especially those that have Intel microprocessors installed. Intel has also made a strategic decision to produce other consumer devices such as portable digital music players, healthcare measurement devices, and educational products. The extensions are close enough to existing businesses to avoid consumer doubts, although in the entertainment category Intel will have a tough time competing with products made by Sony, Philips, and Rio. Perhaps of more importance in the longer term is Intel's entry into healthcare, where its technology is expected to be used by doctors for remote patient health monitoring and other medical uses through new devices.

3. Confidence in the Invincibility of the Brand

While the above reasons are often based on solid market research and a strong degree of common sense, some brands are extended merely on the premise that, because the brand has been successful in one or more categories/markets, it will automatically be a star in others. This thinking may prove to be right in some cases, but very wrong in others. The Virgin Group has suffered from over-confidence in a few areas, such as with its Virgin Vodka, Virgin Cola and Virgin Cosmetics. Thus, while there may be opportunities for stretching a brand, there may also be minefields that can affect a brand's ability to be stretched. Before we look at more examples, I would like to distinguish between what are often referred to as brand extensions and line extensions.

Brand and Line Extensions—Possibilities and Difficulties

Brand extensions involve the use of an existing brand name to move into a new product or service category, while line extensions of a brand use the existing name to offer a new product or service in the same category. Virgin Airlines is an example of the former, and the Mercedes "A" class is an example of the latter.

Examples of where it is possible for one brand, company, or product to line extend include cars, banks, and drinks. Cars can be "flexed" via features such as engine capacity, coupé versions, and so on. Banks can be positioned broadly but be promoted differently to retail, corporate, small and medium-sized enterprises, entrepreneurs, public sector institutions, and so on. Drinks such as Schweppes' soft drinks are flexed via different products such as mixers, mineral waters, and fruit and health drinks, with many flavors to appeal to adults and young people, but all of these remain true to the company's basic positioning of quality soft drinks, and all remain basically in the same category.

Brand extension can also be achieved in taking the brand into another category or industry. For instance, Ford Motor Company once started a Jaguar Bank, and Virgin has moved into telecommunications and finance, among many other categories. The key to extensions of any kind is that the brand must stay true to its original identity. Only in this way will consumers accept the change.

While a company or product can have only one true, strong position, it can be tweaked, adjusted, and flexed to emphasize particular strengths or values that attract different customer groups, as long as it isn't stretched too far. The amount of stretch available is contingent upon knowledge of various market segments. So, multi-positioning can also be seen as line or brand extending, but there are limits to this possibility that mustn't be overstepped.

Harley-Davidson has been successful in marketing its apparel range because it fits well both with the needs and desires of the target audience, and the true personality and positioning of the brand. Associations of freedom, patriotism, heritage, and a macho attitude attract Harley buyers, and the accessories and clothing add value to the consumer experience. They are appropriate to the brand personality and positioning. But even power brands have their limits. The Nike product line extension from footwear to sports apparel was successful, but the step from sports apparel to casual wear wasn't, as the casual wear segments didn't strongly associate with the true Nike position of athleticism, and it appeared that older people didn't feel like *just doing it* anymore. Similarly, Johnson & Johnson's baby shampoo could transfer from babies to children without much problem, but when tried with adults it didn't really make the cut.

On the other hand, Nike seems to have got it right by introducing a line of heart monitors for athletes wanting to monitor their heart rate in order to achieve optimum performance. The data from these devices, and from others that attach to shoes to measure distance covered, download to a wristwatch for training usage. Nike has also introduced watches that allow athletes to capture various training data which can later be uploaded and shared with coaches and training companions over the Internet. For example, TRIAX ELITE HRM allows athletes to enter their training performance data and heart rates into a computer wirelessly. These new training performance products still fit the brand personality of Nike, in terms of passion, commitment, winning, and getting the best out of oneself. The point, therefore, is that as long as the brand extension stays true to the brand personality and therefore matches consumer expectations, it is more likely to be successful.

Another way to analyze the issue of extensions is to look at the nature of the brand in terms of consumer associations, and whether the marketing strategy is to move the brand up or down with respect to associations of price, quality, and, ultimately, value. This is essentially looking at whether a brand can be considered as functional or symbolic in nature.

Symbolic and Functional Extensions—the Fit with the Consumer Mindset

We must remember that brands exist only in the minds of people, and that they can be segregated into two basic types: functional and symbolic brands. This perceptual typology has implications for brand stretch.

For instance, Rolex is a representational brand, as it represents more than just a watch to buyers and occupies a position that is associated with high price, quality, status, and prestige. At the other end of the perceptual spectrum, Casio has a position linked to just functionality—it is low in price, with enough quality in terms of reliability and durability to do the job it is supposed to, but with little association of status or other intangible benefits. However, it has tried to rectify its rather down-market image with some hi-tech innovations.

In extending a prestige brand such as Rolex, the only possibility is downwards. However, a step-down positioning via a product bearing the same name but with lower quality and price will almost certainly damage the original brand image and alienate its existing customer base, even though it might attract a newer clientele who aspire to own that brand. Rolex considered this matter carefully and created a separate brand, Tudor, for the middle market, with no Rolex endorsement. The brand communications are, however, cleverly designed to create an air of familiarity.

For brands already positioned at the high end of a market, the distancing mustn't be so great as to eliminate all the positive associations of the strong, core, prestige brand name. Communications strategies must focus on relating the new product to the favorable aspects of the core brand. Too close a positioning, however, may damage both, again through the cannibalization process. The brand manager's task isn't an easy one in the field of brand extensions, and positioning is critical to success.

Thus, although there is a lot of room for positioning new brand extensions with a prestige parent brand, and the rewards can be substantial, great care must be taken to predict whether there will be any dilution or damage to the core brand image. This is the risk, no doubt calculated, that Mercedes and BMW have taken with their "A" class and 1 series, respectively. The further down the quality/price continuum the extension occurs, the greater the possibility of damage to image, and neither the "A" class nor the 1 series got off to a great start.

Functional brands aren't positioned as high-quality items, and so there is often little room to extend downwards, and any new product introductions will have associations closer to the original brand than would be the case with symbolic brands. The result is that extensions are likely to inflict less damage on the brand image. The downside here is that, because there is less distance between the brands in terms of quality perceptions, cannibalization of sales for both products may occur through customer confusion. Another challenge in trying to extend a functional brand upwards in terms of quality by adding status and value to it, is that consumer perceptions tend to be locked on to the existing brand image and are likely to be very difficult to shift.

The only way that a functional product can really be branded in the symbolic bracket is by distancing the original brand from the extensions through careful positioning. This may well involve the creation of a new brand name, in the same manner described for symbolic brands considered above. For example, Casio had to create new brand names to break away from an image that wouldn't be acceptable to different market segments; hence the introduction of G-Shock and Baby-G. The functionally oriented Toyota brand also had to leave its name totally out of the picture in order to position a new product in the status and prestige category (Lexus). This strategy successfully created a luxury brand without the more down-market associations of its other products. The future of Lexus as a luxury car brand is somewhat questionable, however, as the brand appears to be extending downwards into lower engine capacities and smaller cars. Discipline is therefore necessary in brand management.

The bottom line for brand extensions, then, is that you cannot step away from your basic position or proposition as long as the brand name remains the same, because consumers judge perceptually whether or not there is a good "fit" between the brand itself and the extension of the brand. Although the discussion above has concentrated on the most common elements of quality and price, this judgment also takes into account other elements of importance, such as usage occasions. It is for this reason that some companies are forced to step away from the main brand name and create a product that stands alone. Coca-Cola has done this with Fruitopia and other beverages. Others play down the brand name of the company to give the product minimum association with the parent. Launching new products in such ways helps to position them with highly individual profiles while retaining subtle usage of brand equity from the parent, as with Levi's Dockers and Toyota's Lexus, neither of which would have been as successful as they have been if positioned as another product line of the same major brand.

Corporate versus Product Brand Elasticity

In general, we can conclude that corporate brands are more capable of surviving being stretched or extended than are product brands. Let's take the example of a successful product brand, such as Head and Shoulders shampoo. It has its line extended to provide a range of shampoos under the brand name "Head and Shoulders" for different types of hair and different consumer benefits. However, it wouldn't survive a move into, for example, clothing. I certainly wouldn't be inclined to buy a Head and Shoulders suit or shirt!

Corporate brand names, on the other hand, are more easily stretched because the brand proposition isn't so closely focused and related to a single type of product. They can be successful because they can attach the perceived value of the brand name outside their categories—for instance, Sony has successfully transferred its brand name beyond consumer electronics to entertainment. The perceived value of quality has enabled this to happen in the minds of consumers. The Virgin Group has developed many brand extensions, but it hasn't stepped away from its basic brand proposition. Another great example of this is Caterpillar (see Case Study 18), which has successfully entered vastly different categories. Thus, there is more scope for brand management in corporate extensions, and the current trend is away from product branding to corporate and house (endorsed) branding.

CASE STUDY 18: CATERPILLAR INC.

An Example of Successful Brand Extension

One of the most unlikely, but seemingly successful, examples of stretching a brand into a vastly different industry is that of Caterpillar Inc. The "construction" company has moved into the fashion business. Seen for over 100 years as a supplier of heavy machinery used in construction activities, it has found a new way of building awareness and recognition (not to mention profits) by penetrating the notoriously difficult fashion industry; in the process, it has been accepted by consumers across multi-segments.

This has, of course, been no accident; rather, it was a carefully planned move by the Caterpillar global brand management group, headed formerly by Kimberley S. Neible and now by Jennifer Wilfong. The aim was to boost brand sales among those consumers who also operate Caterpillar machinery products, and to promote the brand to people who wouldn't normally come into contact with Caterpillar.

Caterpillar products have sold well in Europe, competing with the likes of Nike and attracting youth with its edgy attitude. Cat apparel has a worldwide licensee brand in London, and a global licensee for Cat footwear based in the US, but it has its own stores in mind. The first of these was a 5,000-square-foot store in Illinois, near the company's headquarters; this was followed by several more in cities such as London and New York.

The product range itself is astonishing—everything from casuals to luxury goods. For example, you can buy Cat jeans (with five pockets and a yellow patch on the back). Limited edition jeans, at just under US$300, are on the way, along with sunglasses, sandals, and baby clothes. In many countries there are Cat hats, boots, bags, trainers, baby shoes, watches, and sweatshirts. At the flagship store, up-market products such as a US$250 leather bomber jacket and a US$235 timepiece are available. Cat crosses all boundaries, from the irreverent to the traditional, from the young to the over-sixties (and in some quoted cases, the over-nineties!).

CATERPILLAR BRAND PERSONALITY

The secret to the success of Caterpillar's brand extension appears to be the consistent application of the brand "personality," which could be seen as:

- hardworking;
- tough;
- resilient;
- determined;
- bold;
- rugged;
- independent; and
- a good friend when you get to know it.

This personality has been extended into both the product and the shopping experience. For instance, the boots and shoes look tough. The metal band on the Cat watch (over US$200!) looks like a bulldozer's tread lines. The flagship store's interior is decorated in the bold Caterpillar yellow color and features a replica of a Cat-sponsored racing car. Part of the floor is made of wooden blocks similar to those on the factory floor, and when visitors approach a display, reverse beeping sounds are activated. Consistency is key, and Caterpillar's brand management has stuck to the rules; by doing so, it has added considerably to the total brand value.

With worldwide merchandise sales for 2007 of US$817 million, Caterpillar has proven that well-planned brand extensions reinforce and are consistent with the original brand proposition, so that consumers' emotional associations are in tune with the brand personality of the proposed brand extensions.

REFERENCES

Reuters, October 2008
http://shop.cat.com, accessed May 20, 2009
www.usatoday.com/money/advertising/2008-04-15-licensing-chart_N.htm

Increasing Elasticity via Product Innovations

There is sometimes the temptation to stretch a brand via an innovation. This can be a problem when perceptions are very entrenched and consumers aren't ready to accept the innovation. For instance, detergent manufacturers trying to market laundry-soap tablets to people who are used to powders and liquids found market acceptance difficult. The problem appeared to be the nature of the innovation—the product attribute/benefit of the tablet itself, with the attribute being the tablet's compact size and the consumer benefit the fact that consumers no longer have to scoop, measure, or pour. The innovation was aimed at younger working people and small households that essentially don't like doing laundry, and who want to minimize the time taken to do it. However, people seemed to want the option of being able to vary the amount of the ingredient to suit the relative dirtiness of the clothes being washed. The challenge for the brand managers was to convince consumers of the benefits of convenience and time saving, and has been compared to the problem encountered by the proponents of the teabag in the 1950s. Teabags eventually took off, as we all know, but not without considerable investment in educating the consumer. If perceptions are deeply entrenched, companies must be prepared for lengthy and costly advertising and promotion campaigns.

In the detergent case, it might be that research had asked only one of the two vital questions necessary to establish consumer acceptance— "Do you like it?" but hadn't asked the other—"Would you buy it?" This was the same issue that caused Coca-Cola massive embarrassment when the company tried to introduce New Coke. Taste testing carried out with over 100,000 people reassured the company that consumers preferred the new drink, but they just didn't buy it, because their perception of the old Coke as being "the real thing" was deeply entrenched. Anything else was a substitute. When you play around with brands, you are playing around with people's emotions, and brand managers need to understand what these are.

This section concludes with a summary of the advantages and disadvantages of brand extensions.

ADVANTAGES

- Extending the brand is less costly than creating a new one.
- The consumer receives a better choice.
- There is less risk for consumers if the brand is trusted.
- There can be some synergy, and therefore savings in marketing costs.
- They help brand revitalization.
- If successful, they can add power to the main brand image.
- They can keep other competitors from entering the category, and increase coverage.
- They can pave the way for more extensions.

DISADVANTAGES

- If the parent brand has a negative image, it is unlikely that an extension will be successful.

- If not clearly positioned, they can confuse consumers and cannibalize sales of existing brands.
- If not successful, they can damage the master brand image.
- Retailers might not appreciate them.
- All brands have their boundaries, and stepping outside these can dilute brand power.

Whatever the pros and cons, it is possible for a brand to be stretched way beyond its own category as long as it doesn't step outside its basic character and consumers can relate to it. The Caterpillar case above shows how a major brand can extend into categories most would think impossible. Case Study 19 shows how Wrigley extends into other categories via product innovation.

CASE STUDY 19: WRIGLEY

Gum Does Stretch!

Wrigley has been a leader in the chewing gum category since the 1890s and is famous for brands such as Juicy Fruit, Doublemint, and Winterfresh. Extensions have progressed into the sugarless market, where sales have accelerated as consumers have become increasingly health-conscious. New brands introduced into the US market include Extra Polar Ice, Everest (packaged in a tin box), and Eclipse, the company's first pellet gum. Its latest brand, introduced in 2007, is a sugarless chewing gum called "5," which was first available in Rain, Cobalt, and Flare flavors, followed in 2008 and 2009 by additional flavor line extensions named Elixir, Solstace, and Zing. The packaging reflects the flavor color names and looks like a sophisticated cigarette pack design. "5" is aimed at the youth market, but some commentators have remarked that the packaging is more appropriate to an older audience and may not be seen by young people as being relevant to them.

To fuel corporate growth, the company has successfully targeted overseas markets. It currently maintains 14 factories in various countries, and sells its products in more than 180 countries, including the US, Serbia, Mexico, Australia, the UK, Canada, Spain, New Zealand, the Philippines, France, Kenya, Taiwan, China, India, Poland, the Federation of Bosnia and Herzegovina, and Russia. More than 60 percent of Wrigley's sales now come from outside its home country, the US. Deutsche Bank Alex. Brown's analyst Eric Katzman says of Wrigley, which can now be considered a global brand: "Not many companies can have 50 percent of the world market, no debt, very high returns, and that kind of brand awareness."

In 2004, Wrigley purchased the Life Savers and Altoids businesses from Kraft Foods for US$1.48 billion. On January 23, 2007, it signed a purchase agreement to acquire an 80 percent initial interest in A. Korkunov for US$300 million, with the remaining 20 percent to be acquired over time. On April 28, 2008, it was announced that Berkshire Hathaway and Mars, Incorporated would acquire Wrigley for approximately US$23 billion, and Mars is now listed as the owner of the Wrigley Group.

But Wrigley has no room for complacency, as competing brands have powerful owners. Pfizer, Inc. owns the Dentyne, Chiclets, and Trident brands; while Hershey Foods Corp. owns the Carefree and Bubble Yum brands. As of March 17, 2008, Wrigley had a 59 percent market share of the gum market, while Cadbury held 34.5 percent. Cadbury has been catching up after acquiring Pfizer's gum business in 2003, and by launching new products through its Trident brand alongside the 32 gum products sold by Wrigley. In particular, Cadbury has been highly aggressive in focusing on the functional gum category by introducing gums with teeth-whitening features and oral-care properties. Similarly, Wrigley has been maintaining its forefront position with innovative product development, such as its patented Viagra chewing gum.

Wrigley has also moved into other categories, but whether its healthcare and pharmaceutical products will find favor and trust with consumers is another matter. Much will depend on whether Wrigley can manage consumer perceptions well enough to transfer the trust and loyalty it now enjoys into categories where it isn't known to have operated before, and where it will be fighting against already trusted brand names. Wrigley seems determined to win, however, and its costly marketing campaigns have used tennis icons Venus and Serena Williams, entertainer Chris Brown, and other celebrities to endorse the brand.

Although using celebrities can be highly effective, it can also be problematic. Chris Brown's arrest in early 2009 on a charge of assaulting singer Rihanna prompted Wrigley to suspend its Doublemint gum campaign that used Brown as a spokesman. "Wrigley is concerned by the serious allegations made against Chris Brown," Wrigley spokeswoman Jennifer Luth said in a CNN report of February 9, 2009. Nevertheless, the Wrigley brand name is strong, and is likely to overcome this temporary setback.

REFERENCE

www.confectionerynews.com/The-Big-Picture/Wrigley-s-no-longer-a-family-affair

The Great Gamble: Brand Revitalization/ Repositioning

Another great dilemma facing brand managers is when a brand is seen to be going downhill, either through neglect, or because consumers no longer are strongly associated with it, or because competition has eroded the brand position. The decision that needs to be taken is whether or not to revitalize the brand, and if so, how. This process is often referred to as brand repositioning, and what is needed is to convince the target audience to change their perceptions about the brand in a more favorable way with regard to the competition.

Sometimes, brands that have lost their shine and market appeal are allowed to continue without substantial repositioning, or even where repositioning has failed (see Case Study 20), while others undergo tremendous changes aimed at making a low-key brand into a global player (see Case Study 21).

CASE STUDY 20: TAB DIET SODA

The Customer Lifeline

Tab saw its market share shrink to less than 1 percent, and yet it was spared the axe by Coca-Cola. The brand, once so successful, now resides at the bottom of the category heap. It was launched in 1963, and immediately became the drink of the "free" generation, the "Beautiful Drink for Beautiful People." But in 1982 Diet Coke was introduced to add more power to the Coke brand, and Tab began to go downhill. Basically, its demise has been due to cannibalization of sales by Diet Coke and a simultaneous competitive attack from Diet Pepsi and other such carbonated drinks. The company made several attempts to revitalize Tab in the 1980s and 1990s, through various product changes (for example, reducing the content of the carcinogen saccharin and increasing the amount of aspartame; adding calcium; and making a clear alternative), and even by repositioning Tab as the drink with "sass." However, all these efforts have failed to revive the brand.

The big question is, why should a company that is renowned for managing successful brands hang on to one that is certainly underperforming and may even be almost dead? The answer appears to be the fear of adverse customer reaction and publicity. Possibly at the back of Coca-Cola's mind is the terrible mistake the company made in attempting to replace Coke with New Coke in 1985. Customers around the world clamored for the old Coke, which had been positioned so strongly as "the real thing," and New Coke had to be withdrawn.

In this respect, regular Tab drinkers (although relatively few in number) have been very vocal about their brand, so much so that they have been described as "Taboholics." Those who still drink it are very loyal, and have gone to extreme lengths to prove this. Even though few distributors now stock Tab, some customers have reportedly driven far out of their way to find a store that sells it, and have complained vigorously to the Coca-Cola headquarters about the availability problem.

Herein lies another part of the answer to the question as to why the brand isn't deleted. The Coca-Cola distribution system allows the bottlers some autonomy in production, and if they cannot make a profit from a brand they will tend not to produce it. With many bottlers now choosing not to produce the brand, the few that do are meeting the market needs, and Coca-Cola itself isn't out of pocket. It stopped putting marketing resources behind Tab some years ago, but is content to receive a small profit from a select market.

But back to the consumer. What does Coca-Cola say about the Tab situation? Douglas Daft, former chairman and chief executive, said it shows the company cares: "We want to make sure that those who want Tab get Tab." Coca-Cola has remained steadfast in its commitment to the brand, and Tab can now be purchased online— for example, via the Dr Soda website. So, it would appear that some companies, under certain conditions, will continue to support dying brands if the consumers shout loudly enough.

CASE STUDY 21: MAZDA

The Revitalization of a Brand

This case study should be an inspiration to all brand management practitioners. It isn't only about revitalization of a brand; it's about how leading-edge practitioners take a holistic view of brand strategy, from consumer insight, through personality and product, to internal and external communication.

I have always liked the Mazda brand. I have always thought its motor vehicles had style and "class"; it's one of those brands that I somehow feel an affinity with. But Mazda, founded in 1920, is also a brand that makes one think, "It has so much potential. Why hasn't it ever become a world-famous brand?" (This question can be asked of many brands that originate from Japan, where brand management isn't a national strength, and therein lies the answer to the question.) Mazda has always kept a fairly low profile, with little advertising or promotion, and despite obvious talent in its design capability the brand had nearly faded into oblivion by the time it was acquired in 1996. (Ford Motor Company's initial investment in Mazda of 25 percent was made in 1986, with an increased investment to 33 percent in 1996.)

Since that time, the revitalization of the brand has become a significant focus for business attention, and Mazda has now achieved global brand status. However, it is important to point out that the Mazda repositioning and branding is very much Japanese, not Western; the heritage and future would have been blighted by an attempt to impose Western brand values on an Asian brand. It is an example of how Japanese brands are now starting to recognize the importance of brand management, whereas previously they had concentrated primarily on operational efficiency and quality. This case study illustrates how a brand can be totally reconstructed in every way, and how important the role of brand management is in saving a business and then building it up again. The case also demonstrates clearly the many skills a brand manager must have in order to successfully take on this type of huge responsibility, the importance of including all company employees in the brand vision, and how the brand really does drive the business.

THE KEY TO BUSINESS SUCCESS IS THE BRAND

From the very beginning of the business transformation, branding was always at the top of the agenda. Mark Fields, former senior managing director in charge of global marketing, sales, and customer service (and later president and CEO), said to Mazda employees in 1999:

> For Mazda to take a giant leap forward in terms of business profitability, we have set the following goals:
>
> • establishing our brand management strategy;
> • successful launch of new products, and further strengthening of our existing products;

- maintaining our sales momentum worldwide; and
- bolstering our domestic dealer network.

Fields also commented:

To promote improvement of our market share and build our brand image, Mazda must completely understand and satisfy the needs and wants of our target audiences . . . And we must continue to offer higher value and deeper satisfaction . . . The key to this is brand strategy . . . Through our brand strategy, we are aiming at building a brand that differentiates us from our competitors, one that enhances customer satisfaction, improves value—and in the end provides us enduring profitable growth . . . As we go forward, all of our activity will be keyed to our brand.

THE IMPORTANCE OF BRAND STRATEGY

Fields was clear about the importance of brand strategy and what it means to Mazda.

First, the brand strategy is about a relationship with the customer. By enhancing our customer insight we can understand their true needs and wants. Based on this, we should establish an emotional connection with them. It is through this and other touchpoints that we present our brand. Customers who come into contact and grow to love our brand become our assets, and their importance is in no way different from other assets such as profitability and our employees.

Secondly, it is a business growth strategy with a consistent management system. Why? Because branding requires two aspects: communication and products. Both must work in conjunction, and that makes it a management system. Since employees, products, sales, service, and the company itself all come in close contact with customers, everything must be coordinated on the basis of brand strategy.

Finally, brand strategy is a means to generate profitability. A brand with a strong emotional connection with customers can employ pull marketing, henceforth creating an efficient and highly profitable business environment.

Fields further commented:

The will and commitment of top management is, above all, most important. Brand strategy is not a simple matter of image strategy. Therefore, the senior management should take full responsibility and not let PR, marketing, advertising, and other communication groups act separately. The management must lead the entire organization to start brand building and create change.

The next most important thing is the cooperation and commitment of management. They must understand and share the management's direction, and promote coordination and cooperation among different functional groups in the organization, to develop products and services that clearly articulate our brand.

Finally, senior management must lead the organization to generate awareness and passion for what the brand stands for.

PUSH VERSUS PULL IN BRAND DIRECTION

Mazda has taken steps to ensure that its brand image and company profitability aren't damaged by efforts to buy market share through discounting and rebates—the typical "push" approach that many brand managers get tempted into pursuing as a result of competitor strategies. Instead, it has focused on the "pull" approach, which involves giving customers what they really want and engaging them emotionally in the brand–customer relationship. This approach means that the custodians of the brand must understand which particular group of consumers they want to focus on, and then attempt to satisfy their needs, wants, and desires, and to add true value and other motivations.

It is a fundamental premise of branding that brands only exist in people's minds; that companies don't own brands—consumers do; and that it is consumers, not companies, who build brands. Mazda's philosophy is similar. It is therefore of critical importance that brand managers have a thorough understanding of the consumers they hope to attract and retain, and this means gaining consumer insight through research. For Mazda, this means understanding the deep-seated needs of the target consumer, and not just the generic needs that most people have. For example, Mazda uncovered the following deep-seated needs of its prototype target audience:

- Aspires to lead a life that is full of new stimuli and excitement while respecting his personal sense of style.
- Aspires to sustain the sensitivity of a child—moved and excited by the simplest things in life.
- Hates to be constricted by rules and norms, and allows his sensibility and emotions to lead him in pursuing whatever he wants to do.
- Desires to retain his personal uniqueness that invites attention and is respected by others.
- Aspires to enhance his presence as a highly competent person possessing a unique personality and opinions.
- Wants to impress and persuade people around him by expressing his unique values and views.
- By setting high goals for himself, aspires to challenge new possibilities by not adhering to current norms

The Mazda Brand DNA

Mazda takes a life-science approach, which is illustrated by the use of the term "DNA," the very building block of human life. The core of the Mazda brand strategy is the Mazda brand DNA, the essence of the brand, which has two sides: personality and product. The personality side of the Mazda brand can be summarized by the following three characteristics: stylish, insightful, and spirited.

This is the driving force behind the Mazda brand's personality and the foundation of the brand DNA; however, in order to understand the Mazda brand DNA, one must understand that key product attributes are included in it as well. These key product attributes are: distinctive design, exceptional functionality, and responsive handling and performance.

BRAND PERSONALITY

Mazda's brand personality attributes are defined as follows:

- *Stylish*: Every Mazda product should be a self-assured invitation to attention. With this, we acknowledge that Mazda customers are self-confident and truly distinctive individuals.
- *Insightful*: We imply that Mazda has a "street-smart" understanding of its customers' needs and values, and it always takes a creative approach to meeting those needs.
- *Spirited*: We establish that the Mazda brand embodies an enthusiastic and expressive love of life, just like Mazda customers. Together, the Mazda brand personality creates a deep emotional connection with Mazda customers by reflecting how our customers feel about themselves and about life.

PRODUCT ATTRIBUTES

Product is an important part of the equation for the Mazda brand, and the elements are defined as follows:

- *Distinctive design*: The aim for all products is that Mazda products boast distinctive design inside and out; that is to say, they are athletic, youthful, solid, and substantial, both on the interior and exterior.
- *Exceptional functionality*: Mazda requires that its products possess exceptional functionality; this means the most intelligent use of space and functional efficiency with a high-quality fit and finish.

- *Responsive handling and performance*: This attribute is a Mazda legacy and creates a sensory driving experience that translates into significant and noticeable driving satisfaction.

It is the product/ownership experience that expresses brand connection.

While high-level product attributes help in understanding what Mazda wants all its products to represent, they are not specific enough to help planners, designers, and engineers. The company has therefore developed additional tools, the first of which is called *product philosophy*.

The product philosophy is comprised of quality innovation and design policy, as Mark Fields explains:

Our Product Philosophy clearly states our priorities. We wish to be a Leader in these six areas: Design, Craftsmanship, Quality, Stability and Handling, Braking, and Package Innovation. While taking environmental friendliness and safety fully into consideration, our product development aims to take leadership in those six areas.

This hardware exercise is a clear and consistent extension of how the brand DNA is executed within our new products.

The "Design Policy" uses Mazda's design theme of "Contrast in Harmony," a guide to unique and best-in-class design. The new design theme "Contrast in Harmony" aims at creation of Mazda's future products with designs that balance functions and styling harmoniously with each other. "Harmony" refers to the underlying balance and proportion such as details, materials, color combination, configurations, space construction, function, and appearance in our products ... the very foundation of good design.

To further the design direction among products, Mazda has developed the Family Face. The Family Face is a combination of the brand symbol and a five-point grille, and will be applied to all future models to make it a visual expression of Mazda's identity and distinctiveness. For example, some vehicles that are already in showrooms, like the Premacy and the MPV, as well as future concepts, both show Mazda's face—the distinctive five-point grille with Mazda's winged M brand symbol. The body language shows distinctive "Contrast in Harmony" with a clear contrast of sharp and soft. So the Mazda brand strategy is not merely an image strategy; it is a central business strategy that includes product development. New products that embody all the aspects of the brand strategy will be introduced successively into the market.

THE EMOTIONAL CONNECTION

The key element in Mazda's brand strategy is building the "emotional connection" with consumers. The key success factors for brand management are: "Global Perspective," "Listening to the Voice of the Customer," and "Creating an Emotional Connection." Here are a few examples of the initiatives that have been undertaken to make this happen.

In the area of product marketing, Mazda organized the 1st Shohin Ibento, or 1st Product Day, in September 1999 with our key domestic and foreign dealers and distributors from North America, Europe, Australia, Asia, and the Middle East, providing them with the opportunity to view and drive current and future products. Managers in various markets share success and "best practices" regarding new product events and product-focused strategies with the global team. This is a good example of sharing ideas/viewpoints and listening to the customer.

Mazda also ensures global consistency in its brand and marketing strategies through quarterly brand summit meetings with key Mazda marketing personnel from Japan, the United States, and Europe. Fields says:

These meetings drive home a common understanding of the brand and how it is steadily executed in the marketplace.

Clear internal communication is vitally important in developing a consistent brand identity worldwide. A single brand message is required to support the brand globally. Our major market managers participate in this activity, providing input from a local perspective.

In order to establish a lasting emotional connection with the target customers, we need to deepen our understanding of their values. We need a deep understanding of the latent needs that exist in every human being. Only after we grasp this can we establish a strong emotional connection with our target customers. We call this "Deep-Seated Needs" at Mazda. This is what we use to identify our target customer. And it is with this target customer that we aspire to create an emotional connection and encourage a love and passion for our brand.

MAZDA'S VIEW ON ADVERTISING

Mazda has clear views on advertising and on the importance of maintaining a clear and consistent message in the market. However, Fields stresses that advertising is *not* brand.

Advertising is only one aspect of brand. It supports and illustrates our brand identity and makes it clearer to the market. You cannot create a robust brand by advertising alone. Today's customer is far too sophisticated for this type of tactic. What advertising provides is the opportunity to project our brand to consumers in a clear and consistent manner worldwide.

To ensure this, we have developed our "Communication Philosophy." It was developed to manage our overall communications, including advertising. To create tighter advertising consistency with our worldwide brand positioning, we have established a global tagline.

In Japan, our tagline is the same as our brand positioning statement of *"Kokoro o Ugokasu shin Hassou"*; outside of

Japan, it is: "Get in. Be moved." Our global tagline is used in all of our advertisements, and it helps us deliver a consistent message to different markets around the globe. Another innovation to develop a better alignment with our global advertising efforts is our visual identity ending tag, or what we refer to as advertising VI. I'm referring to the last two or three seconds of our TV advertising and how we illustrate our logo and mark at the end of the ad.

This VI was developed and researched with customers to ensure that the visual cues are consistent in delivering the Mazda brand DNA. It is our intention to phase this VI into all TV advertising worldwide in the near future.

Again, I would like to emphasize that our advertising portrays a crystal clear picture of the Mazda brand to convey a consistent emotional message. At its most basic level, our corporate message must support our Worldwide Brand Positioning, while providing relevance to our target customers.

To bring our brand to life, we manage and control not only advertising but all of our communications, consistently guided by our Communication Philosophy. For example, our events, PR activities, and all of our press events and conferences are based on the brand strategy, with information, staging, and the format of press releases all consistent with our brand.

Brand Management Structure and Internal Communications

Following the development of the brand strategy, other initiatives were implemented at Mazda. One of the first innovations was to restructure the marketing organization to enhance the focus on branding. The brand marketing department was established as a part of the marketing division, in addition to the product marketing department. Brand marketing is responsible for consistent planning, implementation, and management of product development through the communication process under the brand strategy. Mazda believes that such an organization is indispensable for aggressive promotion of its brand strategy.

The second initiative was to communicate the brand strategy to every one of the company's employees. Fields says:

> A brand cascade event was held for our 1,400 top managers. These managers were educated on basic knowledge about brand and our brand strategy, which in turn they cascaded when they went back to their respective departments and groups. Check-ups ensured that our message was communicated throughout the organization, and by doing this Mazda succeeded in spreading brand knowledge and creating improved awareness to implement the brand strategy to realize the Mazda brand. By maximizing internal communication activity, goals were shared globally.

According to Mazda, everyone is now reforming his or her daily tasks in pursuit of these common goals, and in this way the company is moving forward with its self-renovation. This provides assistance internally for everyone at Mazda to be responsible for brand development and execution.

A third innovation was a brand cascade kit, which was specifically developed and distributed for internal education. The kit was delivered to all divisions, and brand cards highlighting key words were distributed to every employee. As Fields says, "The brand strategy would never work without a total commitment from every employee. We believe that all of our employees needed to renew their thoughts, and let the Mazda brand direct their everyday job and assignments."

SUMMARY OF MAZDA'S BRAND PHILOSOPHY AND PRACTICE

Mark Fields summarizes the Mazda brand philosophy and practice as follows:

> First, the brand strategy is about a relationship with the consumers. The brand should establish emotional connection

with them, and it is through this and other touchpoints that the brand is presented. Consumers who come into contact with and grow to love our brand become our assets, and their importance is in no way different from other assets such as profitability and our employees.

Secondly, it is a business growth strategy with a consistent management system, because branding requires two aspects—communication and products. Both must work in conjunction, and that makes it a management system. Since employees, products, sales, service, and the company itself all come in close contact with customers, every aspect must be coordinated on the basis of brand strategy.

Thirdly, brand strategy is a means to generate profitability. A brand with a strong emotional connection with customers can employ pull marketing, henceforth creating an efficient and highly profitable business environment. More specifically, this means increased conquest sales, enhanced owner loyalty, and improved market share.

The next most important thing is the cooperation and commitment of management. They must understand and share the top management's direction, and promote coordination and cooperation among different functional groups in the organization, to develop products and services that fully relate to the brand.

Finally, the will and commitment of top management is, above all, most important. Brand strategy is not a simple matter of image strategy and so senior management should take full responsibility and not let PR, marketing, advertising, and other communication groups act separately and inconsistently. Management must lead the entire organization to start brand building and promote change. It is senior management that must lead the organization to generate awareness and passion for the brand.

The Tough Decision: Brand Deletion

Sometimes, there is no option but to kill (whether it is done quickly or slowly) or sell off a brand. In other words, the brand manager decides to remove the brand from the portfolio. This is usually a consequence of a negative reply to the question, "Can the brand be revitalized?" Killing a brand is often called *brand deletion*, and unwanted brands that are sold off are often referred to as *orphan brands*. A brand may be deleted for one or more of the following reasons:

- There is no foreseeable route to recovery when a brand is heading downhill fast.
- The brand is no longer profitable, and isn't likely to become profitable again.
- The brand has been totally outdated by market innovations.
- The brand doesn't rank highly enough in importance, relative to other brands, to justify a place in the future portfolio.
- The brand's customer base has eroded and is unlikely to return.
- Revitalization of the brand cannot be justified in terms of the return on investment.
- Inadequate brand management has caused the brand to move away from its true proposition and character.

Brands are expensive to manage, keep, and revive. In today's world of intense competition it isn't economically feasible to hang on to a large portfolio. Unilever, for example, has reduced its total number of brands from 1,600 to around 400, to concentrate on what it calls its power brands. The financial problems intensify with a product branding approach, as opposed to a corporate branding approach, because there are no synergies in advertising and promotion, and every brand has to make its own way in the marketplace without corporate endorsement. But even when the parent brand is involved in endorsing a brand, markets are so dynamic and consumer tastes so fickle that it is very difficult sometimes to revitalize a brand.

Smart brand managers evolve their brands in line with such changes. Revolutionary changes are often not accepted by consumers and are difficult to sustain, as consumers don't connect with the drastic changes.

The case of Oldsmobile is typical of a brand that has become a casualty through a combination of market changes, inadequate brand management, inappropriate product development, and consumer attitudinal shifts (see Case Study 22).

CASE STUDY 22: OLDSMOBILE

The Final Parking Lot

Oldsmobile was a brand in the portfolio of General Motors (GM), when a decision was taken to phase it out—in other words, to kill the brand. The brand itself was over 100 years old, and possessed considerable heritage, but GM decided not to make any further attempts at revitalization. Previous attempts at breathing life into Oldsmobile during the 1990s had involved a large A&P expenditure and various product improvements. Why was the famous brand axed? There are four fundamental issues that GM had to address in this respect, which it failed to conquer.

1. The name issue

   It isn't advisable to use the word "old" in a brand name. One of the obvious problems for the brand is the name itself, which has proved to be a major consumer deterrent for a few decades, so much so that in the 1960s GM commissioned an advertising campaign aimed at changing the name to "Youngmobile." However, the problem persisted. In the 1980s, GM changed the tagline to "It's Not Your Father's Oldsmobile" in an effort to change the image that people had of a revered but old-fashioned brand. But despite GM's efforts, the brand still couldn't shake off the age association.

2. The product issue

   From the 1940s to the 1980s the Oldsmobile brand heritage and image was one of sportiness and innovation. Its

"Rocket" engines and the long, low designs were renowned and admired. But from the 1980s onwards, product developments moved away from this central brand character. Chevrolet engines were substituted and diesel engines given as an option. Even though these product decisions were tied in with the Arab countries' oil embargoes of the 1970s, when big cars were pronounced "gas guzzlers," they nevertheless had the effect of helping to shatter the brand image of Oldsmobile, and triggered more brand dilution when added to the name problem.

3. The image repositioning issue

   Attempts at repositioning the name as a luxury brand, accompanied by logo changes and product variations to match European competitors, failed, despite US$4 billion having been spent. Major discounting to boost sales worked against these efforts, and consumers were confused. They couldn't accept the widespread transformation of a brand that they perceived was "really not like that," and their associations with the old brand heritage ran deep. Brand sales consequently moved in the direction of fleet purchases and away from individuals.

4. The consumer issue

   The result of all the above—which amounts to inadequate brand management—is that consumers fled from the brand in large numbers, seeing no benefits and no differentiation, and no longer feeling an emotional association. GM at last gave up and bit the dying brand bullet. But like all great characters, according to Hollywood lexicon, the Oldsmobile may not really die; it will fade away, but will still be remembered.

One wonders whether Oldsmobile might have survived if it had been consistent over time with its initial identity, and evolved as a sporty and innovative brand, leveraging on its heritage. The imposed schizophrenia of the brand personality through inconsistent brand communications and product development basically turned people off. Oldsmobile was no longer the trusted and believable personality consumers knew. The emotional association was destroyed.

Deletion by Force

Sometimes, a company is forced to rationalize its brand portfolio and delete or sell some brands. This may, or may not, be a result of its own incompetence. In the case of General Motors, it was partly market forces and partly poor brand management. The process of restructuring the US automobile industry began in early 2009, brought on by the global recession. GM was one of the hardest hit, and filed for bankruptcy in June of that year. In order to survive, and gain government investment, it had to come up with a sustainable plan for a reduced brand portfolio.

The result was that, by June 18, 2009, only four brands remained— Buick, Chevrolet, GMC, and Cadillac; the rest were either sold or marked for deletion. Hummer was quickly sold to a Chinese company and Saab to a Finnish company. Famous brands, including Pontiac and Saturn, were among the victims. GM had too many brands that failed the test of relevance, with too little investment in them. And there was no focus. After the restructuring, Fritz Henderson, chief executive, said in an article published in *The Financial Times* of June 18, 2009: "100 per cent of our product, technology and marketing spend will now be focused behind the four core brands and 34 nameplates. Each one needs to be a hit and that is our challenge/commitment." What GM will also need to do, if it is to avoid further survival crises, is to change the perceptions of consumers toward its somewhat jaded and irrelevant brand image.

When times are bad, only the really strong brands survive—unless they are bailed out by the national government. The success of any brand depends in part on how well it communicates with its target audiences. Brand managers spend a lot of time on communications, and, as we saw from the Mazda case, these are both internal and external. The next chapter deals with the methods of communication used, but doesn't go into detail on advertising, which has been covered in many other books. It does highlight, however, the growing importance of public relations and integrated communications.

Total Communications for Brand Management

There are many options for communicating the key messages you want to be positioned in people's minds; however, the effectiveness of each method is changing very rapidly, as this chapter will show. The main channels of communication are:

- advertising;
- direct marketing;
- sales promotion;
- sponsorships;
- public relations;
- the Internet; and
- integrated communications.

Let's look at how each of these channels can be used in brand management.

Advertising

Advertising is a part of what is called paid mass communications, generally meaning space paid for in a publication, or time on radio, television, or cinema screens, although it may also be taken to include posters, billboards, and other outdoor advertising. Its main purpose is to persuade an audience either to take some action or to develop an attitude toward what is being advertised. Advertising is most frequently used for positioning brands.

Advertising achieves image differentiation mainly through repetition of a particular message, which leads to recognition, recall, attitudes, preferences, and action. It is frequently used by companies, but is also becoming more widespread in its application, being a part of global, regional, and national campaigns where information is less important than the need for exposure and positive perceptions. A good example of advertising-driven brand building is Absolut Vodka, where the personality of the product (intellect, wit, sophistication) has been consistently marketed and advertised around the world, and positioned so that it appeals to the target audience in terms of exclusivity. The brand has enjoyed a successful campaign relating it to different parts of the world. For instance, one advertisement for the product shows the usual clear bottle, but one that was enormously big and fat, with the caption "Absolut Texas."

Advertising can be executed through the various types of media described above, all of which have their advantages and disadvantages; however, creative repetition is the key to its success. The nature and cost of commercial advertising space means that only a limited amount of information can be placed, and so the frequency of an advertisement is also a governing factor in how effective it is. Little perceptual change will be gained by a limited number of exposures. Often, companies complain about the lack of advertising effectiveness, when the real reason is that the campaign was too short in terms of the message frequency. Managers in charge of brand communications need to appreciate that it takes time, and a great deal of repetition, for key messages to strike home and change human perceptions, which evolve relatively slowly. Image advertising, in particular, needs a long-term commitment. When carried out properly, with good emotional and creative input, it can be a powerful aid to positioning.

The Use of Emotion in Advertising: Appealing to the Heart, as well as the Head

There is no doubt that emotion sells. Emotion is still somewhat of a mystery, as far as our understanding of mental processes is concerned, but we do know that it originates in the right brain and manifests as a state of arousal. We also know that emotions trigger the brain 3,000 times faster than do rational thoughts. Emotion can also be positive (as in a state of happiness) or negative (as in a state of fear). As far as brand image is concerned, it is important to establish an emotional relationship with the people who are to be influenced. If positive feelings and emotions can be associated with what we are positioning, there is a much greater chance of attracting people, and altering or producing the perceptions we want them to have.

Emotion is increasingly being used by many organizations, especially service companies who are finding it more and more difficult to differentiate themselves from each other. Life insurance companies, for instance, are not just talking to consumers about the rational aspects of having a policy in terms of investment and returns, but are using emotional questions and statements in their advertising, such as "What will happen to your family if something happens to you?" and "We are offering you peace of mind." Financial services companies are typical of the many service organizations that are trying to persuade consumers that they are different from and better than their competitors in markets that are becoming increasingly commoditized. Fidelity Investments, in the United States, launched a series of advertisements that presented the company as being human and warm, with analysts saying why they like to work for the company and being very helpful to small investors seeking advice. In this age of technology, companies such as Fidelity, with large, dispersed customer bases of millions of people most of whom they might never meet, have to show that they are not just cold, impersonal bureaucracies, but have a human side that cares about their customers.

Some of the ways in which advertising can tap into people's emotions include the use of:

- drama;
- shock;
- fear;
- humor;
- warmth;
- aspiration;
- music; and
- sex.

All of these have their advantages and disadvantages. Any agency creative must be examined very thoroughly to ensure that the emotional response it aims to achieve is in line with the overall position and desired image. *Appropriate* is the key word in creative selection.

Drama

Drama can be powerful in positioning. One brand of coffee ran a series of advertisements that showed a young couple meeting over a cup of coffee, and followed them as the relationship developed through its ups and downs. It was like a mini soap opera, and audiences loved it. The coffee was always present, being a part of their everyday lives. Drama was created by means of a story, but demonstrations and narrative can also attract audience attention and brand recall. However, care must be taken not to offend. In 2008, Snickers ran a TV commercial featuring Mr. T of the TV series *The A Team* saying: "Speed walking. I pity you, fool. You a disgrace to the man race. It's time to run like a real man!" Although the ad was intended to be amusing, the gay community in the UK found it offensive and Snickers eventually removed it.

Shock

Shock tactics can also be powerful influencers, but the line between a positive and negative response can be fine. Some non-profit organizations use images of starving children and distressed, abused animals to boost their position, but these tactics can easily alienate viewers. In 2007, in an effort to discourage smoking, the British government launched anti-smoking posters featuring men and women with fish hooks through their mouths, and TV advertisements showing people being dragged along the floor by a hook embedded in their cheeks. The campaign received nearly 800 complaints from viewers who claimed the visuals were offensive and distressing for children. However, the whole purpose of the campaign was to shock people into giving up smoking.

Fear

Closely related to the above is the use of fear. Volvo has used images of people who were involved in horrific car accidents, but who lived because of the car's safety features. The "Volvo Saved My Life" club helped the company to establish its position as the safest car, a position it still owns today. Since the terrorist attacks in the United States and London of September 11, 2001 and July 7, 2005, respectively, some insurance companies have been heavily promoting the element of fear and peace of mind in their corporate and product marketing communications, which, while being reassuring to some people, may irritate others.

Humor

Humor can be a double-edged sword. Ethnic and minority jokes can offend, even though many people enjoy them. Care must be taken to ensure that the surprise element of the humor is followed by pleasure, not pain. Humor, when used well, relaxes audiences and reduces their resistance to key messages. Cadbury's "eyebrow" advertisement, which shows a young boy and girl moving their eyebrows in rhythm with the soundtrack, has attracted a lot of favorable attention around the world.

Warmth

Warmth also relaxes audiences and creates positive mental attitudes. Images that project love, patriotism, friendship, caring, and other warm behaviors can be of great assistance to positioning. Johnson & Johnson advertisements for baby and other products have built an amazingly powerful and unassailable positioning of gentleness, care, and love, which is represented in the company's global market share. Even sporting events such as the PGA Tour introduce warmth into their advertisements, with golfing celebrity Nick Price describing, with the help of emotion-building images, how the tour has helped many underprivileged people. The commercial ends with the tagline, "Anything's Possible."

Aspiration

Aspirational advertising can be a great motivator. Nike's "Just Do It" campaigns are all about self-improvement and success, and advertisements featuring successful sportspersons such as Tiger Woods help to reinforce this position. Aspiration as a means of bringing out people's emotions is often executed in advertisements through the use of children and well-known personalities.

Music

Music is frequently used in advertisements on television and radio, whether as jingles or background. If memorable, it can aid recall of the commercial, but it can also be a source of irritation. Up to 50 percent of all advertisements include music in some form. It may be used to arouse sentimentality, as was done so successfully in advertisements for the Hovis brand of bread where a northern English brass band played a very sentimental tune; or to illustrate fun, excitement, seriousness, and other emotions that fit the desired positioning and perception. Music is liked by every possible segment and can be used to stimulate emotions in all age groups, but it is particularly appropriate for younger audiences. It can, however, be a non-differentiator, as is the case with so many car television commercials playing the same kind of dramatic, classical music as the products weave their way through hills, rain, and difficult terrain. A lack of creativity in both scenes and music can cause consumers to take the opportunity to briefly leave the room.

Sex

Caution should be exercised when using sex to sell a product. There are no adequate guidelines here, but research indicates that sexual images should be linked clearly to the product benefits, and are received better by consumers if linked also to humor and respect, and are used suggestively rather than explicitly. Sometimes, brand management steps over the mark and risks damage to the image of the brand, as Calvin Klein did when featuring children dressed only in underwear. Other brands are more subtle. A Martell advertisement for its liquor brand features a glamorous woman saying suggestively, "All great discoveries begin with a question. Like, can you come out and play?" and "If you shouldn't, you should." Similarly, in an ad for Chivas Regal's successful, but enigmatic, "When You Know"™campaign, an exceptionally attractive model, dressed in very little, is shown with the caption: "Yes, God is a man."

In recent years, the European advertising "watchdog" bureaus have clamped down on what they call "Porno Chic," where the use of sex and nudity in advertising by some brands is considered offensive and in-decent. One advertisement that was withdrawn after bureau criticism in France was produced by DDB for the clothing brand La City. A young woman wearing only underwear was shown on her hands and knees beside a sheep. The tagline read, "I'd like a sweater." Subtlety is key to the use of sex in brand communications.

Direct Marketing

Direct marketing is where consumers deal directly with manufacturers or suppliers when buying items, with no intermediary such as a retailer involved. Techniques used here include:

- direct mail;
- telephone selling; and
- press, television, and radio advertising.

To be effective, direct marketing has to be clearly targeted or it can damage a company's image through unwanted solicitation, as with "junk" mail. If done well, it can be highly effective, not just in sales terms, but also in building a strong position. Its specific advantages are:

- It is effective in targeting well-defined segments.
- It can help build relationships over time.
- It is interactive, thus involving the consumer.
- It is easily measurable in terms of responses.
- It is easily customized to provide specific messages to specific people.

It is critical for positioning and image building that the personality and identity of the company is visible and consistent, and that the correct values are projected. Dell Computer has built its entire brand identity and position through this means, establishing a first-rate image with low-cost, high-quality products and speed of delivery.

Sales Promotion

While advertising tends to occupy a large part of the communications budget for many companies, especially those involved in consumer goods, sales promotion techniques are often used to get new products off the ground and establish positions, to acquire new and lost customers, or to speed up the buying process. Included in sales promotion techniques are:

- free gifts with purchases;
- redemption coupons;
- contests;
- samples;
- price reductions;
- discount coupons;
- self-liquidating premiums;
- "buy one, get one free" offers;
- gift packs; and
- privilege cards.

The danger with sales promotion activities is that consistent promotional activity may weaken brand image. Some experts argue that they shouldn't be used for brand building for this reason, but companies such as American Express, Citibank, Carlsberg, and others have found them to be useful in increasing their customer base (mainly by getting people to switch brands), increasing individual customer spend, and speeding up the purchase decision. As a general rule, it is better to avoid the price discount type of promotion and go for the added value type. Adding more value to the brand offering, rather than subtracting from price, gives consumers good perceptions about value without losing quality perceptions. Perceived value for money is rarely a reflection of price alone.

Sales promotion activities are liked by retailers and salespersons, and can provide a company with a short-term competitive advantage, but there is always the tendency for competitors to wade in with their own similar promotion, so the results may be short-lived.

Sponsorships and Endorsements

Sponsorships and endorsements are now becoming a fact of life for many brand managers, as more and more companies try to boost their brand images by tying up deals with celebrities. The main things to watch out for in this area of brand management are that they are relevant to the audience you are targeting, and that they are appropriate to the personality of your brand. The following examples are mainly from the world of sport, but other examples can also be found.

Brands and Sports Sponsorships

Sport has universal appeal. It is one category that attracts virtually everyone in the world—a universal audience. Sports sponsorships give corporate brands an advantage over advertising, by offering them a better chance of standing out from cluttered communications and addressing huge, targeted markets. It is little wonder, then, that the big brands are equally attracted, and want to be in on the major sporting events and activities that can give them global reach—and that they are willing to pay the substantial prices necessary to get there. An example is Barclay Group. Becoming the name behind the change from the English Premier League to the Barclays Premier League (BPL) cost Barclay Group US$130.65 million between September 2006 and the end of the 2009/2010 football season. Barclay's wealth marketing director Ian Ewart says, "More than 600 million people in 204 countries watch the BPL, and roughly 1,000 hours of Barclays Premier League time is broadcast around the world every week."

Arguably the world's largest and most valuable football brand—Manchester United (MU)—was reported in June 2009 to have signed a four-year shirt deal with the insurance giant Aon Corporation that was reputedly worth £80 million over four years. Aon said it hoped that its relationship with MU would help to improve its brand recognition. Aon had noted that AIG, a previous sponsor of MU and a casualty of the global financial meltdown, had become the 47th most recognized global brand and had jumped from 84th to 30th position on *Barron's* list of most respected companies. Another example is Norwich Union, the British insurer, which renewed its contract to sponsor UK athletics in 2007 through to 2012 for around US$100 million, according to head of sponsorship Tanya Veinguard.

No mention of sports sponsorship would be complete without reference to the Olympic Games. Olympic revenue now exceeds US$4 billion over the four-year Olympics cycle, and a great deal of this comes from the power brands. The turning point was the Los Angeles Olympic Games held in 1984, when the cost of sponsorship and broadcasting rights accelerated tremendously. ABC paid US$225 million for the US rights, and the number of brands allowed to become official sponsors was limited. As a result, a payment of US$4 million got sponsors exclusivity in their category. Coca-Cola paid US$12 million to be the official soft drink of the Games. Nowadays the premiums are far higher, and the big brands compete savagely for global exposure at the world's greatest sporting event. For example, Adidas became the third sponsor of the 2012 London Olympics when it signed a deal in 2007 worth more than US$201 million. Adidas will be the official sportswear partner for the Games and provide clothing for the 70,000 volunteers and officials. The deal also covered sponsorship for clothing and equipment used by British athletes for the 2008 Beijing Games, the 2010 Vancouver Winter Games, and the 2012 London Games. When six billion people are watching, it's worth it.

Sports Personalities

Sports personalities have become very popular with companies seeking global exposure and recognition, boosting the image of the brands (but not in all cases, as shown below) with their endorsements. Here are one or two well-known examples.

Reebok: Venus Williams

In 2000, Venus Williams became the first African-American to capture the Wimbledon singles title since Althea Gibson in 1958. At the end of 2000, Venus Williams capped a great year with a massive present from Reebok in the form of a US$40 million contract to represent the brand, the most lucrative endorsement deal ever for a female athlete up until then. Reebok had been losing out to Nike, watching the world leader in sports shoe and apparel products sign up many top athletes and sports personalities, including Roger Federer, Maria Sharapova, Christiano Ronaldo, and Tiger Woods. Although Reebok has been associated with Williams since she was 11 years old, the company regarded the five-year contract extension as both a relief and a triumph, with chief marketing officer Angel Martinez saying at the time: "There's no better athlete, no better individual in the world who is better suited to represent our brand. Our goal is not to show Venus as a tennis player but Venus as a lifestyle icon, someone inspiring with the power of her presence." The price tag lifted the earning power of women athletes to new heights. As Williams said, "For women's sports and women's tennis, it's just so great." Not bad for her bank balance either.

Nike: Tiger Woods

Other personalities are getting big fees, too, but few can match the estimated US$100 million forked out by Nike for Tiger Woods in 2000 for a five-year extension to his existing contract, the largest endorsement fee in the world at that time. Woods not only excels at his sport—in his case, being the world number one in golf—but is also regarded as a role model for young people. This alone guarantees him the money, because great sportspeople aren't necessarily perceived as great human beings. Woods himself realizes why he is worth the multi-million-dollar attention of Nike when he says he is a role model who embraces the responsibility of influencing others positively. It is now estimated that Woods will reach the US$1 billion mark through tournament winnings and endorsement fees by 2010.

Other Personalities: The Good, The Bad, and The Ugly

Apart from reminding us that there is big money in sport these days, the following examples show how the branding of sports products revolves around brand personality, and the personalities who represent the brands. Maria Sharapova is a popular athlete, endowed with both athletic skill and beauty. She was the highest-paid female athlete in 2008, with earnings close to US$26 million. Her youthful and athletic personality tends to appeal to a young audience, which makes her a suitable role model for many youngsters and a sought-after endorser for many brands. Currently, she has lucrative brand ambassador contracts with top global brands such as Nike, Tiffany & Co., Tag Heuer, Canon, and Sony Ericsson.

Relevance and appropriateness are everything when it comes to personality endorsements. Most of the big brands get involved in this form of promotion, and not just the sports brands. Admittedly, sports watch brand TAG Heuer has used Formula 1 racing drivers Kimi Raikkonen and Lewis Hamilton, but we also see this type of endorsement with other brands and non-sports personalities, such as Omega (Chinese film actress and singer Zhang Ziyi) and Rolex (Canadian crooner Michael Buble). TAG Heuer has used actor Brad Pitt, and basketball player Yao Ming has enjoyed lucrative deals to appear in advertisements for Apple, Visa, and other brands.

With the correct endorsements, the returns are there; but if things go wrong, the brand reputation may suffer. Pepsi once had the misfortune to have endorsement deals with Michael Jackson, Mike Tyson, and Madonna when all three entertainers were having their own reputation problems. Pepsi also had problems with Britney Spears. Hertz Rent-a-Car tied up with O.J. Simpson, who was charged with murder, and by trying to distance themselves from the association brought even more attention to it. Other personalities, such as former footballer Diego Maradona, have also caused extreme embarrassment to associated sponsors, as has basketball superstar Kobe Bryant, who was charged with rape while under contract to McDonald's. Michael Phelps, the hero of the 2008 Olympics US swimming team, lost his endorsement contract with Kellogg's after a photo of him smoking marijuana was made public. Of course, you can never tell what will happen when famous personalities are intertwined with the brand, and the public does tend to forgive and forget, but care is essential when choosing the "face" of the brand. It is sometimes easy to grab at opportunities to reach millions of people through personality endorsements without taking the time to look at the possible downside. And even thorough analysis cannot predict how people are likely to behave in the future, so there is always an element of risk in this strategy.

This subject leads us naturally to what is arguably the most stressful part of the job for all top and brand managers: public relations and crisis management.

Public Relations and Crisis Management

I often think of public relations (PR) as the "Cinderella" of brand management, because it works so hard but receives few accolades when brands are successful. While advertising and sales promotion are very visible and tend to get the spotlight, PR is often the unsung hero, capable of achieving a great deal of perception change, yet getting very little recognition for the role it can play.

PR departments are often referred to by a variety of other names, including "corporate affairs," "corporate communications," and "public affairs." The basic work of PR is communicating and developing relationships with various target publics, including:

- the media;
- employees;
- shareholders;
- business partners;
- industry analysts;
- local and foreign investors;
- governments;
- the general public; and
- customers and potential customers.

Advantages of PR

PR is heavily media-related and communicates to these audiences through press releases, press conferences and interviews, advertorials, newspaper/magazine columns, receptions, sponsorships, and other events. Because PR can speak so widely through so many channels, it is critical to the brand-building process, although, surprisingly, many companies don't purposefully use it to do this. I would suggest that more brand managers use PR in a strategic way to build and protect their brands, as opposed to relying on it in a reactive way, as happens with crisis management.

It is surprising that PR isn't used more widely in brand building and management. Although it often uses mass media, unlike advertising, it doesn't pay for the space, a fact that might be of great appeal to the thrifty. In many cases it is free, and can both influence public opinion and build/maintain brand reputation and image at zero cost! It is for this very reason that PR often has more credibility with the public than does advertising. I am not suggesting that PR is a total substitute for A&P activities, but that it should be in every brand manager's armory, as it can provide valuable support to those activities, just as they can act as a support to PR.

Another advantage of PR is that, unlike advertisements, news tends to be read. The proliferation of advertisements in newspapers and magazines tends to result in readers largely ignoring the messages they contain, merely giving them a cursory glance. Similarly, television commercials are often given short shrift by viewers, sometimes because they are of poor quality, but mostly because they have no relevance to them. The tendency of advertising to irritate and alienate people, via whatever medium, is well known. But PR presents messages in a more engaging, newsworthy way that captures people's attention.

Disadvantages of PR

The work of PR is no easy task; it involves a lot of time invested in meeting and talking with the target audiences, and persuading them to listen to a certain point of view, and to adopt particular attitudes toward a variety of situations and circumstances. It also involves managing the media; getting people such as journalists, in particular, to report or say favorable things about the client when many competitors are also seeking comment, especially at times of great importance, such as new product launches. PR is an ongoing process, as opposed to a one-off campaign.

The stories that are generated by PR and sent to the media must be significant and newsworthy. Nine out of 10 releases/stories that journalists receive never get into print—they are just not different or interesting enough. PR contributions must therefore be both timely and interesting, and the more expert PR practitioners will generate what in reality are releases that contain ordinary information, but also give the material a special twist to make it rise to the top of the editorial in-tray.

Because of the above, the PR professional must have well-honed skills. In fact, the success of the PR effort depends on the strength of the PR practitioner's networks and oratorical skills—how they convey their ideas creatively and persuasively.

Points to Note

Most large companies have corporate communications departments whose tasks include looking after public relations. Some companies and individuals hire agencies to do this for them, whether on a retainer basis or for particular projects, or in times of crisis. Some points to note that have relevance for brand management include:

- Most press releases never see the light of day in the media, and should be used sparingly. Inundating journalists with them isn't going to get results. They look for really newsworthy items, and routine releases are usually filed immediately in the wastepaper bin. Journalists only consider press releases when there is something significant to say that consumers will want to hear about. They are only interested in stories that sell and have a human-interest angle.
- Treat journalists as strategic partners in your business. Relationships are very important, and good relationships are only earned over time. Buying journalists the odd lunch won't buy you media space. It is more important to listen to their views, because they are the ones who are constantly in touch with the public and know what they will want to read, see, or listen to. Also, don't try to be everyone's friend. Choose carefully those few journalists who you believe will, in the long run, be the best choice for your strategy and future situation, and be prepared to invest a lot of time in talking to them.
- Make the best of opportunities that present themselves. An important development in the industry can give you the chance to comment and make your name known. One bank positioned itself as the "Knowledgeable Bank" and managed to get a regular column in an influential newspaper, where it wrote about financial developments affecting people around the world.
- If events are being planned to boost the image of the company or its brand(s), ensure that they are a good "fit" with the company's positioning strategy. The same applies to sponsorships: they have to be to be appropriate to, and in character with, the brand personality or identity to be projected. When Mattel organized The Barbie Doll World Summit event for charitable purposes, it brought together children from over 27 countries—an event that was totally in line with the brand's personality and positioning strategy. When Rolex sponsors sporting events, the company chooses only those top tournaments that reinforce the status and

prestige of the brand name. And, of course, with both these examples, they were and are sure of getting the right media coverage targeted at the right target audiences.

Public Relations and Crisis Management: You Can Expect the Unexpected, But Can You Prepare for It?

Every CEO and brand manager fears a crisis that can influence market and consumer opinion in such a way that it sends the share price rocketing downwards and does serious long-term damage to the brand image of the product or service and the company that owns it. It is also a nightmare for PR specialists, because, when a crisis occurs, everyone else in the organization suddenly seems to distance themselves from the problem and to hand the "hot potato" over to PR. Poor handling of a crisis can spawn more crises and ruin a brand's image. A good response, on the other hand, can save and even enhance it.

PR specialists are skilled in handling awkward and potentially image-damaging situations, and some are capable of turning a crisis into an opportunity. The problem with a crisis, of course, is that you don't know when it is going to materialize. Nevertheless, many companies are wise enough to develop crisis management manuals and procedures that try to anticipate every disaster situation and prescribe what the response should be. However, although crisis scenario planning is carried out by many leading brands, it is nevertheless simulation, and often doesn't resemble the real event when an actual crisis occurs. However good these preparations are, there is always the chance of something unexpected happening.

Unfortunately, there are no rules for crisis management. But we can look at some unfortunate situations that companies have had to face, and glean from them valuable information about what can go right and wrong, and what can be done or should be avoided.

The Speed Factor

In crisis management, the speed and type of response is critical to maintaining brand image. Sometimes, the public initially knows more about a problem or disaster than the company itself, as news teams tend to be quick on the scene. In such cases, the company is faced with a lack of information, and yet hard questions are being asked which require answers. As a brand manager, it is imperative that you put out a media statement of some kind as soon as possible, acknowledging what has happened. You may not have all the details, but you must say what you know. Failure to do so can seriously damage your brand image.

In times of crisis, brand managers have to move swiftly, and yet it is surprising how often avoidable mistakes are made, even by the famous brands. Coca-Cola made a huge PR error in 1999 when it failed to make any media statement for three days after a poisoning scare occurred at its canning/bottling plant in Belgium. While people were being poisoned and the media all over Europe were drawing damaging conclusions, Coca-Cola's head office made no attempt to communicate with the public. By the time it issued a statement, it was too late. This wasn't only poor PR and brand management; it was irresponsible. Had the crisis happened to a brand of lesser stature and power, it could have suffered permanent and fatal damage. There is little doubt that this decision, taken at the highest level in the company, was partially responsible for changes in management not long afterwards, and that it caused considerable damage to the reputation of the world's most famous brand.

In August 2008, melamine-contaminated milk produced by China-based dairy producer Sanlu caused the deaths of six babies in China, while another 300,000 fell ill. New Zealand dairy giant Fonterra, which had a 43 percent share in the joint venture company, made no comment for several weeks after learning of the contamination. Angry consumers finally forced the company to take responsible action and recall the product, but the delay damaged its reputation with its customers.

Other companies have demonstrated a quick response, as in the famous case of Tylenol—Johnson & Johnson's leading analgesic brand. The speed of withdrawal of the product from the market after poison was found in some of the product probably saved the company from catastrophe and demonstrated how concerned it was about public safety. Its re-entry into the market with tamper-proof packaging reinforced the critical attribute of "We Care."

The "Ostrich Syndrome": Denial

One critical issue with crisis management is whether or not the crisis should be denied. Many companies opt to deny that there is a crisis until either they work out their response or things become so much worse that they have to admit it. This is the fastest possible way to destroy a brand image that it has taken time to create. Generally, the best advice is not to deny that there is a crisis situation, even if you think it isn't really significant. What must always be remembered is that you are dealing with human perceptions, and these are very fragile, easily influenced, and difficult to change once entrenched. The message for PR here is that if consumers *think* there is a crisis and that it is important, then there *is* one and it *is* important, especially if those people are from the media. Perceptions can be fact or fiction, but they exist in people's minds; and to those people, their perceptions—which cumulatively form the brand image—are reality.

Maintenance of Trust

The world's most powerful brands enjoy the trust of their customers, and this trust creates brand loyalty. In a crisis of any proportion, maintenance of that trust is vital to continued brand loyalty. Reassurance is an essential part of the PR response, and failure to quickly regain trust can mean that the brand image fails just as fast.

The case of Singapore Airlines (see Case Study 25) demonstrates how a company can avoid many of the pitfalls in crisis management and retain the trust of the public. However, before we look at that case, we will examine two cases that illustrate both quick and slow PR responses aimed at preventing damage to a brand's image.

CASE STUDY 23: HELLO KITTY

Damage Limitation: Quick Response

Hello Kitty, from Sanrio, has enjoyed a great deal of success with many age groups. The little cat with no mouth has managed brand extensions on a huge scale, but the Hello Kitty brand managers are always on the lookout for incongruent exposure. In late 2000, Sanrio learned that two films were to be made in Hong Kong that would tell the story of a woman who was tortured to death. The persons responsible dismembered the corpse, cooked the body parts, and then stuffed them in the head of a Hello Kitty doll. Mr. Soji Nyoi, general manager of the company's distributor Sanrio Hong Kong at the time, said that both films would run against the corporate ethics of the company. "Our whole corporate ethic is based on social communications, with love, friendship, and happiness," he said. Sanrio was concerned to the extent that it said, "We formally state that we do not support the production of these films, nor do we accept the use of Sanrio's characters." The company was concerned that the tragic event would be used for entertainment and so damage the brand image of Hello Kitty.

CASE STUDY 24: McDONALD'S

Damage Limitation: Slow Response

In Singapore, Hello Kitty unintentionally caused a problem for someone else's brand. In 2000, McDonald's co-branded with Hello Kitty for a sales campaign that blew out of all proportion. The subsidized Hello Kitty figures given away with burgers caused pandemonium on the streets of the island state, with people queuing for blocks to get their favorite little cat. Fights broke out about queue positions, and people who became violent were arrested. To cap it all, customers were entering McDonald's outlets, purchasing huge numbers of burgers in order to get quantities of the Hello Kitty dolls (in one case, 150!), and then throwing the burgers into the waste bins and making off with their feline prizes. A lack of supply of the little animal at some outlets exacerbated the tensions of customers. The adverse publicity damaged McDonald's image, but this brand management crisis was poorly handled at the time. In defense of brand management, there was little chance of forecasting the disaster, but the physical customer problems and media response could have been managed more effectively. Luckily for the fast-food giant, the brand image damage proved to be temporary, and in 2001 it resumed its co-branding activities with Snoopy characters, altogether a safer bet and a better brand fit. McDonald's is currently running another co-branding promotion using cartoon characters from the movie *Ice Age 3*.

Another implication here is the issue of distribution channels. As an example, McDonald's franchises its brand, and when any company allows this, there is always the danger that the brand won't be represented in the way the brand owner would wish. For those working in brand management and PR, there is the additional problem of helping maintain the consistency of the brand in many markets when those entities representing your brand are not under your total control. Many top brands, such as Gucci, have bought back their brand franchises at significant cost, in order to control the total brand experience.

CASE STUDY 25: SINGAPORE AIRLINES

Thrust into Disaster—PR in Action

The alpha-numerics "SQ 006" commanded worldwide media attention and created emotional concern when an aircraft from one of the world's most famous airlines and international brands, Singapore Airlines (SIA), crashed in Taiwan on October 31, 2000. This case illustrates how a brand can be put under the spotlight by public opinion and the world's media, and describes how this top brand dealt with this unexpected disaster, which tested its brand integrity.

THE SCENE

A foggy, bad-weather environment at Taiwan's Chiang Kai Shek Airport. Visibility is low and the winds are high. Aircraft are allowed, under international rules, to take off on the decision of the pilot with airport guidance. SQ 006 moves toward the designated runway, and turns left when it reaches a runway with some of its take-off lights illuminated. (This is a normal scenario for a bad weather take-off.) There are no barriers to the runway; nothing to suggest anything unusual to the pilots. The pilots request approval for take-off from the airport traffic controllers, and this is given. The airport controllers cannot actually see the runway because of the poor weather conditions. The plane accelerates, but hits unseen objects on the runway, later classified as construction equipment. The plane has turned off on to the runway before the correct one; the wrong runway has repairs being carried out. The disaster results in the loss of 83 lives.

Taiwanese reporters have free access to the airport, and their crews are quick on the scene to film and report the burning wreckage and casualties. SIA learns of the disaster only when the world's media break the story.

SIA's CRISIS MANAGEMENT RESPONSE

There is complete and utter shock at an airline that has the world's trust and confidence. SIA is a major international brand with global aspirations. The company has a crisis management center that immediately swings into action, with its PR staff assigned to work around the clock in two 12-hour shifts. They answer media "hotline" questions without delay. In an immediate response, they announce that they acknowledge what has happened and are searching for more details. They give out what information they have and advise what they don't have.

They promise that they will update the media at every opportunity. This wasn't just a promise made by a company about information, but a promise made by the brand itself. What SIA did was to reassure the media that they were acknowledged as being important. When global calls are constantly being received, the PR team has to give out what information it has, and promise to deliver every piece of information as it receives it.

The SIA website was switched immediately from its normal condition to the "crisis site," which replaced all corporate information with crisis information, so that anyone hitting the website would be privy to sharing the media releases in real time. All the communication channels started to operate in the same way. This was good crisis management planning. Also planned was that one person only was to address the media, so the airline spoke through and with one voice, leaving no room for error. This person— receiving all reports and constantly interacting with the chief executive officer—gave out not only up-to-date information from the airline's point of view, but also reports of what was known, who it was affecting, and what plans there were to deal with these dynamic issues. All media coverage was captured, analyzed, and released to keep the brand promise.

All stakeholders, including employees and investors, were informed and kept up to date, also via the company Intranet, as were market analysts. The SIA PR approach was one of total transparency.

DEALING WITH THE PUBLIC

A brand has only one opportunity to keep the faith and trust of people when a disaster strikes, and SIA made sure it did the right thing. As soon as the disaster was known, the CEO publicly admitted that the accident had occurred and said that the company took full responsibility for it, as it was its plane. This was a brave and thoughtful decision, made when no one knew the cause of the accident. It gained SIA a lot of respect in the world community, and ensured that it kept the world's trust. SIA also recognized that in situations such as this, those affected need empathy, not sympathy. Examples of how this was done included a 100-day period of mourning for the dead passengers and crew. During this period no advertisements were run by the airline, and the letterhead was altered to omit its famous tagline, "Now More Than Ever, A Great Way to Fly."

All in all, the PR response from SIA was remarkable, and showed how the initials "PR" can, when disaster strikes, become synonymous with "public responsibility."

Whenever disasters occur, there are always PR opportunities at both the national and corporate levels. Out of sadness can come hope and resolve; for companies, a crisis can offer opportunities to improve their brand strength.

The Internet and Integrated Brand Communications

The Internet is now a vital component of brand management and market communications, as discussed in detail in Chapter 7. Often, however, outside assistance is needed for Web-based and other communications. The trend now is toward integrated communications being offered by single agencies, which can provide companies assistance on various fronts.

In the past, brand managers have had to rely on different agencies, or parts of agencies, to deliver brand communications via a variety of means, but this inefficient and often inconsistent approach has given way to new ideas on integrated communications that bring consistency to the way in which the brand is presented. Brand managers I have talked to welcome this trend, because consistency builds great brands.

New Global Marketing and Media Realities

The marketing and brand communications industry has seen some significant shifts over the last decade, driven by the managers of brands and the consumers that actually build the brands. First, there are many more competitors, and many more media opportunities, than before—for instance, there are now hundreds of cable TV channels in the United States. Second, more money is now being spent on promotion, as opposed to advertising, than in the past. Mass media is becoming less impactful, and therefore less fashionable. Brand managers are realizing that in the world of mass customization, mass-media approaches are less successful. Third, consumers are much more discerning and choosy, and less tolerant of traditional media attempts to influence them.

The traditional agencies have responded to these global and media realities by producing communications solutions that give brands and consumers more choice and relevance. The latest developments in brand communications are concerned with bringing together many communications platforms to create a bigger impact on target audiences, and to add power to the projection of the brand identity. Many agencies are combining their separate units and divisions to create improved and more cost-effective "packages" for their clients.

Interactive A&P and Consumer Touchpoints

Television and print are still the primary media for advertising, but the growth of the Internet and the digital world promises to give companies more opportunities for targeted and one-to-one advertising. The power brand companies are now developing interactive strategies that cover all possible consumer communications touchpoints. For example, as well as carrying out all the traditional means of advertising and promoting its watches, Swatch has its own club, with an online community, for whom it provides social networking opportunities and a means to share common interests and photos, and to engage in discussion forums. It has blog features where Swatch club members can share their brand

Figure 6.1 Brand touchpoint wheel: Traditional

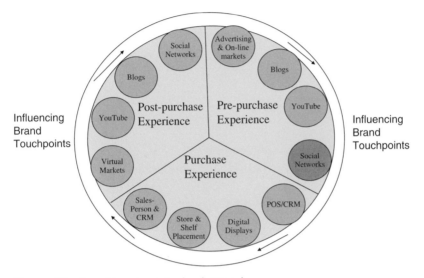

Figure 6.2   Brand touchpoint wheel: Digital age

experiences and opinions. Through this experience, Swatch generates many more touchpoints with consumers and ensures that its brand communication is a two-way street and not a one-way dead end.

If we compare the traditional methods of A&P with the new methods that take advantage of digital innovations, we see differences like those shown in Figures 6.1 and 6.2. The increasing shift toward the use of digital as well as traditional media ensures that the brand receives maximum exposure. Such interactive strategies also ensure that consumers are involved with and can communicate with the brand. Chapter 7 contains analysis of some of the digital brands that are being used for this form of brand communications, such as Facebook and YouTube.

Analysis of Brand Communications Copy

One final important element of brand communications is the copy used. Brand managers need to be able to distinguish between creative that is "on brand" and that which is "off brand." Too often, the tone of a company's brand communications copy fails to match the personality of the brand.

It is critical to speak to the audience in the way the brand as a person would speak to people. Case Study 26 provides an example of how a thorough analysis might be carried out of brand communications copy and appropriate tonal adjustments made to create copy that is "on brand."

CASE STUDY 26: MALAYSIA AIRLINES

Analysis of Advertising Copy for Perceived Brand Personality

Malaysia Airlines has won several awards for its in-flight service, a fact that it occasionally mentions in its advertising copy. In this case study, I was asked to analyze some advertising copy produced for the airline. (Although the ad itself isn't shown here, use of warmer colors might also have proved beneficial.) The original wording of the materials is given, followed by my analysis and suggestions.

What do you do to the airline that was voted number 1 as Asia's Best Business Airline for three consecutive years? Better it.

Our luxury fleet of B747-400s and the "super ranger" B-777s have two world firsts on board. They are the business center with a laptop computer printer and fax machine and an air to ground retail transaction service.

Receiving the highest honour in the airline industry can only mean one thing: to provide service at a higher level of excellence.

For reservations or information, call your travel agent or Malaysia Airlines.

General Comments

In general, the advertisement has a somewhat dismissive, arrogant, and self-congratulatory tone. It doesn't involve the reader in any way, or provide any reason for the customer to be at all interested in this award. There is no warmth or friendliness in the ad. In tonal quality, the airline stands well apart from and above its audience.

Further, it presents a somewhat perplexing line of argument—namely, "We are number one but determined to be better. We have the most modern planes with some special business facilities. Getting the award means a determination to be better. For more, call your travel agent or us."

The headline provides no reason for readers to move on to read the body copy, the concluding sentence of which, frankly, is insulting to their intelligence.

Specific Comments

Headline: The traits suggested are: assertive, disinterested, and pseudo-sophisticated.

Paragraph 1: The brand personality traits suggested are: efficient, manufactured, and systemized. There is no explanation of what an air-to-ground retail transaction service might mean to the consumer.

Paragraph 2: This assertive statement requires a tortured leap of logic.

Paragraph 3: This just states the obvious.

In summary, the personality traits communicated by this ad are:

- assertive,
- disinterested;
- efficient;
- manufactured; and
- systemized.

They add up to a personality that is arrogant and dismissive. Here are my suggested adjustments to the copy to encourage a different perception of brand personality.

Wow!

They say you said we're number one!

When *Business Travel World* told us Malaysia Airlines had been voted Asia's "Best Business Airline" for the third year running, we paused for a moment to think about what we might have done to deserve it.

Yes, we have all the Business Class features, facilities, space, and services you'd expect of one of the world's most sophisticated airlines. But three years in succession? When we asked around, we found a very simple, gratifying answer.

It's all about you. It's the way you respond to our people and make them feel. Malaysians are genuine, gentle, and caring at heart, and you have a way of bringing out their natural best. Yes, we train intensively, but an inherent attraction of personalities isn't something that can be "trained for" or "systemized"; it's the way people are.

It's curious, isn't it, that the key difference we're told makes us Asia's "Best Business Airline" is not confined to Business Class at all—but there for everyone who flies our airline. To all our friends, a heartfelt "Terimah Kasih."

The key to this suggested copy is that it claims ownership of the award *on behalf of the customers*, in a modest way, while making it relevant to *all* those who fly the airline, not just to Business Class travelers.

Specifically:

- *Headline*: The "Wow!" is disarming, moving far away from any impression of arrogance. "Wow!" is a happy expression, in line with the airline's personality. Reader curiosity is intensified by the impression of Malaysia Airlines' "surprise" at winning the award for the third time. Subliminally, this very powerfully increases the sense of value of the achievement.

- *Subheadline*: "You said" immediately involves the reader. In a single line, the airline claims leadership with no sense of arrogance. It puts the conferring of the award firmly into the hands of a third party—"They." It also creates curiosity, leading the reader into the subsequent elements of the ad. Tonal qualities present a much nicer personality.

The personality traits communicated by the revised ad are:

- *Paragraph 1*: Natural, modest, approachable, interested, caring.
- *Paragraph 2*: Genuine, natural, modest, approachable, interested, caring.
- *Paragraph 3*: Helpful, approachable, genuine, natural, modest, interested, caring.
- *Paragraph 4*: Helpful, approachable, genuine, natural, modest, interested, caring.

Summary

The tonally revised text still achieves the very important objective of communicating the "win." And in itself, the conferring of the award automatically communicates a modern fleet, sophistication, provision of a very high standard of service, and so on. This leaves us free to sell the far more important, differentiating personality benefit, not only to Business Class passengers but also to the market at large.

From a tonal standpoint, we have:

Original copy	Suggested copy
Assertive	Modest
Disinterested	Interested
Pseudo-sophisticated	Approachable

(Continued)

Original copy	Suggested copy
Efficient	Caring
Manufactured	Genuine
Systemized	Natural
Immodest	Happy

The airline is still blowing its own trumpet, but in a way that now endears it to, rather than separates it from, its customers.

I would suggest that any advertising copy that is proposed to be sent out to consumers, via whatever means, be subjected to an analysis similar to that carried out in the above case study.

Emotional Brand Communication: Example of a Simple, Emotion-Packed Advertisement: Mercedes-Benz

Some of the best advertisements are those that use few words, but are filled with emotion in both pictures and copy. The following is an excellent example.

Source: Courtesy of Mercedez-Benz. Used with permission.

The product attributes are clearly shown and referred to, as is the element of human desire. The advertisement is headed:

"The New C-Class Sports Coupe. Let your feelings go."

The copy says:

How wonderful it is to dream. Of capturing the rush of youth. Of accelerated heartbeats and boundless enthusiasm. Of butterflies in your stomach. Of the pure driving pleasure of a lowered sports suspension that brings every curve and corner to life. Of the commanding power of a supercharged Kompressor engine. Of giving in to temptation.

This advertisement is a perfect example of how a brand makes the emotional connection with consumers and slips in rational areas of competitive advantage. It has a wonderful visual and terrific copy.

What You Say, and How, Depends on What You Know

It is probably clear to you by now that it is critical to understand the target audience well before attempting any communication with them. Some brands go to extraordinary lengths to get to know their customers, and base all their communications on the insights they gather. Once they understand the way the target audience thinks and behaves, then they tailor what they say, and how they say it, to that audience.

In Case Study 27, we see how Chivas Regal cleverly communicates values derived from market research that are highly relevant to the brand name and to the emotional needs of its target consumers. Case Study 28, on Procter & Gamble, a company that has a long history of successful brand communications, shows that even within one target market, there may be opportunities to communicate the same message very differently to different segments of that market.

CASE STUDY 27: CHIVAS REGAL

"Live with Chivalry"

Chivas Regal: A Brand with Heritage

Chivas Regal is a brand with almost 200 years of history and heritage. It is a highly regarded brand in the premium scotch category and is sold in over 100 countries. The brand was acquired by Pernod Ricard in 2001 from Seagram and currently ranks as one of its top 15 brands. Some 4.5 million nine-litre cases were sold in 2008, the highest volume ever recorded by Chivas Regal.

New Marketing Campaign

In 2008, Chivas Regal launched a 50 million Euro global marketing campaign that had as its anchor the tagline, "Live with Chivalry." The campaign was targeted at discerning 28- to 40-year-old males and aims to encourage them to aspire to *be* more and not just to *have* more. It is closely aligned to the brand's values: Chivas Regal is a drink representing honor, integrity, and passion, and was originally created by the two Chivas brothers to be shared.

The campaign was the result of a worldwide market research study to comprehend key values that appeal to most people. From the market research, it was found that 71 percent of the respondents believed they would have a far better quality of life if people around them chose to live by the values associated with the notion of "chivalry." This result indicated that chivalry is a major motivational value that is appealing and with which most people could connect.

Chivas Regal's brand director, Sophie Gallois, says: "This was a fascinating survey for us to carry out. The results showed some really interesting contrasts in attitudes to chivalry between the different countries. Despite these variations, the message was overwhelmingly that people around the world wish to see those they know and those in the public eye acting with the values of chivalry."

From the market research insights, Chivas Regal developed a marketing campaign that goes about celebrating gallantry, brotherhood, honor, class, sophistication, freedom, bravery, and courage to do the right thing. These traits associated with chivalry were emphasized across various communication channels, promotions, and marketing events. As part of the campaign, several marketing activities were carried out to invoke the values of chivalry. They included:

- TV and print advertisements;
- the introduction of computer games at airports in Singapore and Hong Kong that reward gamers who play according to the values of chivalry;
- promotional events at pubs (for instance, the Euphoria by the Ministry of Sound in Malaysia) with themes consistent with chivalry.

LEVERAGING "LIVE WITH CHIVALRY" TOWARD CORPORATE SOCIAL RESPONSIBILITY

The "Live with Chivalry" campaign functions as a double-edged sword for Chivas Regal. On the one hand, it has an appealing image for its customers, while on the other the values of chivalry can be used by Chivas to drive its CSR agenda. To portray the values of chivalry, Chivas Regal held events to raise funds for the needy and underprivileged. For instance, in its first "Live with Chivalry" musical event in Shanghai, Chivas invited popular Hong Kong performing artists such as Jimmy Lin, Charlene Choi, Chilam Cheung, and Alice Liu to perform in order to raise funds for the earthquake victims of Sichuan.

In another instance, Chivas Regal leveraged on its "Live with Charity" campaign to raise funds for the Dubai Duty Free Foundation, a charitable foundation established to help worthy causes. In this charity drive, Chivas Regal made a donation to the Foundation for every bottle of Chivas purchased between December 2008 and January 2009. This initiative was also part of Dubai Duty Free's 25th anniversary celebrations. So, both brands gained in the co-branding exercise.

"The ideals of the Chivas brand emphasise strong values such as respect, brotherhood, passion and humility. This is a great partnership for the brand and we are excited about being involved in an initiative that gives a little bit back," said John O'Sullivan, marketing manager for Pernod Ricard Gulf.

REFERENCES

Pernod Ricard Annual Report, 2007/08
"Chivas turns Chinese whisky fans into modern knights," *AdAge China*, December 10, 2008
www.moodiereport.com/document.php?c_id=31&doc_id=19395
www.moodiereport.com/document.php?c_id=31&doc_id=19569
www.marketwire.com/press-release/Chivas-Regal-918634.html

CASE STUDY 28: PROCTER & GAMBLE

Cross-Cultural Insights Shape Brand Communications

Procter & Gamble (P&G) has global brands with the same brand positioning and central message. It manages to communicate this single message, while also localizing it for each distinct market in which it operates, by really understanding each country's socio-economic situation and the aspirations of its consumers. This gathering of consumer insights is critical to how P&G tailors its communications to local audiences, while at the same time projecting a consistent brand proposition. This case is a good example of a brand that adapts *what* it says to its consumers—and *how* it says it—based on what it knows about them.

TARGETING WOMEN

Many of P&G's brands are targeted at women, and we will look at two examples of its women's brands, Pampers and Always. But first, P&G regularly takes a long, hard look at its target market, to see if there is anything changing in the lives of its prospective customers that must be reflected in its brand communications.

P&G says that women, as a target market, are changing in many ways. They are reinventing themselves. They are becoming more independent, more demanding, more questioning, more self-reliant, more aware of their power, and more connected. And the increasing pace of globalization, driven largely by technology, has united them in how they live their lives, using social networking and mobile media. P&G found that the use of mobile text messaging (SMS) is increasing rapidly, particularly where young women and teens have little privacy at home. In Saudi Arabia, for instance, teens use Bluetooth technology to bypass the laws that prevent them from communicating with the opposite sex.

Technology is now a vital part of women's lives, and they use it in different ways, but women as a whole have one ideal in common—personal fulfillment. As with the use of connection technology, P&G found that the expression of this ideal also differs in different cultures and markets. In Western markets, women see the pursuit of independent non-work activities and passions as their gateway to happiness; whereas women in emerging markets seek to find a balance between achieving their potential and gaining financial independence, and complying with traditions and the obligations of family. These insights have led P&G to look closely at how women's basic ideals are shared, and how different expressions of them, filtered by cultural norms, can influence their decisions to purchase its women's product brands, such as Pampers and Always.

PAMPERS BRAND

Pampers is what P&G and other brand owners call a "power brand," having achieved more than US$1 billion in sales. In fact, sales of Pampers have topped US$8 billion, and the brand has a presence in almost every country in the world. Pampers has become the generic name for diapers in its category, similar to Colgate in the toothpaste category, and consumer understanding is the secret of its success.

Although motherhood is universal, and a mother's concerns are similar wherever in the world she might be, P&G targets the Pampers brand based on women's different aspirations. The brand stands for the same central idea everywhere in the world: caring for a baby's development. However, according to Nada Dugas, associate director, corporate affairs:

The way we communicate differs with respect to who we are addressing. There are mainly three groups of mothers that exist in all countries, but the predominance of each group depends a lot on the socio-economic situation and the economic development of the country.

The first group is more related to developed countries and affluent classes (but is not limited to them), and their aspiration is to have achievers (children such as the early music learners and experimenting kids). The key motivators for a mother belonging to this group are:

- Self-reliance, and creating a nuclear family
  - seeing herself as a person—not just a mother
  - having contact with people outside the family, but
  - with a sense of belonging that comes from a smaller circle

- Enabling development, tracking progress, and coaching for success
  - the mother sees herself as a coach
  - is able to track development goals
  - seeks a competitive edge to reach her milestones

- Discovery, seeing the child as an individual, and building independence
  - sees the child as a little person; a "self"
  - views the world as a safe place, if one is prepared
  - teaches children to make their own choices
  - learns through experience and discovery

- Newer and better, looking forward, and being prepared for the future
  - views things with a longer time horizon
  - believes in progress; wants the newest and the best
  - focuses on tomorrow, and has a plan to get there

For this group our communication focuses on "hero-ing" the baby, showing his progress and development.

A second group is focused on relationships and the physical and emotional contact with the baby. This segment is focused on:

- Building bonds, belonging, and the extended family
  - her world is defined by the extended family
  - she lives in a community of families
  - traditional, generational influences (her mother, her grandmother, etc.)
- Being there today
  - of life goals, "Mom" eclipses all others
  - more likely to be a stay-at-home mother
  - wants to enjoy every day while her children are babies
- The desire to protect
  - sees the child as very dependent on her
  - the world is different from the one in which she was raised
  - may fear the day her child leaves the nest
- Everyday moments
  - focuses on "now"; not eager for separation
  - memories made of the missteps as well as achievements
  - enjoying the "roller coaster" of life

For this group, again, we tailor our communication to reflect the closeness of the mother to the baby and her caring for him.

Finally in the less affluent countries, what matters is being practical, healthy, and buying a product that performs and represents good value for money. Women in this group are motivated by:

- Healthy development, day-to-day living, physical health

- illness is more likely
- baby's physical health is an accomplishment
- can impact on emotional and economic status
- puts family at risk

- Value, responsibility, balance, and practicality
  - life happens
  - solo parenting
  - makes trade-offs
  - takes pride in making good choices
  - each choice is important

- Positive self-image, confidence, and the belief in good
  - optimistic outlook makes today happier
  - gets confidence from the black and white
  - stands up for herself...and especially for kids
  - believes in things that are "good" and "right"

- Hope and a better tomorrow
  - dreams are free
  - for her children, she wants happiness, health, education, and "to have it better"
  - feet planted on the ground, but can indulge in fantasy
  - believes things can change at any moment

For this segment, we target our communication by showing the performance of our product and its value.

The role of consumer insight in brand communications is to enable brand managers to address the target audience in terms that are relevant and suitable to them.

Another example of P&G's discerning insights into consumer thinking is the Always brand. Nada Dugas explains:

The Always brand stands for women's empowerment, but empowerment is perceived differently, and so our communication differs accordingly.

For example, in countries like Pakistan, Egypt, and the Arabian Peninsula, women's accomplishment is through family status: marriage and children. In this case, our communications focus a lot on the married woman and her family environment. In Russia and other countries, women's self-realization is through a good job and economic independence. The external signal is very important. In this case, we focus more in our communication on the role of the woman as an independent and self-assured woman.

So, although P&G has global brands and global communication, it constantly adapts its marketing to suit local needs and the nuances of local cultures. What it says and how it says things to people depends very much on how well it gets to know them.

Summary

This chapter has dealt with the more traditional aspects of brand communications, and has introduced some new ways of communicating. As mentioned briefly, there are some radical changes taking place in the way brands communicate with customers, and this is changing what brand managers have to do. These changes are driven mainly by innovations in the use of the Internet. The next chapter looks in more detail at the impact of the digital world on branding and at some of the new kids on the branding block.

Relationship Management, Relationship Brands, and the New Digital World

Introduction

Since the first edition of this book was published, the world has changed in terms of the management of brand relationships and the appearance of relationship brands. If we consider a brand to be a relationship, which is as good a definition as any, then, like relationships, brands need to be managed well. Many companies still don't employ customer relationship management (CRM), or employ it inadequately. It continues to concern me that there are few good corporate role models in this area.

Less than 10 years ago, the Internet was just starting to be used as a small part of the brand manager's touchpoint analysis and development. Today, we are firmly in a digital world, where sophisticated online brand strategies are an accepted part of the brand manager's toolkit. I have therefore dispensed with text from the first edition that covered the principles of building a website. However, the most fundamental change in how we use the Internet relates to the fact that it is becoming much more "real time." Some of its applications enable users to know what is happening *now*—not several hours or a day or so ago. This huge step forward has empowered people who use the Internet for social, as well as business, purposes, and has enfranchised many who previously didn't use it. We have witnessed the birth and development of a number of Web-based relationship brands, and you will read some case studies on these in this chapter.

The above changes are a direct result of the new digital world—or Web 2.0, as some call it. The rise of this "new world" has spawned many brands that exist to facilitate relationships between consumers, a bit like hosting a continuous party of friends. Traditional brands not only have to harness the power of these brands as strategic alliance partners in their online strategies; they also must manage their relationships with customers in every way, and this is the focus of CRM. While CRM is empowered by technology, it is a fundamental part of both online and offline brand management and it is to this subject that I turn first.

Customer Relationship Management

The development of new and improved software applications will continue to revolutionize 21st-century brand building, especially on the Internet. Any company wishing to develop a great brand must have both an online and an offline strategy, and these should be very consistent in what they offer and how they appear. One of the great assets that companies now have in managing the brand experience in both the physical and virtual worlds is the innovations that have occurred in CRM.

What is Customer Relationship Management?

One of the most worrying things about CRM is that there are still a great many people who don't really understand what it means and how it can be applied. This section explains briefly what CRM is and how everyone in the organization has a role to play in a CRM program. Customer relationship management is sometimes called customer relationship marketing, or relationship marketing.

Traditionally, marketing textbooks have suggested that "all customers are equal." But does that old adage really make sense? We all know about, and subscribe to, the Pareto principle (the 80:20 rule). So, if 20 percent of your customers represent 80 percent of your revenue, or 10 percent represents 90 percent of your profits, it is clear that all customers are *not* equal. CRM recognizes that different customers represent different values to your organization. But CRM takes this knowledge one step further by suggesting that, if this is the case, then they *shouldn't be treated equally.*

The purpose of CRM programs, then, is to recognize and hold on to the best customers by increasing your understanding of their needs as individuals, meeting the expectations they have of your organization, and making a difference to their lives.

Profitable and Nonprofitable Customers

CRM is also about looking at customers who may not be big spenders now, but could be if they are encouraged by a really good brand experience. While the economics of focusing on your most profitable customers are compelling, a good CRM program shouldn't ignore all the others. Although it makes sense to pay more attention to more-profitable customers, the same CRM principles can apply at all levels.

There is no doubt that by turning your organization into one that is centered around the customer, every single customer will ultimately benefit in one way or another. Once you begin to alter the culture of an organization and your people get used to thinking "customer first," it is virtually impossible to go back to the old way. So, even though a particular customer ultimately may not be among the elite ranks of your "Premier Customer" group, or may not hold your "Titanium" card, he or she will surely be enjoying the benefits of all the positive changes that have percolated their way through your company.

Share of Wallet versus Share of Heart

Some people talk about the aim of CRM as being to capture "share of wallet"—in other words, trying to increase the portion of each customer's spend that comes to you. It is a mistake to think in these terms; you might build up short-term sales by this type of thinking, but not enduring relationships. I prefer to think of it as capturing "share of heart"—that is, creating an emotional bond with your customer such that they pledge allegiance to your brand. If you achieve this, "share of wallet" will be a natural by-product. But what is important for your long-term business is that, if you appeal to the hearts of these customers, they will themselves become part of your best sales force—by being your happy and loyal customers and advocates.

Loyalty Schemes and CRM Programs

In their practical application, CRM programs can take many shapes and forms, but it is useful at this point to draw a distinction between a "loyalty scheme" and a CRM program.

Most people today are members of loyalty programs—or points schemes, as they are sometimes known. Just about every type of retail outlet in every city in every developed and developing country has a loyalty program. It's pretty hard to live life without being part of one. You buy groceries–you earn points; your fill your car with petrol—you earn points; you fly—you earn points; and so it goes on—hotel stays, car hire, even surfing the Internet now earns you i-points or mouse miles. If it's not points or miles, it's in the Starbucks or TGI Fridays mould of collect six stamps and the next coffee or meal is free.

Points programs such as these are designed to keep you coming back for more, and it is true that they might influence brand loyalty to some extent, although the degree of influence is debatable. Do these programs constitute CRM? My view is that they don't, but they can certainly provide a solid foundation upon which to build a CRM program. Normally, these programs have a mechanism—for example, a brief sign-on questionnaire—used to collect a little data about the customer and their purchasing habits, but all too often they fail to take the next quantum leap that makes the difference and turns a loyalty program into a CRM program. That leap is achieved by capturing that data, turning it into knowledge, and using that knowl-edge in some way to tailor the product or service you offer that cus-tomer to make it more relevant, more suited, and more specific to their needs. Without this customization a loyalty program is just a process of "earning and burning" points, and although consumer habits may be affected momentarily, competitors can merely offer more points with the result that the "loyal" customers you thought you had will disappear.

Let's illustrate this point with an example of a commonly seen marketing initiative that contains elements of both a standard loyalty program and a CRM program. Frequent flyer programs typically have an "earn and burn" element, which means customers earn points when they travel and, once they have enough points, they redeem them for free flights. The idea is that customers will pick one airline over another on the basis of the accumulation of more points toward their flights. However, many of these programs are in fact "disloyalty" programs that punish passengers who don't redeem their points by deducting them. This has happened to me. A "Privileged Passenger" of a well-known international airline, I'm tired of having points deducted for non-redemption. On one occasion, upon trying to redeem my points for a flight two weeks in advance, I was told I couldn't do so unless I put in my request two months in advance. "The system doesn't allow for such short-term redemptions," I was told. I never know exactly where I will be in two months' time, so the result is that not only is it made very difficult for me to redeem my points, but I'm punished further by having points deducted.

The airlines claim that frequent flyer programs are CRM programs because the more points people earn, the more benefits they get—for instance, use of the express check-in counter and the executive lounge, with free food and drink, extra baggage allowance, and a good chance of an upgrade (though I have never managed to get one). Once customers have flown a qualifying mileage, they are invited into the upper tiers of the program. Here they will receive a range of program-specific benefits designed to make life easier and more comfortable for them. Airline staff are sometimes trained to recognize customers at this level by sight, and to refer to them using their preferred name. The best programs are multi-tiered, with a so-called Chairman's Club, or similar, at the very top. Here only the most valuable customers get invitations to exclusive events, have direct lines of communication to the chairman's office, and never have to stand in line for anything. If it actually worked like this, it would be effective CRM; however, the "earn and burn" mentality has the opposite effect and damages brand image.

The following sections address some questions that are commonly asked about CRM and how it differs from traditional marketing activities.

Is CRM Different from Advertising?

TV commercials—or TVCs, to use the advertising trade jargon—are an effective way to create general corporate and product awareness and, to some extent, to build a brand. They are big broadcast messages, but using them makes it very difficult to target specific groups of customers, not to mention individual customers.

Invariably, TVCs are based on a monologue; they make a statement, but don't particularly call for a response. Some TVCs included a freecall telephone number where a specific product is being promoted, but this hardly constitutes direct-response TV advertising. With the global move toward digital television broadcasting comes an increasing ability to know who is receiving a particular broadcast, for that person to interact with the TV set, and therefore, implicitly, the likelihood that TV advertising will become more interactive within the next few years.

Ultimately, the aim of CRM is to communicate and interact with an audience of one. It is vitally important that marketers, and indeed the agencies that support them, bring CRM into the overall media mix used by their company.

Turning now to some other forms of advertising, there are a number of potential opportunities to create "interaction" between the audience and the advertiser. A simple method is to include a response coupon, or even just a phone number, in newspaper or magazine advertisements. Many marketing executives run a great advertisement—people like what they are saying or what they are offering—and that's it; the process grinds to a halt. By including a response mechanism, they will:

- gain some idea of who is interested in the product;
- make their marketing spend (ads) work harder; and
- begin to build a database of people who have at least expressed an interest in their company or product (the beginnings of a marketing database).

Is CRM Different from Direct Marketing?

Direct marketing at its worst can involve "cold mailings" to a list of names, sourced from a bureau, about whom the marketer knows very little, other than that they apparently conform to the specification he or she supplied to the bureau. The brand manager has no idea whether or not these people are interested in buying the product he or she is selling.

A good direct marketer will segment the list into control groups and try different creative styles and different incentives in an effort to find the magic formula that generates the highest response rate. But even the best direct marketing campaigns run in this manner may achieve only a 1–2 percent response. Not surprisingly, the consumer normally regards this type of marketing negatively, because the chances of it being something they need, and of it being delivered at a relevant time, are pretty remote. This type of mail-out has rightly earned the label of "junk mail"— because, for most recipients, that's precisely what it is.

Having said this, those direct marketing campaigns that are run by a company trying to sell more to an existing customer can enjoy significantly bigger responses to a well-thought-out campaign. Campaigns have seen percentage response rates ranging from the mid-20s to the low 30s, by sending offers to those customers who have already bought from a company and are happy with the product and service, and who know that the company has taken the trouble to offer them other products that are relevant to them. Again, think about human relationships—if someone you do not know asks you out on a date, what is the likelihood that you will go? Compare that with a situation where this is someone you've known for a while, you know that they can be trusted, and you have some idea of their personality—isn't it far more likely that, in those circumstances, you would accept the date?

Is CRM Different from Customer Service?

CRM and customer service are very closely related, because CRM is all about building brands by giving customers wonderful experiences. In fact, product and service quality are at the center of all the great brands. Traditionally, customer service has always been an important part of brand building for every company, especially for service companies. It has offered great opportunities to companies to get close to their customers, and to build long-lasting relationships with them.

Unfortunately, many companies have failed to take advantage of these opportunities and have damaged their brand images as a result. Instead of leveraging on the brand experience by giving excellent customer service, they may have treated the customers poorly. They may not have listened to them, or they may have been unable to help because someone else dealt with the customer last time, or they may have been unable to answer queries that aren't in their area, or they may have been under so much pressure they have made the customer feel unwelcome. We all come across poor customer service stories on almost a daily basis. But each time customer service fails to delight the customer, it is another nail in the coffin of the brand; nothing kills brand value faster than poor customer service. Even the millions spent by some companies on training their staff in customer service techniques still only manage to inculcate generic interpersonal skills at the end of the day. So, how does CRM work to one's better advantage than the activities mentioned above?

How Does CRM Work?

CRM works by:

- *Creating a continuous communication loop between your brand and your customer:* This can be phone-based, face-to-face, by mail, the Internet, or any combination of these. But the critical thing is to open the communication channels and make it easy for the customer to interact with you.
- *Getting to know the customer:* Use this new-found communication channel to get to know your customer—not just their name and address, but also:
  - Who they are.
  - Who is in their family unit.
  - What they do for a living.
  - What their ambitions are.
  - Their likes and dislikes.

You can get this information by:

- Using existing customer data, such as:
  - how often they buy from you;
  - how much they spend when they do; and
  - the last time they bought from you.
- Asking the customer what they want from you:
  - What might they buy from you if only you supplied it?
  - What do they like about your brand?

- What do they dislike about your brand?
- Establishing the unlocked potential by finding out:
  - what competing brands they buy;
  - why they don't buy everything they need from you, if you offer it; and
  - what you would have to do to persuade them to buy more from you.
- *Creating the knowledge*: Marry all the foregoing data to create the most powerful database in your entire organization. This database will now drive every single piece of targeted sales and marketing activity to your customer base.
- *Reusing the knowledge time after time*: Each and every time a customer interacts with your brand, make sure that the person the customer interacts with has the knowledge in front of them and can thus talk to them like a friend they have known all their life. It is this concept of intimacy that really helps in the brand-building process.

The Concept of Lifetime Value

Since the 1960s, supermarkets have only been interested in transactional data—how many units of product have been sold today. Banks are just the same. Only now are they beginning to realize that, by understanding more about the actual person buying the product, they can make more profit. Lifetime value of customers is a reflection of how often a customer buys from you, how much they spend when they do buy, when they last bought from you, and what they are likely to buy from you during their lifetime.

The Concept of Brand Intimacy

Knowledge is power. If you can get to know your customers, then you can really become close to them and deal with them on a one-to-one basis. It is the ability to create this degree of intimacy between your brand and the customer that will lock out the competition and maximize the profit for your company. It means concentrating on, and streamlining, all your marketing efforts so that the customer and your brand become one.

In Asia, relationships are a fundamental part of social and business life. Some companies realize this. Jakob Meier, president of Giorgio Armani Asia Pacific, has said: "In Asia, the personal relationship with the customer is more important. We work much harder with the database in Asia. We try to capture more about the customer, how he reacts to different products. The relationship becomes quite close."

Getting closer to, or becoming more intimate with, your customer means you are going to be in the best possible position to sell them something at the time they need it. You will be their best friend, the person they turn to when they need help, guidance, and, ultimately, someone to buy from. This isn't pressure selling, but quite the reverse. It is sound brand strategy. And by using your customer knowledge base, you will be putting offers to your customers only at a time when you already *know* they will need you. Your advances will therefore always be welcomed. You are constantly adding value to your brand proposition, and not being a nuisance. Consumers like intimacy, but not intrusion, and good relationship management can make the difference between whether your brand is perceived as a really close friend or an unwelcome visitor.

CRM: A Growing Trend

Job titles such as "product manager" or "brand manager" or "chief marketing officer" indicate that a company is entirely inwardly focused. Where is the "customer manager" or the "chief relationship officer"? We have seen some companies take the step of including a "channel manager"—but what does this really mean? Who is at the end of the "channel"? Is there really such a reluctance to recognize the existence of customers?

Happily, some major organizations such as Procter & Gamble and Unilever are taking the lead and creating "customer managers." And if they can do it, so can you. If Unilever, a company with several hundred brands, can recognize that customer managers may be more important to long-term profitability than brand managers, then shouldn't you be giving it some hard thought? It's not that brand management is now considered of less importance. On the contrary, these companies are saying that the best way to build strong brand equity and value is by focusing their efforts on the consumer, not the product. So, CRM helps brand management look from the outside in, rather than the inside out.

Effective CRM is about applying your knowledge of your customers every time they interact with you, in such a way that your knowledge of them increases each time. In this way, your interaction can better meet their needs. In other words, you add value to the interaction between you and the customer by reusing information they have previously volunteered to you. By building up that body of knowledge over time, you can increase the degree of tailoring of your product or service, strengthening the emotional bond between the customer, your brand, and your company.

Good Brand Management Needs Consumer Focus

For brands to be successful, there needs to be a total shift toward consumer-centricity. In other words, the consumer should be the sole focus for all brand initiatives. So, whether it is the website, product development, advertising, the CRM program, or anything else that will influence the brand image, all activities must reflect the brand consistently and appropriately. In many cases, this means that companies have to change their structure to make it easier to be close to the customer, and with CRM this is usually inevitable. The results will be worth it. You can build an outstanding brand very quickly. The companies that have developed the most powerful brands have done so by always thinking from the outside-in, starting with a thorough understanding of what consumers need, want, and feel.

Becoming a "Customer Manager"

In order to become a "customer manager," a brand manager must be prepared to become more immersed in the brand–customer relationship, with the aim of assuming responsibility for the way in which the whole company deals with customer relationships. It is essential, then, that brand managers are given responsibility, not for a product or range of products, but for *all aspects of delivery* to a selected group of customers. Look at the way management responsibilities have changed in companies such as Tesco, the supermarket chain based in the UK. For years, the store manager's key responsibilities were the day-to-day store operations— making sure the shelves were stocked, that the delivery orders were placed, and so on. Now, this is all delegated activity. Today, the store manager's primary focus is getting to know each of the store's highest-value customers by name. Store managers make phone calls on a regular basis to ensure that their highest-value customers are happy with Tesco: Is there anything they are not happy with this month? What could Tesco be doing more of? Why? How? Tesco has realized that these top customers represent 80 percent of its profits, and that if any of them are dissatisfied and take their business elsewhere, Tesco's profits are walking out of the door at the same time, decreasing the value of the brand name in the process.

Brand Management Must Be Both Macro and Micro

The end-result of the new innovations that are sweeping across brand–consumer relationships, enabled by the sheer power of technology, is that those responsible for managing brands have to be prepared to manage them from a macro point of view—looking at markets and groups of consumers—as well as from a micro aspect: building individual relationships between a brand and each individual customer. This is no easy task, and requires that brand management be prepared to work more closely with all functions of the organization.

The Branding Opportunity

CRM represents a great opportunity for brand management, because the CRM technology that is now available allows a company to gather more and more details about each individual customer, such as their preferences, dislikes, and so on. Importantly, it gives every brand manager the capability of interacting with each customer individually, and of treating each customer differently with customized offerings. Unfortunately, this one-to-one approach has rarely fulfilled that potential, because companies have rushed into buying technology without thinking through what information they want to collect and what they want to do with it. In other words, they have failed to develop a CRM strategy.

The toolkit in the appendix at the end of this book contains a complete list of questions for companies to consider when embarking on a CRM program. Those of you who are interested in the details of implementation are advised to read *Romancing the Customer: Maximizing Brand Value through Powerful Relationship Management*, which I co-wrote with Martin Trott (John Wiley & Sons, 2001).

We have seen so far how good brand building focuses on building the relationships between customers and brand owners. Taking this idea, new companies have, in the last half-decade or so, extended it to create brands that focus on enabling relationships between their customers and other people. These are what I call "relationship brands." In the new digital world, they are predominantly called "social networking sites." They facilitate relationship building, and are now giving brand owners the opportunity to use their social networking skills to build corporate brand–customer relationships.

Before we look at some case studies in this fascinating area, it is appropriate to take a look at the profound changes that have taken place in the digital world and enabled a social revolution on the Internet.

The New Digital World

There is no longer a digital divide. In the years since the publication of the first edition of this book, the gap between those people who were frequent users of the Internet and those who had little access, skill, or willingness to use it has largely disappeared. Now, nearly all age groups are computer-literate and Internet-savvy, from four-year-olds to adults in their golden years.

The Internet and its applications have revolutionized the way in which humanity communicates and does business. I don't know of a company these days that doesn't have a website, and many are even using "podcasts" to promote their brands. Many individuals have their own personal websites or blogs (Web logs, or diaries). But for hundreds of millions of individuals who use the Internet, social networking sites such as Facebook and MySpace do the job just as well of telling the world who they are, and enabling them to communicate with potentially millions of others. Privacy settings allow users to choose who can see their details or contact them. An increasing number of sites, not just social networking sites, allow users to post vlogs (video blogs, often taken with a mobile phone camera). Reality TV no longer has a monopoly on instant viewing (seeing things happen in real time) as viewers can do their own reality programming via their own chosen channels. This isn't just a one-time digital revolution that has taken place; it is ongoing, with more and more sophisticated services emerging that make life easier and enable us to do things faster.

Symptomatic of the swiftness of the change that is taking place is the rapidity with which Internet search engine Google displaced decades-long holder of the honor, Coca-Cola, as the world's most valuable brand. As of April 2008, according to a survey conducted by Millward Brown Optimor (www.millwardbrown.com/sites/mboptimor), Google (see Case Study 34, later in this chapter) was the world's most valuable brand for the second year running, valued at approximately US$100 billion, an increase of 16 percent from 2007. Brands such as Google, YouTube, MySpace, and Facebook have become legendary in less than eight years, and are transforming everything from politics to personal relationships, from finding things to finalizing deals, as we will see in the case studies in this chapter. Companies that haven't yet embraced the Internet will find themselves at an increasing disadvantage, as nowadays an online brand strategy is just as important as one that is offline.

The Speed Factor

It took 89 years for telephones to reach 150 million users, television 38 years, mobile phones 14 years, the iPod seven years, and Facebook just four years. This new digital world is characterized by enormous and increasing speed; not just marketing speed, but the speed of innovation and availability. The development of the Internet has made commercialization so fast that it is hard to keep up. It is both a brand manager's dream and nightmare: you can become a star overnight but a has-been a short while later. For some, an idea may be good, but it may take too long to make a profit, and the idea becomes obsolete. Whatever happened to WordPerfect?

Fundamental Change

Technological innovation of the kind referred to above is producing game-changers in all areas of the Internet. In the case studies that follow, we will see how this fundamental change is playing out. We will see how, in a relatively short time, social networking has made its entrance and totally changed the global communications landscape. These new channels are providing everyone with the opportunity and ability to know instantly what is happening around the world, and to get involved. The new digital world allows users to be interactive with anyone, anywhere, and at any time in *real time*.

This chapter is about this new digital world, and about some of the companies that are changing the way we live. We will look at new "cool" brands such as Facebook, and new communications channels such as Twitter, and we'll see how people's insatiable appetite for information has propelled Google to the top of the world brands list.

But before we look at those cases, let's take a look at how the new digital world is impacting on some of the more "traditional" brands, including repositioning them, as is the case with MTV.

CASE STUDY 29: MTV

Will Internet Kill the Video Star?

MTV is struggling to gain a foothold in the digital world. In my book *The Branding of MTV*, I traced the history of MTV from its birth to the present day. MTV invented music television and repositioned the business of radio music with music videos; however, MTV itself is now in danger of being repositioned by Internet digital websites such as YouTube. Here is a closer look at this case.

THE REALITY OF TECHNOLOGY CONVERGENCE

The real challenge for the business and the brand of MTV comes not so much from the more traditional areas, but from the rise of digital and Internet technology, which is revolutionizing the world of music. It is important to analyze this challenge, and MTV's response, in some depth.

The traditional boundaries between content and distribution are fast disappearing. Digital technology has been embraced most rapidly by the youth, who are always on their mobile phones and love moving between platforms. Connectivity is a part of their everyday lives. The huge opportunities arising from the Digital Revolution are changing at lightning speed, and only the most agile companies with the right kind of talent can take advantage of them.

The face of entertainment is accordingly changing rapidly, and this poses a distinct challenge for MTV. The success of the brand has been largely due to a complete victory in the medium of television. Even the name "Music Television" and the famous initials "MTV" represent this past dominance. But we now live in a digital world, where everyone, especially the youth, is looking for and finding new forms of access to entertainment and music. The fight has now moved significantly from cable television to the Internet. The winners will be those who dominate digital space, and the Internet medium that gives them access to it in new and exciting ways. Where television is basically a one-way channel, the Internet provides consumers with two-way communications capabilities.

MTV has an apparent disadvantage here that it is trying to rectify, with large numbers of organizational and staff changes. The MTV supertanker has to change direction without losing speed, a task it acknowledges. As MTV president Christina Norman says, "MTV has a history of surrounding the consumer with both long-form and interstitial content, and I think we can deliver on a two-way relationship with our audience." How is MTV adapting strategically to the new challenges?

CONVERGENCE IS HERE NOW

Since the proliferation of broadband Internet access and the falling prices of data storage, people are beginning to put all aspects of their life into a digital format. Music, movies, video games, and television shows are already piped into their laptops, cell phones, cars, and living rooms. There is a huge global trend away from TV to mobile centricity, in particular. The annual global spend by young people is around US$106 billion, with US$16 billion spent on music.

MTV has to create a digitalization edge if its expansion and growth are to meet internal and external expectations. Since the turn of the century, it seems to be doing so. From its programming, to hiring of staff, to its content distribution throughout the world, MTV has become increasingly fluid, efficient, and responsive through the use of the Internet, mobile phones (3G, 4G), and newer platforms such as Microsoft's Xbox 360. But is this enough, and is it fast enough?

There is no doubt that TV has become a large part of people's lives, and that mobile subscriptions have reached, in some countries, a saturated level, notable exceptions being China and India. The result is that convergence of technology for TV and mobile became an organic process, with interactive TV as an extension for advertising purposes. Therefore, it came as no surprise when MTV took advantage of this, crafting content for mobile TV users such as the latest *Head and Body* "mobisodes" (mobile + episodes).

Technology market research firm In-Stat estimates that with the emerging availability of mobile TV, whether it be a mobile video phone or a broadcast TV handset, the number of mobile TV users will increase from 1.1 million in 2005 to over 124.8 million users worldwide in 2010. The driver of all the trends mentioned is that each person wants his or her own individual choices to be instantly available.

Mass Individualized Customization

MTV has responded to the mobile challenge and now airs some of its shows first on mobile, then on TV. Also, with the acquisition of online video company IFILM, MTV can now distribute huge numbers of videos to mobile users. In fact, MTV has over 63 partnerships globally with mobile operators to deliver digital content, and the capability to deliver video games to mobile with its Game One offering. The result is that MTV is rapidly moving into the business of mass customization.

A new benefit for all sides, whether it is MTV or advertisers or consumers, is that technology has fueled the possibility of not just mass customization, but individual customization. Technologically-savvy and enhanced persons are now able to download anything that interests them, and edit and eliminate what they don't want, thus setting their own "play list" and, now, "video list" as seen implemented on MTV's broadband channel, MTV Overdrive. Furthermore, they are able to interact with MTV directly about what they want.

Users won't just have access to digital entertainment in their rooms; in the near future, it will be available anywhere they want it. It's no wonder that the age of digitalization has really pushed the brand forward to further enhance MTV's slogan, "I want my MTV!"

The intangible personal deliverables the viewer receives, whether it is hearing the kind of music they like or finding and interacting with others with similar tastes, translates to personal empowerment. The convergence of music and technology provides the viewer with the unique connection to music and inventiveness.

MTV GETS THE URGE

The Urge digital music service was jointly launched by MTV Networks and Microsoft in early 2007. This music store initiative competes to some degree with iTunes from Apple (it cannot be used to download music to iPods), and with Napster, Yahoo!, and RealNetworks' Rhapsody.

Unlike iTunes, Urge is a fee-based subscription service that allows people to listen to vast amounts of music via the Microsoft Windows Media Player 11 beta software, although other online music stores can be browsed through Windows software without installation of Urge. In addition, Urge allows viewers to visit a main MTV, VH1, or other pages, and to create custom play lists. MTV videos are also available, but Urge is still in its infancy and much more development work is needed. As of March 2007, it was only reachable in the United States and US territories and possessions. In August 2007, Urge was merged with Rhapsody and its life as a separate music service came to an end.

PROVIDING PEOPLE POWER: THE COMPETITIVE LANDSCAPE

The MTV brand has more than proved its capability to endure and reinvent itself during the last three decades, but the advent of new media typified by providers such as MySpace and YouTube has caused management to re-think the brand's future. People want more power and control over what they do online, and with whom they do it.

For example, people can now not only go online to discuss and share with others videos and other information about themselves, but also the music business model has changed. For instance, traditionally a music band would need to get a contract with a music label, get airtime on radio, and then, hopefully, it would take off with plays on the best TV channel in the world—MTV. Now, a band can go from nowhere to the top independently of these channels, merely by posting itself on the Internet.

Google's YouTube and News Corporation's MySpace have taken an outright lead in giving online youth what they want. In 2005, Rupert Murdoch's News Corp. bought Intermix Media, owner of MySpace.com, the fifth most viewed Internet domain in the US, and of other sites, for US$580 million. At the time, it was thought the networking site would drive traffic to Murdoch's Fox TV sites. MySpace.com users connect to the site for the purposes of making friends, professional networking, dating, and sharing interests.

Are Digital Players Moving MTV Down the Value Chain?

MySpace has injected a lot of pace into the digital music race. As a very successful social network, it is now set to offer what many observers see to be an Internet version of *MTV Unplugged*, by inviting musicians to choose a studio location and the songs they want to perform on its new program, *Transmissions*. MySpace will show and offer for sale videos of the artist's performances. The difference between this and the traditional *MTV Unplugged* is that

MySpace gets revenue immediately, whereas *MTV Unplugged* released such products months after the event.

MySpace also offers instant gratification to consumers, as downloads are available immediately. The advantage to the artists is that they can choose their distribution channel. The first singer to appear was James Blunt, who was impressed by the flexibility of the process. "Through MySpace, I can get songs heard that are any length I choose, that are any format I choose," He said. This kind of competitive move puts a great deal of pressure on MTV to stay in touch with consumer trends. For example, in October 2007 MySpace became the third-largest music website, with 17.9 million unique visitors, behind Yahoo Music with 22.4 million and ArtistDirect with 19.1 million. However, the MySpace website enjoyed the highest increase in traffic year-on-year, at 42 percent.

If artists are looking at new channels as a means of breaking into the music elite, MTV is in danger of being moved down the value chain. Another example of how digital Internet competitors are repositioning MTV can be seen in the rise to stardom of Colbie Caillat, a 22-year-old singer from California. She "made it" on MySpace in 2007 after friends uploaded her music. As a result of this almost-instant fame (three million visits and 10 million plays), she was signed by Universal Music, and only subsequently appeared on MTV and VH1, with recordings following at the famous Abbey Road studios in London.

Furthermore, if we look more broadly at competitive challenges, we shouldn't overlook the possibility that global innovators in music and communication such as Apple might well try to make a move into mobile video music content. Such a move would pose a serious threat to any player, including MTV.

The speed of growth of these new digital channels that give the youth freedom, self-expression, and instant music gratification will continue exponentially over the next few years. In truth, MTV has been a little slow to adapt to the above changes, but it is now moving rapidly to address this critical brand management issue.

One response from MTV's parent, Viacom, was to ask YouTube to remove thousands of video clips from Viacom's programming. Content from MTV, along with other channels such as Comedy Central, Nickelodeon, VH1, CMT, Spike TV, and BET, were included in a takedown demand of around 160,000 clips. Negotiations broke down on the issue of sharing of revenues, and Google didn't remove content as fast as Viacom wanted. In March 2007, Viacom issued a US$1 billion lawsuit for copyright infringement by YouTube. The outcome of this suit is unlikely to be known before this book goes to print, but this is a response to what has happened in the past.

A more interesting and forward-looking business initiative was to develop a strategic partnership with Joost (pronounced "Juiced"), the Internet video service that is under development by the founders of Skype. Although not launched at the time of writing, Joost had its soft launch in August 2007, with high hopes for success. It had positioned itself as the go-to destination for professionally produced video. However, in early 2009, the company had to restructure its services as it failed to operate as an independent, ad-supported online video platform. A major factor instrumental to its failure is that it had virtually no access to exclusive content. Furthermore, users were compelled to download the Joost player to watch videos, instead of streaming in videos via a Web browser as with YouTube. As such, it consistently lost market share to rival services Hulu and YouTube. Although it eventually offered Web browser streaming services, it was already too late. In July 2009, Joost announced that it would be dropping its consumer video focus and reinventing itself as a business-to-business Web-TV platform provider. This Internet video platform will enable lots of Viacom-owned "television and theatrical programming" to be viewed, such as MTV's *Real World*, *Punk'd*, *Laguna Beach*, and *Beavis and Butthead*. Viewers will be able to watch Viacom content free of charge, and to utilize its Web discussion, social networking, annotation, and community features. Philippe Dauman, Viacom's president and CEO, said:

We're extremely pleased to be working with Joost, and couldn't be prouder to be a key partner in the launch of the next generation in broadband video technology. We're determined to keep pushing and growing our digital presence and bring our programming to audiences on every platform and device that they want... We will continue to seek out partners like Joost, which has created an exciting breakthrough platform that represents not only a fantastic user experience, but one that is built on a compelling and sustainable business model that respects both content creators and consumers.

In addition to Joost, Viacom has established agreements with Warner Music Group and production company Endemol.

There is no doubt that MTV will have to become a major player in the digital and Internet space, and it seems determined to do so. However, responding with technological advances is one thing; to be really effective, MTV must understand the changing needs and wants of its customers with respect to interactive content.

REFERENCES

David Carr, "Do they still want their MTV? A changing format" (www.iht. com/articles/2007/02/19/yourmoney/mtv.php)

Accenture Global Convergence Forum, 2006.

"Mobile video is a tough sell according to In-Stat" (www.in-stat.com/press. asp?ID=1407&sku=IN0502050MCD)

Eric Sylvers, "MTV comes to small screen for T-Mobile users" (www.iht.com/ articles/2006/03/07/yourmoney/mtv.php)

"MySpace set to show and sell music videos," International Herald Tribune, December 5, 2007

Anne Broache and Greg Sandoval, "Viacom sues Google over YouTube clips" (www.news.cnet.com/Viacom-sues-Google-over-YouTube-clips/2100-1030_3-6166668.html)

Andrew Orlowski, "Joost—the new, new TV thing," January 17, 2007 (www.theregister.co.uk/2007/01/17/joost/)

While MTV and other brands are trying to safeguard their future from competitive attack, the very same competitors are adding a new dimension to the mix; not just involving music, but the sharing of friendship in all its forms. Social networking has arrived and is here to stay.

The Rise of Social Media: Social Networking

Social networking is probably the most significant innovation in the last decade of online branding and is challenging all previous methods of brand communications. In Case Study 30, we will look at how a relative newcomer to the Internet has revolutionized the concept of social networking.

CASE STUDY 30: FACEBOOK

See You There!

Facebook's membership is around the size of a large country and growing. In January 2009, it grew at the rate of five million new members per week and by February of that year, it was 175 million people. This compares well with MySpace, which has flattened out at about 135 million members. Facebook was originally aimed at the 14–18 age group, but the fastest-growing segment is now women over 55. This fact demonstrates not only that the site is user-friendly, but that it is suitable for everyone.

Facebook founder and CEO Mark Zuckenberg's original plan in setting up the site was to enable users to build up an online version of their real-life relationships. In real life, people have different levels of relationships and reveal different sides of themselves—different "faces"—to different people. Facebook's sophisticated technology and user-friendly tools also make this possible online.

As a result of its success as a social networking site, Facebook has managed to achieve that elusive indicator of a good Internet website—"stickiness." The average log-on time for its users is 169 minutes per month (news sites average only around 10 minutes), and therein lies its potential as a marketing vehicle. Zuckenberg's original aim was for Facebook to become the future platform for personal communication; however, from a marketing perspective, the "stickiness" factor has created much more value than simply that. Companies love sites that attract people, but they need them to stay on a site to get them interested in their products and services.

MANAGING CUSTOMER RELATIONSHIPS

One gray area that has to be managed on social networking sites is what to allow users to post, and what to censor. This is a tricky business, as there are no real rules in the new digital world except those concerning pornography. And in between the clearly acceptable and the illegal, is a variety of "maybes." But the issue has to be addressed, and Facebook evidently has 150 out of its 850 employees doing just that—making decisions on these "iffy" areas. Their tasks are to work with law enforcement organizations to uncover crime, regulate and censor user postings, and limit spammers. They have generated a few amusing categories and related policies concerned with mischief the company must deal with in its censorship repertoire, such as the "Fully Exposed Butt Rule," the "Crack Rule," and the "Nipple Rule." In addition, Facebook has to combat other perceived/imposed irregularities, including the illegal use of registered names and trademarks, such as "Batman," and enforce its "real-name culture." For example, in December 2008, Facebook disabled actor Lindsay Lohan's alias account, where she appeared under a false name.

There are many such brand management dilemmas for Facebook, and the employees who deal with these issues are given a great deal of freedom to solve them. Nevertheless, just like the brand management discipline imposed by the world's top traditional brands, social networking brands have to find relevant and socially acceptable solutions to the above issues, which can affect their very existence. And while they are dealing with these programming issues, they also have to deliver on the numbers.

WHAT ABOUT THAT UGLY WORD "PROFIT"?

To date, Facebook hasn't managed to make a profit. Zuckenberg argues that profit isn't a priority at this stage, where the objective is still growth and development, and that the returns on investment will come later. But there has to be a "later," and Facebook has to figure out how it will turn a social networking site into a money-spinning machine. Traditional online advertising hasn't really worked on social networking sites such as Facebook, because brand and marketing managers know that people who visit such sites mostly ignore their promotional material.

Some sites aren't attractive to marketers because they cannot track user behavior, but this isn't the case with Facebook. When a member logs on, Facebook can trace where they spend their time on the site, and send them relevant information that suits their preferences. One issue is that the information members give Facebook depends on their privacy settings and the feedback they give to the site. A second is that, because it is a social networking site, members tend not to want to be the target of advertisements. Users feel uneasy if they believe their information is being sent to commercial companies. This became evident in 2007 when Facebook introduced Beacon, a tool that allowed people to see what websites their friends were visiting and some of their online purchases. Users protested, arguing that the tool didn't allow them to control what they shared and that they hadn't given Facebook permission to use this information. The global media homed in on the protests, leaving Facebook to apologize and allow users to opt out of Beacon.

Facebook is now trying out another such tool, called Connect, which allows members to go to company websites using their Facebook log-in details, and this can be sent to friends via "feeds." With friends seeing friends visiting websites, they may visit them, too, or be invited to do so by their friends. This tool seems to be a better option than Beacon; it gives users an opt-in choice before any information is shared, and it still allows brand managers to interact with Facebook's database.

The big revelation is that, today, users of the Internet can watch live events from around the world and discuss and comment on them with their friends during the viewing. The power of this tool was demonstrated during Barack Obama's inauguration as US President, in January 2009, when Facebook linked with CNN. com Live using CNN's video feed to show the historic event online, enabling members to interact while watching. Facebook had some 27 million hits that day, with 8,500 status updates a minute when the new president started his address. CBS and Starbucks have also used this service, but there is as yet no revenue sharing for Facebook, and so no bottom-line benefit.

If this tool eventually makes money and satisfies all parties, it will have the end-result of pleasing both users, who can decide what information they are willing to share, and marketers, who can see and use that information. For Mark Zuckenberg, this step forward would fit with his overall ambition and vision for Facebook, which is for the site to become *the* global communications and marketing platform; the gateway to the digital world—a global digital phonebook, if you like.

Confidentiality still remains an issue for Facebook. On February 17, 2009 the site had to change its terms of use, again concerning the liberal use of member information. Zuckenberg said, "Over the past couple of days we have received a lot of questions and comments about these updated terms and what they mean for people and their information. Because of the feedback we have received, we have decided to return to our previous Terms of Use while we resolve the issues that people have raised." The issues he was referring to were to do with Facebook's new policy, which claimed that its right to use and modify a user's content didn't expire if the user removed the content from the site. Essentially, this potentially could mean that even if you ceased to be a member, Facebook could keep your information!

Other efforts by Facebook to satisfy the needs of both consumers and marketers include making use of applications. Intel has used this technique to promote a DreamWorks movie called *Monsters v. Aliens*, which used Intel technology, and to enable users to create their own monster. Also on trial are engagement techniques, where users can respond to events or send virtual gifts to their friends.

For social networking sites such as Facebook, the investment is big but the returns are unproven. The challenge is to harness the valuable database of information provided by users in a commercial way without alienating them. It is clearly a dangerous path to tread, but there is pressure to get a return. The amount that Facebook or similar sites can charge for an advertisement will depend on its ability to leverage member information for the benefit of brand owners. The interaction between user and business partner traffic is the key to future success.

Signs are appearing that this strategy is beginning to work, as more brands are "personifying" themselves as individuals in Facebook. Facebook provides them with an avenue to build and reinforce their brand personality, and to build relationships with their customers or fans, as is the case with JEEP, Victoria's Secret, Coke, Toyota, Prada, and other brands.

Even more good news appears to be heading Facebook's way, as it appears to have found a more solid and substantial source of revenue through the introduction of an internal payments system. Basically, this will allow Facebook users to buy "credits," which can then be used to buy virtual goods from third parties running their applications on the site. The largest such application running on Facebook to date is games provider Zynga, whose 42 million users produced annual revenue of US$100 million for them in 2008. Facebook's business model will allow it to take a percentage of all virtual sales on its site, and it could transform over time into a shopping portal. For applications developers, it means a faster distribution network.

Facebook is now the number one social networking site globally, and this has put the rival it overtook—MySpace—in a difficult position. To counteract its slide in popularity, MySpace will have to reinvent itself.

CASE STUDY 31: MYSPACE

A Site That Needs to Reinvent Itself

MySpace used to be *the* social networking site, but things change quickly in the high-speed digital world. In 2005, MySpace was bought for US$580 million by Rupert Murdoch's News Corp. It was the first social networking site that could claim to be a mass-market medium, reaching over 50 million users. Since then, it has been overtaken by Facebook, whose popularity has exploded, as the case study above shows.

MySpace has also fallen short of its revenue targets. Partly in order to address this issue, and that of its social network standing, MySpace is trying to reinvent itself as a *social portal*, a site where users can gain access to a great deal more content than just friendship networks. As a part of this transformation, MySpace is entering into new space.

For instance, marketers and brand managers can "takeover" a part of the MySpace home page, which gets around 45 million views per day, in order to get their brand messages across. MySpace has helped generate competitions among users to create jingles and videos for McDonald's, and has linked up an insurance company with young consumers via a music concert series that featured pop group Linkin Park. MySpace is pushing hard on the music front, and claims to have helped many artists to reach stardom, including Lily Allen.

MySpace says its focus on adding new content genres will give advertisers and users more flexibility, having realized that only a small portion of advertising expenditure goes to social networking sites. Also of interest to advertisers is information about consumers and what they buy; Facebook, for example, says it has more data than companies such as Google.

It appears that MySpace is looking to adopting a YouTube business model. As well as MySpace Music, it has developed MySpace TV, with programs such as *The Simpsons* and *National Geographic*.

All these developments have begun the reinvention of MySpace, but it remains to be seen whether it can break into the competitive space occupied by huge brands such as YouTube, Apple, and Google. MySpace still hasn't answered the revenue challenge. Revenue at Fox Interactive Media, the unit that is mostly MySpace, fell 11 percent in the three months ending March 31, 2009, forcing parent News Corp. to activate some restructuring that involved reducing its workforce by around one-third—about 420 employees. The layoffs were announced in June 2009, as was the fact that the social networking site's executive team was to be replaced.

REFERENCE

The Wall Street Journal, June 18, 2009

CASE STUDY 32: TWITTER

A Simple Idea Really Soars

One of the more recent additions to the social networking scene is Twitter, which was launched in 2006. The original idea for Twitter came from Jack Dorsey, who simply wanted a way to know what his friends were doing at any particular time.

Twitter is like a mini-blog, and its success lies in its simplicity. Many great ideas are simple, and are often obvious in hindsight, but because they meet previously unmet needs, they become hugely popular. In this case, it is the basic human need to keep in touch with what other people are doing.

According to www.twitter.com, Twitter "is a service for friends, family and co-workers to communicate and stay connected through the exchange of quick, frequent responses to one simple question. **What are you doing?**" Users can send updates on what they are doing at any time, using no more than 140 characters. The process is simple and fast. According to Twitter, "[E]ven basic updates are meaningful to family members, friends or colleagues—

especially when they're timely. So, if you're going to a party, visiting someone in hospital, attending an important event, or whatever, you can let the right people know at the right time." The ease of use is enhanced by Twitter's ability to accept messages from any mobile texting, instant messaging, or Web communications platform.

Users are not obliged to send responses, as the messages are merely updates of what others are doing; they can choose either to ignore or get involved in message interactions. The company says this is a major advantage: "**Twitter puts you in control** and becomes a modern antidote to information overload." Anyone using the service can also set quiet times, when they don't want to be interrupted.

REAL-TIME DATA

With Twitter, users get instant news. It is built on an open-source platform, which means that anyone can search for and extract data from the service, and can mix this with data and applications from other open-source systems, a process called "mashing." This enables them to create new forms of data never produced before, such as weather maps across a region or country using data generated from friends and other users.

THE BRAND NAME

One thing about Twitter that immediately strikes a branding note is the brand name. Good brand names are usually short, memorable, meaningful, and relevant. Twitter fulfills all four criteria. It is short and easy to remember, and because it describes the communication pattern of birds, it is both relevant and meaningful. Birds are usually moving around and telling other birds where they are and what they are doing by "twittering" either on their own or in groups; hence the name—a clever choice.

BRAND MANAGEMENT APPLICATIONS

Twitter is interesting in that it can be used in different ways to create different applications. In its most basic form, tweets can be used to send out brand information or to respond to comments, which can help in shaping your brand's image. However, there are other interesting uses, too. For example, there is the opportunity to monitor what others are saying about your brands using search. twitter.com or desktop applications such as TweetDeck. With tweets, a brand manager can see not only what customers or potential customers are talking about, but also, importantly, how they are expressing themselves using specific words and phrases. This data could then be used to design better products, services, and media messaging. Additionally, by creating hash tags for branding initiatives such as promotions, brand managers can encourage consumers to discuss them and get feedback. They can use this to manage the conversations people are having about their brands. With Twitter, because many people might follow one person, who might not follow others, brand managers have the opportunity to identify the key opinion leaders in target markets and engage them in discussions. As is the norm with innovation, what appears to be a simple idea can be a game changer. Real-time, user-generated data like that made available by Twitter applications is now beginning to make search engines look old.

TWITTER'S FUTURE

Twitter has certainly got the attention of the global media, and is used by many celebrities and other well-known personalities, even being the medium through which major news events and happenings are reported. Most notably, the Iranian presidential election aftermath brought huge awareness and publicity for Twitter. On June 15, 2009, the US State Department asked Twitter not to close its site for maintenance of its global network, as this would have cut off information about the protests. With other means of communication apparently blocked by the Iranian authorities, the Iranian people were using Twitter to inform people outside Iran of what was happening in the country in terms of rallies, protests, and crackdowns by the Iranian government. Twitter, almost by default, had become an instrument of foreign policy.

Even US Secretary of State Hillary Clinton got drawn into the issue. After acknowledging that she is technologically disadvantaged—"I wouldn't know a Twitter from a tweeter"—Mrs. Clinton went on to say that it was important to keep "that line of communication open and enabling people to share information, particularly at a time when there [were] not many other sources of communication. . . . It is a fundamental right for people to be able to communicate."

The fact that Twitter, a brand that didn't even exist four years previously, was acknowledged by the US government as a critical component capable of influencing situations in Islamic countries, gave the brand a huge global public relations boost. But importantly, it confirmed that, in the age of e-diplomacy, social networking websites not only have a great deal of influence; they have also given birth to a new model of democratic empowerment.

But let's not get too carried away. Despite its meteoric rise in global brand awareness, Twitter still has the same major challenge faced by other social networking sites: how to make money. The company says it is still investing in research and development, and will work out its business model at a later stage. This innovative social networking site is definitely one to watch for the future if it can manage to earn revenue.

REFERENCE

The Straits Times, June 19, 2009

Brands Using Multiple Digital Media

Many of the big brands are now paying a lot more attention to digital branding and marketing strategies. For instance, Coca-Cola uses multiple platforms, as shown in Figure 7.1.

Coca-Cola has a MyCoke website and a virtual world called Second Life, and endorses on its websites other major brands relevant to its target market, such as *American Idol*. It has its own corporate blog site

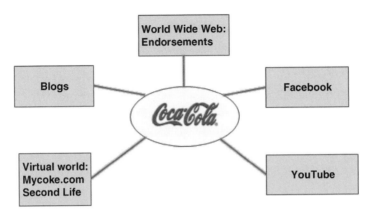

Figure 7.1   Coca-Cola: Branding in digital space

and one for fan blogs, plus a social networking page on Facebook, where members can exchange pictures and videos, and conduct discussions. Coca-Cola also features on YouTube. The company clearly sees social networking as a major part of its online brand strategy.

Many other companies haven't got this far but are experimenting with social media. For example, Carphone Warehouse, Comcast, and Virgin Media have used Twitter to respond to customer service questions, and Dell offers discounts to people who follow it on Twitter. Nokia has used LinkedIn to assist in reaching over 5,000 professionals, and H&M, Reebok, and Victoria's Secret have all used Facebook.

In China, online games are offered by website operators such as social networking site Kaixin001, which lets people who play the game "park" cars in virtual car garages. Volvo, BMW, Shanghai General Motors Co., and Shanghai Automotive Industry Corp. are all represented. By clicking on a particular car brand model, users can see features and information about their choice. Shanghai General Motors vice president Terry Johnsson was quoted in *The Wall Street Journal* of April 9–13, 2009 as saying: "We will definitely do more on social-networking sites." In 2009, he said, 10 percent of the company's overall media budget is allocated to the Internet. This trend is apparent in most industries, with many companies shifting budgets away from traditional media and toward new media.

In the battle to promote smaller cars, Ford is also using new ways of marketing on the Internet. According to the same *Wall Street Journal* article, 100 young drivers who are frequent users of the Internet were selected from more than 4,000 video submissions viewed more than 640,000 times online. The company rated applicants on their "social vibrancy" (how much they were followed online across a number of platforms) and on their creativity, video skills, and ability to hook a viewer within 5–10 seconds. Successful applicants were asked to drive the new Ford Fiesta sub-compact model for six months, and to post their views on social networking sites YouTube, Twitter, and Flickr. Ford hopes that these 100 people will be "opinion leaders" and build a "collective of digital storytellers."

Many more companies are turning to these new and exciting ways of developing relationships with existing and potential customers, and are using the experience to understand how consumers react with each other. Some are still trying to work out how to use social networking to their advantage without alienating consumers by being too intrusive. It is important to note, however, that social media are still only a part of the quest to really understand what motivates people, and should be used in conjunction with other ways of developing consumer insight, such as those discussed in Chapter 2.

What Does the Future Have in Store?

These days, it's difficult to predict what will happen six months ahead, never mind a few years, but we can draw some conclusions.

First, we will see the decline of traditional advertising and one-way communications in favor of two-way communications and greater consumer involvement.

Second, this doesn't mean that brands will cease having offline strategies, but they are much more likely to ensure they have both. This approach can be highly effective, as the strategy used by Barack Obama during his US presidential campaign proved. Obama used all the techniques of branding, but his online strategy was very powerful in reaching all his target audiences, as Case Study 33 shows.

CASE STUDY 33: BUILDING BRAND OBAMA

Using Online and Offline Strategies

Barack Obama has offered the world a master-class in brand creation. He has built a global brand in less than two years—a phenomenal achievement, but one nevertheless accomplished using the methods of all successful international brands:

- *A central vision:* Branding is all about consistency and emotional appeal. Obama's vision was "Change for the Better," a vision given emotional power by such universal triggers as "Yes We Can" and "Hope." These words are forcefully repeated in all Obama's speeches.
- *Powerful values:* Underpinning brand visions are core brand values, both emotional and rational. In Brand Obama these were *honesty, openness, integrity, professionalism, passion, patriotism;* all complemented by a powerful brand personality—that of Obama: *approachable, caring, understanding, warm, firm but fair, visionary, cool,* and *cosmopolitan.*
- *Understanding the target audience:* Obama's soaring aspirational rhetoric was plentifully salted with down-to-earth practical understanding of the customer (that is, the voter): for instance, the pain and helplessness they might have experienced, or the hope they carry for their children.
- *An overarching and empowering message:* Obama reached out to all his target audiences with a single powerful message embracing vision, values, and competitive positioning: "Yes We Can! And Yes You Can!" In addition, his brand communications strategy cleverly exploited the fact that no consumer can resist an approach that talks about *them* and helps *them* feel they are in control. Obama would say things like, "This election is not about me; it's about *you*" and "I'm asking you to believe. Not just in *my* ability to

bring about real change in Washington. . . I'm asking you to believe in *yours*."

- *Multiple touch*: Communicating via all channels relevant to target consumers and creating a great brand experience for them at every touchpoint is vital. Obama reached out to all communities and every demographic and psychographic target group, brilliantly exploiting a mix of traditional media and modern technologies.

Offline, his events have been magnificent spectacles, choreographed to perfection, presidential in presentation. His retail outlets ("Obama branches") covered the whole of the US, offering accessories and memorabilia such as his "Change the World" T-shirts.

Online, his strategy had something for everyone—tools for organizing locally, talking to voters, forming local groups, finding events, raising funds, and blogging. Browsers could connect via the website to Facebook, MySpace, YouTube, Flickr, and many other social networking sites, or click on Barack TV to see videos about the man and his life. Even his website sign-off enshrined a key emotional message ("Powered by Hope and supporters like you").

Supporters could also contact the Obama campaign by mobile by just texting "HOPE" (that word again) followed by the number. Advertisements were even placed in electronic games to catch young, newly franchised voters.

Barack Obama has used these established techniques to attract friendship, loyalty, and trust, and to create a compelling and attractive image that few can resist. By so doing he has changed perceptions in unprecedented ways, not just in America but globally, about America. The American Dream has been brought to life, and like a global brand, Obama has made everyone feel they can have a piece of it.

Third, we will see more transformation of Internet usage. Although much of this will be via new websites, such as social networking sites, we will see Internet usage swing more toward the mobile networking industry, as devices become more efficient and capable of providing all online usage in a mobile environment.

Finally, it is inevitable that the consumer will become the prime driver in the development of the Internet. Brand managers must understand that they will only be able to provide the meeting places for consumers; it is the users who will decide if, and how, they use them. Kent Wertime and Ian Fenwick provide a good overview of what brand and marketing managers need to know about the possibilities that exist in the new digital world in their book, *Digimarketing: The Essential Guide to New Media and Digital Marketing* (John Wiley & Sons, 2008).

It is a fitting to conclude this chapter with a case study on Google, a brand that signifies speed, growth, and innovation in the digital world.

CASE STUDY 34: GOOGLE

"Never Settle for the Best"

In 2008, Google was the world's most valuable brand, valued at approximately US$100 billion, an increase of 16 percent on 2007, according to a survey conducted by Millward Brown Optimor. People no longer search for something on the Internet; they "Google it." In other words, *Google* has become the generic name for conducting online searches. It is worth looking at how this giant company has grown so quickly in such a short time.

According to the company's website (www.google.com):

Google is a play on the word *googol*, which was coined by Milton Sirotta, nephew of American mathematician Edward Kasner, and was popularized in the book, *Mathematics and the Imagination* by Kasner and James Newman. It refers to the number represented by the numeral 1 followed by 100 zeros.

Google's use of the term reflects the company's mission to organize the immense, seemingly infinite amount of information available on the web.

Google Inc. was officially founded and registered by Larry Page and Sergey Brin in 1998 (although the two met in 1995 and were working on its development from January 1996). In that short time, Google has become a household name. Google's meteoric rise to fame is legendary, yet the concept isn't complicated—provide people with information they want. In fact, Google's mission is to organize the world's information and make it universally accessible and useful.

INSPIRATION AND ETHICS

Google is an inspiring and ethical brand that is typical of the brands that are being created by the youth of today who respect transparency, accountability, and social responsibility. In 2007 it became the world's most valuable brand, worth approximately US$86 billion and dislodging the seemingly invincible Coca-Cola, which had held the position for over a decade. Google was also ranked by Fortune 100 as the number one company to work for in 2007 and 2008. Gaining global brand status and admiration without losing internal brand appeal is no easy accomplishment. The brand culture that has been paramount since Google's inception, and despite its tremendous growth, is based on the 10 things the company values most.

Google makes it clear that it will "Never Settle for the Best." Google co-founder Larry Page says on the company's website, "The perfect search engine would understand exactly what you mean and give back exactly what you want." This is the basis of Google's culture, accompanied by its philosophy, which embodies the values that permeate the organization and drive the brand in the form of "10 things Google has found to be true," which are:

Focus on the user and all else will follow.

- It's best to do one thing really, really well.
- Fast is better than slow.
- Democracy on the Web works.

- You don't need to be at your desk to need an answer.
- You can make money without doing evil.
- There's always more information out there.
- The need for information crosses all borders.
- You can be serious without a suit.
- Great just isn't good enough.

BRAND ARCHITECTURE AND ACQUISITIONS

Google has a huge number of products and services grouped into five themes that continue to expand with tremendous speed, each one a call to action:

- Search
- Explore and Innovate
- Communicate, Show, and Share
- Go Mobile
- Make your Computer Work Better

Google has acquired several other brands as a way to increase its reach, all of them compatible with its core business. These include YouTube (a major acquisition, bought for US$1.66 billion in 2006), MySpace (see Case Study 31 above), Adwords, Picasa, and DoubleClick.

From a brand architecture perspective, Google follows the trend of corporate, as opposed to product, branding. Many of its products therefore don't have names of their own and just have descriptors, such as Google Desktop, Google Maps, Google Calendar, and so on. There are exceptions, where the master brand endorses a product brand—as is the case with GMail, by Google—but the color properties and fonts are the same and easily recognizable. The only cases where Google doesn't associate itself visibly with its brands are the major acquisitions, such as YouTube, MySpace, and Picasa. The reason for this is almost certainly that Google doesn't want to disturb these brands' strong brand/customer equity, at least not at this stage. Google might later decide to link them to its corporate brand name in some way, in order to gain greater leverage for its corporate brand, but this is highly unlikely as it risks over-exposing Google. For instance, there is the possibility of alienating customers of the social networking brands who may not want one company (Google) having access to all their details from MySpace, Facebook, and other sites.

GOOGLE'S CULTURE CELEBRATES DIVERSITY

"Diversity and inclusion are fundamental to Google's way of doing things. We strive to be a local company in every country that we operate in and we understand that our users all have different cultures, languages and traditions. It drives the projects we work on, the people we hire and the goals we set ourselves. We go to great lengths to create products that are useful to our users wherever they are and we've found that this commitment to diversity and to our users has been key to our success," says Nikesh Arora, president, EMEA Operations and vice president, Google UK Ltd., on the company's website.

Google aspires to be an organization that reflects the globally diverse audience that our search engine and tools serve. We believe that in addition to hiring the best talent, the diversity of perspectives, ideas, and cultures leads to the creation of better products and services. The diversity of our employees and partners serves as the foundation for us to better serve our diverse customers and stakeholders all over the world.

Google considers diversity a business imperative. We actively support diversity through our pre-university outreach initiatives, support of university students, partnerships with professional organizations, and continually working to perfect a work environment that is inclusive, collaborative, and innovative.

Here are some things that you might find in a Google workspace:

- Local flavor, from a mural in Buenos Aires to ski gondolas in Zurich, expressing each office's unique location and personality.

- Bicycles for efficient travel between meetings, dogs, lava lamps, and massage chairs.
- Googlers sharing cubes, yurts, and huddle rooms (few single offices!) with three or four team members.
- Laptops in every employee's hand (or bike basket), for mobile coding and note-taking.
- Foozball, pool tables, volleyball courts, assorted video games, pianos, ping pong tables, lap pools, gyms that include yoga and dance classes.
- Grassroots employee organizations of all kinds, such as meditation classes, film clubs, wine tasting groups, and salsa dance clubs.
- Healthy lunches and dinners for all staff at a wide variety of cafés, and outdoor seating for sunshine brainstorming.
- Snack rooms packed with various snacks and drinks to keep Googlers going throughout the day.

Eric Schmidt, chairman and CEO, says on the website:

Our products and tools serve an audience that is globally and culturally diverse—so it's a strategic advantage that our teams not only encompass the world's best talent but also reflect the rich diversity of our customers, users, and publishers. It is imperative that we hire people with disparate perspectives and ideas, and from a broad range of cultures and backgrounds. This philosophy won't just ensure our access to the most gifted employees; it will also lead to better products and create more engaged and interesting teams.

GOOGLE: FRIEND OR FOE?

During 2009, Google became the focus for regulatory concerns, with several separate probes. Lawyers for the company were forced to defend a settlement made with authors and publishers that would make millions of books available on the Internet. This, some argued, would reduce competition for digital books. Federal probes were also under way into Google's hiring practices, and whether it, along with other companies, had an agreement not to poach each other's managers. Additionally, the Federal Trade Commission was looking into the role of Google CEO Eric Schmidt, who had a presence on both the Apple and Google boards. The US Justice Department had also criticized Google's policy on advertising, when it said, as reported in *The Wall Street Journal* of June 12–14, 2009: "Internet search advertising and Internet search syndication are each relevant antitrust markets and Google is by far the largest provider of such services, with shares of more than 70 percent in both markets." These probes are still under way at the time of writing.

When companies grow as fast, as big, and as successfully as Google, they automatically attract regulatory attention. Microsoft has had similar issues to deal with, and has been penalized heavily, especially by the anti-trust regulators in Europe, for behavior associated with the prevention of competition.

Despite all of the legal reviews, it is clear that the Google juggernaut will continue to roll on. The continued success of the Google brand will depend on the number and quality of the future businesses it can bring under its wing, how well it can control them, and whether it can maintain the same Google culture. In other words, it will depend on how effectively Google manages its brand.

"Long Live the Brand!":
Creating a Brand Culture

Moments of Truth

Moments of truth determine success or failure, weakness or strength, loyalty or desertion, resolve or retreat. Moments of truth are not defined by companies or brands, but by everyday people whose experiences impact on their lives.

The really smart companies in the world of branding accept that powerful brands are the only route to survival and differentiation. Occasionally, there are defining moments of truth on a global scale, in the form of a major crisis, such as those described in Chapter 6, but smart brands recognize that they also face moments of truth every day in terms of the brand–consumer relationship. As brands exist only in the minds of consumers, every contact with a consumer can potentially be a moment of truth. Former CEO of Scandinavian Airline System (SAS) Jan Carlsson once told his entire workforce that 12 million customers a year, and an average contact rate per customer of five SAS people during a single journey, translated into 60 million moments of truth—that is, 60 million opportunities to get the brand experience right or wrong. His message was that *all* touchpoints with *all* consumers count, and that companies need to look closely at how they can manage these. That's brand management thinking.

"If Only It was That Easy!"

Many people with responsibility for company and brand image might respond, "If only it was that easy!" If we study Carlsson's strategy, we can see that it wasn't just rhetoric; he changed structure, systems, and technology, among many other things. Importantly, he empowered

Figure 8.1   The brand management wheel

front-line staff to take decisions that impacted immediately on the consumer's brand experience. He succeeded in bringing the SAS brand to life by motivating and empowering employees so that they saw their contribution to the value of the brand and the business. In short, he created a massive organizational change project based around the brand–customer relationship and involving every function in the company—no easy task.

The big challenge for CEOs such as Carlsson, and for brand managers in charge of major corporate and/or product brands, is to bring the brand(s) to life through strategy and change, and to motivate people to deliver on the brand promise. This is particularly important for those involved in any business that uses a corporate- or house-endorsed branding approach. This chapter examines how this can be achieved through careful management of the brand management wheel, shown in Figure 8.1.

Brand Management Wheel

The brand management wheel shows how every aspect of the consumer experience, every touchpoint, must be carefully managed. Few companies do this well. Most lack a strategy that drives brand management from the center out to the "spokes" of the wheel. The inner part of the wheel, labeled "brand strategy" in the figure, guides everyone in the organization as to how to manage the brand in each area of responsibility. If a company has a clear brand strategy, then it is much easier to manage the outer areas.

Without clear guidelines on brand personality and positioning, there is little hope for brand consistency among the different areas (the "spokes" of the wheel), as these will be managed on an ad hoc basis. This usually results in a confused, mixed, and relatively poor brand image. The absence of a clearly defined brand strategy means that advertising agencies commissioned by a company to promote its brand will have little idea of what it stands for, what its brand platform is, and what the key messages should be when addressing the different target audiences. For instance, one of my clients asked me to find out why its advertising agency wasn't portraying its brand messages the way the client expected. When I asked the client company if it had given the agency a proper brand brief, they answered "yes." But when I asked to see the brief, the client said it had been verbal, not written. The client hadn't clearly defined its brand positioning or personality for the agency, and so the advertising creative team's interpretation of the brief was very different from the client's expectations, leading to a history of continuous misunderstandings between the agency and the client.

Below I describe each of the "spokes" of the brand management wheel as they relate to the brand manager's task.

Advertising

It is difficult not to use advertising in some form, but companies are often lured into using tactical advertising, instead of image advertising. It is advisable to use a combination: tactical advertising to deal with changing competitor moves and brand features, attributes, and innovations; and image advertising to build a consistent brand message.

Sponsorships and Endorsements

Ensure that all sponsored activities related to the brand, every co-branding opportunity, and every endorsement made by external parties and individuals, is appropriate to the character of the brand. For instance, Marlboro's brand character is one of strength and independence; it wouldn't, therefore, sponsor synchronized swimming. However, for many years it has sponsored Formula 1 racing, particularly through its relationship with Ferrari. Although on-car advertising is now rarely seen, due to stringent advertising regulations, Marlboro's red-and-white packaging is a good brand fit with the Ferrari racing colors.

Promotions

Use promotions sparingly so as not to dilute the image of your brand. Frequent "special offers" and other promotions can make the brand appear cheap. Ensure that any co-branded promotions are relevant to your customer base and appropriate in terms of brand fit.

Packaging and Design

Design is increasingly becoming an important differentiator in the brand proposition, as really attractive design generates emotional power. Design can also be used as a strategic competitive advantage, when defining first-mover product features and benefits, as with the case of Apple's iPod and iPhone. Packaging follows design, and attracts customers, helping a company's products stand out from the crowd, especially in outlets where the shelves are filled with competing brands.

Channel Management, CRM, and the Internet

I have discussed CRM and the Internet at some length in Chapter 7, but with regards to channels of distribution, beware when putting your brand in the hands of other parties. Ensure that they represent your brand properly, and focus on fighting other brands in the market, rather than fighting other distributors who are also offering your brand on the basis of price. Poor representation by channels has led some companies, such as Gucci, to buy back all their franchises.

Public Relations

Public relations is a good source of brand building, as was discussed in Chapter 6. Use every means of PR at your disposal to get your brand name out in the market, and be quick to respond if a crisis occurs.

Corporate Events

Corporate events held by your company, or outsourced to an event management company, are an effective way of raising your brand's profile. However, it is imperative that such events are meticulously managed so as to maintain the right image.

Physical Premises

Even your buildings and offices represent your brand, so ensure that they are appropriate and in line with your desired consumer perceptions.

Product Performance and Development

To build a strong brand, the product or service must be of the highest quality. Also, these days, innovation is a basic requirement, not a luxury. Ensure that you achieve both.

Service Standards and Behavior

Service quality is one of the most difficult elements of brand management to get right, but also one of the most essential. Poor quality service can permanently damage a brand. It is essential to monitor closely all aspects of customer service. Regard it as a never-ending process and not just a one-off training course.

HR, Employee Morale, and Brand Culture

As discussed in this chapter, the whole brand has to be brought to life. An organization's culture needs to be appealing to its employees if they are to have good morale that encourages them to go the extra mile to support your brand initiatives. All aspects of human resource development and management must be involved.

Word of Mouth

One of the most powerful ways of building brands is through word-of-mouth recommendations by happy customers. Yahoo! initially built its brand in this way, rather than through advertising; Google and many of the social networking brands have done the same. Customer advocacy can only come from a consistently great brand experience, and so we come full circle. Do all the other things right, and word of mouth will become your biggest brand-building weapon.

Great brands are built on consistency, including consistent and appropriate behavior in all areas of operation; however, consistency can only come from a clearly defined brand strategy. This is where brand managers need to be especially skillful. Take a hard, analytical look at the "spokes" of the wheel, and ask yourself and your colleagues:

- Is our brand vision and platform clearly articulated in written statements?
- What is currently happening in each area that is affecting our ability to manage the brand consistently?
- What needs to be done to improve our management of the brand in each area?

Every "spoke" of the wheel is vitally important, although some might be more relevant to your brand than others. Develop an action plan incorporating any necessary or relevant improvements, and review it frequently with those people responsible for managing and guarding your brand.

In the following section we consider some practical ways to build a strong brand culture.

Living the Brand: Developing a Strong Corporate Behavior and Culture

Companies are judged by their behavior. Everything they say or do affects their image and reputation. In order to build a powerful corporate brand with a positive image, the company's behavior must be controlled and shaped in such a way that people's perceptions of it are always favorable. Good customer relationships will be jeopardized if the company's behavior is perceived negatively. One of the crucial roles of brand guardianship is therefore to manage corporate behavior.

The ideas presented in the brand wheel must be applied to products, services, and companies. However, to develop a powerful corporate brand image, where the company is the center of attention and customers interact frequently with the company's representatives, a whole brand culture has to be built around the brand's personality and values.

Corporate Image, Branding, and Culture

Corporate culture is a much-discussed topic these days, as companies try to accommodate modern work practices and management styles. Many sophisticated training and organizational development initiatives are implemented by both internal and external specialists to suit current corporate cultures, and to help promote efficiency and effectiveness for the future. Corporate culture, in its crudest form, is described as "the way we do things around here." Essentially, it is a complex blend of employee attitudes, beliefs, values, rituals, and behaviors that permeate a company and give it its unique style and feel.

Corporate culture can have a profound effect on both staff and customers. For staff, it can mean the workplace is either an invigorating, stimulating, and exciting place to be, or a dismal daily experience. It can empower people or enslave them. Because culture is ubiquitous, it inevitably has an impact not just inside, but also outside the organization. Customers who come into contact with staff can sense the organization's culture through the employees' morale, attitudes and comments, body language, and service standards. Since corporate culture impacts considerably on corporate image, it needs to be controlled.

A company that is trying to develop and maintain a good brand image, whether it be for a corporate brand or a service brand, must create a culture that is appropriate to, and reflects the essence of, the brand. A culture is based on values, which provide behavioral guidelines. Branding is a very positive and well-received way of changing the culture of an organization, for reasons that will soon be discussed.

One of the most successful ways to build a brand is to create a personality for it that summarizes what the brand really stands for. A brand platform that is based on certain personality characteristics or traits is easier for consumers to connect with and become attracted to. Once these personality characteristics have been chosen as the building blocks of the brand, the culture of the company must conform with that personality.

Corporate versus Brand Values

Most companies that decide to commit to building a brand already have some corporate values defined in the organization, although staff may or may not be well versed in them. A word of caution here: too many values may cause confusion among the staff. There is a consequent need to explain the difference between corporate and brand values to every employee, and this is usually accomplished through a combination of brand literature and training.

One way to explain the difference is to use the analogy of a building. In the construction of a building, a strong foundation is critical. Without a strong foundation, the building is likely to collapse. In a corporate sense, the "foundation" is the organization's *corporate values*; they define the ways in which the members of the organization will work together. They include beliefs about teamwork, and commitment to quality, integrity, and customer orientation. But once the foundation, based on those values, has been built, the focus switches to the style and appearance of the building. In corporate terms, this is how the company wants to be seen by the outside world. This external face is represented by the organization's *brand values*, or personality characteristics, which influence how the organization is perceived by those outside it.

If the company already has a set of corporate values at the time it embarks on a branding exercise, then decisions will have to be made on which of the existing corporate values to retain, and which to replace, in order to create the new brand personality. If the corporate values are somewhat similar to the brand values, then they can be retained and the brand personality used to reinforce and strengthen the practise of these values. For example, if *reliability* is a corporate value, then the brand personality characteristic of *dependability* would translate into roughly the same message. On the other hand, if the old corporate values are far removed from the brand personality, some or all of those values can be discarded in favor of new ones based on the brand personality. The company may choose to retain some of its old values that it considers still to be relevant (for instance, *quality*), and there is no harm in doing so as long as the value doesn't conflict with any brand personality characteristics. Indeed, some companies have a mixture of conventional values and personality characteristics. The important consideration is that the people working in the organization aren't confused by the existence of conflicting values.

As every brand change agent knows, brand values must be defined and explained at every level of the organization. This involves helping business units apply the brand values strategically to everything they do, by integrating the brand into both their business planning and employees' jobs. These activities are now discussed in more detail.

Developing Brand Strategy Plans for All Business Units

Business units, divisions, and departments within companies will find it useful to develop plans for the short and medium term with respect to how they will deliver on the brand values. It is critical to include support services in this activity, as unless they also change the way they do things, it will be difficult for those departments that impact directly on consumers to implement their plans. For example, it may be difficult for a marketing or sales business unit in a telecommunications company to improve performance on the value of *friendliness* if customers continue to receive separate bills for fixed line, mobile, Internet, and other services. Customer-friendly billing would give them just one bill covering all their transactions. So, it is often necessary to change systems and procedures in order to provide a total impact on, and change in, consumer perceptions.

With this in mind, all divisions or departments—such as information technology, finance, research and development, human resources, production, credit control, logistics, marketing, corporate communications, and others—will need to develop strategic and tactical plans to demonstrate to top management how they intend to implement each brand value. These plans shouldn't contain vague statements of intent, but rather concrete action plans detailing timing and accomplishment criteria.

Brand strategy workshops are the best way to help departments articulate these plans. Once managers get used to developing such plans, it becomes easier for them to establish and control the brand, and for departments to define people's jobs more clearly in terms of the brand.

As an example of brand strategy execution, let's take *innovation* as a key brand value or personality characteristic. Many firms have this brand value, but they execute it in different ways to ensure that their products and services are truly innovative. Gillette does so through its policy of insisting that over 40 percent of its annual sales come from products introduced in the last five years; 3M has a ratio of 25 percent to help implement the same value. Kao, the Japanese personal-care-product company, concentrates heavily on innovation, and approximately 2,000 of its 7,000 employees are dedicated to research and development—around three times the number employed in R&D at giant Procter & Gamble. Kao's aim is to become a global player, but it states it can only achieve this through producing a constant stream of new products to aggressively seize international opportunities.

Disney Corporation has created a section called "Imagineering"—a think-tank employing over 2,000 people devoted to developing innovations for the organization's six divisions. Within this section are highly paid scientists with expertise in fields such as flight simulation, artificial intelligence, cognitive psychology, neuro-anatomy, mathematics, and neural networks, among other disciplines. Their task is to create a future where, for example, there will be virtual theme parks, or where a child's wished-for a toy can be conjured up on the Disney website. This is an example of a company living its mission of making people happy.

The message, then, is that every brand value or corporate personality characteristic has to be very carefully defined, not just at the corporate level but also at departmental and job-specific levels. The brand has to live in every strategic way possible, including being brought to life by every employee in the organization. The following case study on the Virgin Group describes how the brand value of *fun and cheekiness* is brought to life in one of its businesses.

CASE STUDY 35: THE VIRGIN GROUP

Let's Have Some Fun!

Inspired by the freedom of the 1960s, Sir Richard Branson has developed his brand consistently over the last 30 years. This is a prime example of how the founder of a company can create a brand in his own image, and whose charismatic style has influenced his various businesses and their people to "live the brand!"

The extent of the Branson empire is an interesting example of brand stretch from a corporate brand viewpoint, which I mentioned in Chapter 5 as being easier than extending product brands. From its not-so-humble beginnings as Virgin Records, the Virgin brand has now extended into many different enterprises and industries, including cola, bridal wear, cosmetics, rail travel, financial services, mobile telecommunications, Internet-related businesses, wines, and air travel.

Although not highly successful in all its business initiatives, the Virgin brand has largely been able to accomplish this amount of brand extension through single-minded commitment to its values, which are:

- the best quality;
- innovative;
- good value for money;
- a challenge to existing alternatives; and
- a sense of fun and cheekiness.

To get a sense of what this means commercially, consider that although Virgin management is inundated with requests for joint ventures and 90 percent of the projects it considers are profitable, none gets a green light unless it satisfies at least four of these five values. Virgin's values don't in themselves constitute what I would call a "brand personality," but Branson himself adds that dimension, so that the brand's personality is a reflection of his own personality, particularly with the values *sense of fun and cheekiness* and *challenge to existing alternatives*—the underdog role he plays so well. *Quality, value for money,* and *innovation* are now regarded as "must haves," and no longer as differentiators. However, companies such as Virgin incorporate these values as reminders of what their brand stands for and what they believe in.

We can see the values applied meticulously to all consumer touchpoints, as in the case of the value *sense of fun and cheekiness,* examples of which are given below in regards to Virgin Atlantic and other brands in the stable.

BRAND VALUE: SENSE OF FUN AND CHEEKINESS

Product: The airline has been the first to introduce product innovations such as personal massage, live rock bands, and casino opportunities for fliers. Even the top-price seats are cheekily called "Upper Class."

Service: In-flight staff are friendly, happy, and fun-loving; they enjoy joking with customers and generally creating a fun atmosphere. They will also go the "extra mile" when necessary. (Once while traveling with the airline I tore my trousers as I got up from my seat. One of the cabin crew sat me "trouser-less" in the galley while she personally repaired the embarrassing tear, much to the amusement of my fellow passengers and the other crew members!)

Website: On one occasion when I accessed the Virgin Atlantic website, a plane in Virgin colors crossed the screen and a little hand waved at me through a window. Another element of fun was the reference to the "Cyber Espionage Centre," which invites visitors to "report back" on their findings. There is always something amusing to be found on Virgin's websites and in its offline communications.

Public relations: Branson uses every opportunity to put across this brand value of *fun.* When he was about to climb into a hot-air balloon in an attempt to break a world record that nearly got him killed, Branson was asked by an observant reporter why the balloon capsule contained a

British Airways (BA) seat, rather than a Virgin Atlantic one. Apparently, Branson quipped that there would be less chance of him falling asleep in a BA seat.

Events: At the announcement of the signing of a joint venture deal between Virgin and Singapore Telecom to form Virgin Mobile, the journalists and other media representatives were treated to a lion dance, the traditional way of celebrating in Chinese culture. After a few minutes the dance stopped, the lion removed its head, and there was Branson. He had taken the trouble to learn how to perform the dance in order to produce the unexpected and create a sense of fun. At the press conference later, a more serious Branson told the audience that Virgin and Singapore Telecom were not forming a company, but were creating a brand together. When launching the Virgin bridal-wear brand, Branson dressed in drag as a bride; on another occasion, he ran naked from the sea. When a deal with Singapore Airlines (SIA) was being finalized, Branson passed a note to the CEO of SIA that read something along the lines of: "I agree to the figures, but who's paying for lunch?" These are just a few illustrations of the *fun* value extending into even the most serious of business discussions at Virgin. (By the way, SIA apparently paid for the lunch.)

Brands that live their values attract not just customers, but partners, too.

WHAT WILL HAPPEN WHEN BRANSON GOES?

This is the big issue with brands that are based around their founders. Of course, we hope that Branson stays around. But retirement comes to everyone, and it will be interesting to see if, as with Walt Disney, the legacy and the brand values will continue to be brought to life at Virgin, enhancing the consumer's experience of the brand and carrying the company to further successes.

Defining Brand Values for Every Employee

It isn't good enough simply to select brand personality characteristics and then announce that they now exist. Personality characteristics must be closely defined at two distinct levels.

First, each characteristic or value must be defined generically at a corporate-wide level, so that employees understand how they fit into the goals of the organization. If we continue with the innovative brand value example, this could be broken down into the three key behaviors of "creative," "resourceful," and "proactive." It is important that all employees are informed of the brand values and the reasons for bringing the brand to life, and why the behaviors included in the definitions are so important to the branding process. This step alone calls for a substantial awareness and briefing effort on behalf of the company, and may take the form of many short training programs or a significant brand launch event.

Second, and importantly, the personality characteristics must be defined at a job-specific level. The biggest obstacle to realizing brand potential is a lack of clarity about the brand, what it stands for, and what it means to the individual. For a company to brand itself properly and meet its moments of truth successfully, everything it does must reflect the brand personality characteristics. This means that every employee, from the CEO downward, must understand and attempt to live that personality in the job that he or she does. If they don't know how to apply the brand values to their own job, then they are unlikely to take the whole exercise seriously, which will mean the customer is unlikely to feel much impact. Thus, brand management must work closely with the human resource function to ensure not only that staff are aware of and understand all the corporate personality characteristics, but also that they know how to apply these values to their particular jobs.

There are No Short Cuts

In the case of a characteristic such as *caring*, the company would need to explain through training what this brand value means to a customer-service assistant, a receptionist, an IT manager, a production supervisor, and so on. If one of the brand characteristics is *innovation*, the company must educate all its van drivers, salespersons, accounts clerks, human resource executives, and every other individual in the company, in terms of what that characteristic means for them in carrying out their jobs. Only then will they know what specific behaviors, attitudes, and relationships to adopt in order to make that personality come alive. There is no short cut to brand building; the more time and effort taken, the more successful the brand will be. For instance, Dupont, which has *innovation* among its values, has put 26,000 of its people through innovation training programs, in the belief that everyone can come up with good ideas. Another example is Disney, which has four brand values. Every Disney employee, from cleaners to the CEO, undergoes a two-day values training program on entering the company. Each value is defined in terms of each job, so that every employee knows how to apply the values to his or her job.

The training of staff in the job-specific implications of a brand isn't optional. It has huge implications for human resource management, development, and training. It is vital to a company's performance and the achievement of brand consistency that everyone gets involved. For companies that pursue this course of action, the rewards can be spectacular. In my experience, staff take easily to personality-based values, and can understand why those values will differentiate their company from the competition. Applying their brand's personality can give them a sense of purpose that they may not get from other training and project initiatives. This is because they are used to dealing with personalities, and have a tendency to judge companies/brands they come in contact with in personality terms.

Developing Extensive Training for Brand Values

Training is an integral part of achieving good performance on brand values. As explained above, it is very important to brief staff on the company's brand strategy, and to identify how they can apply the values to their jobs. But, staff may need to learn new skills in order to perform well. It is important to look at each value and decide what skills are required to apply it. One way to do this is to analyze the behavior of employees who have been identified as performing to a very high standard on a particular value. Look at critical incidents where a staff member had to bring that value into action; find out what they did and how they did it. Also, interview other people who know about or were involved in the incident. This research can be very revealing in terms of identifying not just the skills associated with particular values, but also the organizational implications for helping staff to bring that value to life. As an example, the following is the result of a series of interviews with employees of an Asian bank on the value of *caring*.

Personal Skills Required	Organizational Implications
Showing empathy	Encourage openness and honesty
Emotional resilience	Improve coaching and counseling
Suspending judgment	Train more in interpersonal skills
Listening	Develop teamwork
Giving positive and negative feedback	
Self-discipline	
Openness and honesty	
Combining formality and informality	

In this example, it was found that it wasn't easy to really care about others (including staff, subordinates, customers, suppliers, and others). It is an attitudinal-related skill that goes much deeper than just being friendly and can be extremely stressful. An intensive coaching and training effort is required if all employees are going to be able to live the value of *caring* and bring the brand personality to life. Yet, this is absolutely critical to corporate vision, mission, brand strategy, and credibility. Some companies go to extreme lengths to ensure that their employees understand and apply their brand values, as the following case study illustrates.

CASE STUDY 36: INTEL CORPORATION

Training for Maximum Brand Performance

In the 1990s, Intel made serious inroads into training all its employees in how to apply its values in their jobs. For each of Intel's six brand values, the company defined the associated behaviors, trained staff in those behaviors, and specified how performance on that value would be judged. The following summarizes how Intel trained its people to apply one of its values: *risk taking*.

Intel used internal communications to link all its values to the company's mission, objectives, and strategy. In addition, everyone in the company undertook a one-week training program, where senior managers explained how the values were inked to Intel's success. They also stressed the importance of people becoming role models on the values.

Risk taking was found to be a difficult value for people to understand and apply. Employees found themselves being punished for taking risks that failed, despite the good intentions of their managers. Problems also occurred in the practical application of some of the company's other values. As a result, an Intel Values Task Force was formed, which identified five key behaviors for each value. For *risk taking*, these were:

- embrace change;
- challenge the status quo;
- listen to all ideas and viewpoints;
- encourage and reward informed risk taking; and
- learn from our successes and mistakes.

Intel found that employees were still unsure about some aspects of risk taking, such as: "How can I take a risk when it might be detrimental to quality?" Intel provided additional tools to help its employees judge when risk taking was appropriate behavior. For example, a self-assessment survey evolved into a 360-degree core management survey that was used around the world. Under each key behavior for each value, employees had to rate themselves and have others rate them. For instance, for the key risk-taking behavior of *encourage and reward informed risk taking*, employees were rated on how often they acted in the following ways:

- failed to clearly define expectations and limits;
- rewarded only successful activities;

- communicated that failure is not tolerated;
- provided insufficient time for implementation;
- criticized employees for pre-approved risks that failed; and
- insisted on clear ownership and accountability.

THE USE OF ROLE MODELS AND TRAINING KITS

Intel searched for role models—people who demonstrated success in the values. Their behaviors and skills were analyzed in a similar fashion to that used in the bank example on page 258. Risk taking was the top priority for Intel, and was the first value to have its own training kit featuring 10 items that included team and individual exercises, written and video interviews with role models, advice on specific issues of concern, and a list of further resources to use.

VALUES "OWNERS"

Intel appointed an "owner" of the role model strategy, and the "owners" of a value or value process had to prove they could implement it and recruit others who wanted to be co-owners. Laurie Price was the owner—or values champion—and she produced courses for employees that were based around the following two questions:

- Do you know what the values mean?
- How does your behavior match them?

Pre- and post-testing of results was used, and the results showed not just greater awareness of the values, but also significant improvements in performance. Eventually, the whole program was offered to all employees via Intel University.

THE ROLE MODEL ADVOCATE AWARD

All nominations for this annual award are accepted, but the selection process is rigorous, with only three or four awards a year being given out. Winners must demonstrate not only that they are role models for all values, but also that they are outspoken advocates of them.

Intel is itself a role model. It serves to remind us that there are no short cuts in getting people to "live the brand"; it requires well-planned hard work. Companies must use whatever means necessary to help their employees create a brand culture. They must also be prepared to undertake the difficult task of assessing what constitutes good and bad performance on the brand values.

Rewarding and Recognizing "Brand Performers"

However loyal and enthusiastic a company's employees are, whenever it introduces a new process they will want to know what is in it for them. Employees will always perform better if they gain some kind of recognition and reward for changing their work practices. Therefore, to accelerate the acceptance of personality characteristics into corporate culture, it is a good idea to think of ways by which employees can gain recognition and rewards.

Rewards

It is not unusual for companies to allocate a certain percentage of their employees' remuneration packages based on values performance. General Electric, for example, links 50 percent of its incentive compensation to performance on values, while Toro links 25 percent and Levi Strauss one-third. Poor performance on brand values is a career killer at Levi's, leading to loss of promotions and increments. Putting brand values into performance management and appraisal schemes ensures that the values are translated into corporate behavior, so that the consumer sees and experiences consistency. This influences their perceptions and has a major impact on the brand image of the company. Further, it increases profitability. Harvard Business School research reveals that companies implementing "performance-enhancing cultures" achieve profit growth of several hundred percent more than those that don't.

Recognition

It is not only financial rewards that can motivate employees to perform well on brand values. Here is a list of ideas that have been applied successfully by client companies with which I have been involved:

- *Role models*—seek out people who perform outstandingly well on all values, as well as those whose performance is outstanding on individual values.
- *CEO awards*—reward outstanding brand values performance with special certificates or memorabilia.
- *Competition awards*—reward teams, departments, business units, and so on, for performing well on brand values.
- *Public acknowledgment*—use company newsletters and magazines to publicly acknowledge people whose outstanding performance you want to expose to everyone in your own company, as well as to companies you deal with.
- *Customer recognition awards*—highlight people in your company who have helped delight customers by giving them outstanding brand experiences.
- *Peer group awards*—involve peers at different hierarchy levels in nominating and choosing winners of best-in-class awards related to brand values.
- *Outstanding team awards*—reward innovative contributions to the development and practice of brand values.
- *Brand ambassadors*—select people who are really committed to the brand, and who enjoy the respect of others in the organization, and give them opportunities to talk about the brand, and to share their thoughts on best practice and success stories. Wherever possible, ask senior managers in every market the company operates in to make recommendations to top management for improving brand execution.

The company has an obligation to help people understand the brand and bring it to life. In addition to the strategy facilitation and training described so far, corporate literature can help in the creation of a brand culture.

Brand Manuals and Corporate Identity Manuals

Some companies have manuals that set out clear guidelines on what can and cannot be done with the company's brands. They usually refer to the visual aspects of the brand, and are often referred to as corporate identity manuals. Such manuals are essential for day-to-day brand management, and as a reference for advertising, promotion, and other agencies. Some decisions, however, cannot be prescribed in advance, such as whether a particular television commercial best reflects the brand personality and positioning. In such cases, the decision should be taken by an experienced senior manager; while the highest-visibility decisions must be taken at the top.

Brand Manuals are For All Employees

Brand manuals are intended for all employees, with the purpose of explaining what the brand means for all jobs within the organization. They are often distributed at a brand launch initiative or a brand-related training event, where employees are given the opportunity to ask: "What does the brand mean in terms of my job?" and "How can I incorporate the brand values into my everyday work?"

Brand manuals typically include:

- a message from the CEO about the central importance of the brand to the future of the business;
- a definition of brand;
- examples of powerful brands and the benefits they bring to companies and employees;
- an explanation of the brand values chosen by their company;
- examples of how they can bring the brand to life in their work;
- questions for people to answer relating to what actions they will take to "live the brand."

Brand manuals that invite employee interaction, by including quizzes and other activities, are generally more effective than purely descriptive text. If well-designed, with good use of color, they will stay in sight and in mind, and employees will tend to refer to them more often.

Brand manuals are best supported by training at the departmental/ section level, so that every employee knows what each brand value means in relation to his or her job and understands how to implement them in his or her everyday work.

A Special Note on Customer Service

The role of customer service in brand delivery is absolutely critical, whatever business you are working in. Customer service is all about staff attitude and values performance, as opposed to public behavior and "customer first" scripts. Customer service training should therefore rely not on generic interpersonal skills courses, but on dedicated values performance courses. The brand values should be layered on top of the generic behavioral skills. Companies such as Singapore Telecommunications, for example, are training their service staff not just in how to deal with customers, but also in how to enhance the perception of trust through the use of certain words and phrases and appropriate body language.

Also essential for outstanding customer service is empowering employees so that they can deal with problems. What use is there in training people to understand and appreciate customers' problems, if they then have to refer the problems to higher levels to be resolved? Many companies are now allowing front-line service people to take direct action, including spending up to specified amounts, to solve problems on the spot.

But customer service isn't confined to the interaction between front-line staff and customers. Many other things make up the total "service value package" in the minds of consumers. They include:

- warranties;
- speed of response following a breakdown;
- employees' dress and personal presentation;
- employees' tone of voice and verbal style;
- written response times and style in letters and emails;
- employees' product and service knowledge;

- retail layout and window presentation;
- customer-friendly telephone response system (with a minimum of menu options before speaking to a customer representative); and
- call center practices.

All such factors that affect the brand–customer service experience should be benchmarked against best practice.

The Technical Assistance Research Programs Institute in Washington, DC once published some alarming statistics showing just how significant customer service problems have become:

- Complaints about service had increased 400 percent since 1983.
- Ninety-six percent of customers will never tell you they have a problem. They will simply take their business elsewhere.
- For every customer with a problem a company knows about, there are 26 others that it doesn't know about.
- The average customer with a problem talks to 9 or 10 other people about it.
- Thirteen percent of the customers with problems will tell as many as 20 other people.
- For every customer with a problem, there are 250 people who have directly or indirectly heard negative comments about the supplier.
- One of the primary reasons customers switch loyalties is because of perceived neglect or indifference—68 percent, in fact!

On the other hand, the Strategic Planning Institute in Cambridge, Massachusetts, found that companies noted for outstanding quality and service:

- charge on average, 9 percent higher prices;
- grow twice as fast as the average company;
- experience yearly market share increases of 6 percent, while the average company loses 2 percent a year; and
- receive an average annual return of 12 percent. (The average during the research period was 1–2 percent.)

Companies therefore need to communicate and live out their brand values in both words and actions. For instance, AT&T Universal Card:

- collects and analyzes daily more than 100 measurements of customer delight;
- uses these to produce company-wide and departmental indices;
- gives all employees a bonus on days when global numbers exceed targets;
- gives the bonus based on total company indices, so that all departments co-operate with one other; and
- makes 5,000 customer calls per month for follow-up interviews.

Why do companies go to such great lengths to build cultures based on values and to ensure that their customers are happy? The results below will help explain.

Rewards for Creating A Values-Based Culture

Kotter and Heskett, in their book *Corporate Culture and Performance*, argued that "performance-enhancing cultures" such as those based on the principles I have identified above bring enormous bottom-line benefits to companies. Covering 200 companies in 20 countries over four years, their research revealed that companies with a strong culture based on shared values outperformed others by huge margins, as the following shows:

	Average Growth with a Performance-Enhancing Culture (%)	Average Growth Without a Performance-Enhancing Culture (%)
Revenue	682	166
Stock price	901	74
Profit	756	1

The message is simple: define your brand values carefully and reinforce them with consistency, repetition, and rewards.

Who is Responsible for Brand Management?

Many people ask me, "Who is responsible for brand management?" The answer is "everyone" because, as I hope I have made clear, everyone can make an impact on it. Every department and every employee can, and should, help to manage and guard the brand. Nevertheless, the CEO must drive the efforts.

The Role of the CEO

Although CEOs cannot be made solely responsible for brand management, they must drive branding from the top and help create the conditions necessary for strong brand management to take place. Without forceful leadership at this level, brand managers will find life very difficult, as they generally lack the power to influence the other functions upon which their success often rests, such as human resources. One of the best ways to ensure that the brand culture is built properly is for the CEO to be involved in the brand process by way of boards of management and other control committees. Case Study 37 describes a forward-looking CEO who understands the need for a good brand guardianship and management structure, and has ensured its implementation.

CASE STUDY 37: PHILIPS

Brand Philosophy: Making Brand Guardianship Happen

Gerard Kleisterlee, president and CEO of Philips, has clearly stated his commitment to value creation through a strong Philips brand. He doesn't believe that building business value and brand value are different processes. He believes that the way to create value is to understand consumers better than the competition can, and argues that this skill is at the heart of the marketing function.

A big part of the current effort in building brand value at Philips has been in strengthening overall marketing competence right through the company. This is done structurally, as well as individually. Philips believes that the brand is important because it can deliver a potent promise with the power to make people choose its products, its jobs, and its stock, in preference to those of other players on the market.

The Philips brand values are summarized by the promise of "sense and simplicity." As explained on the company's website:

> Technology exists to help make our lives easier and more productive. So why is it so often such a hassle, full of complexity and frustration? At Philips, we believe that technology should be as simple as the box it comes in. It's this very simplicity that transforms a task into an opportunity, a burden into a pleasure. Which is why we are committed to delivering products and solutions that are easy to experience, designed around you, and advanced. Simplicity can be a goal of technology. It certainly is the goal at Philips. It just makes sense.

This represents the company's ability to enhance people's quality of life with its wide range of products, as well as by the jobs it creates, and the way Philips tries to become part of the societies in which it operates. In this way, Philips feels it clearly differentiates itself from other brands in the market.

BRAND MANAGEMENT STRUCTURE

The Brand Equity Board (BEB) has been set up as the highest marketing body within the company. The BEB has the task of clearly setting out the company's fundamental values, and then creating the means for them to be applied consistently right across the company. The BEB's "agreed" definition of brand equity is "positive associations that drive the net present worth of a brand's sustainable or potential contribution to profits and market valuation."

Philips is now charting a course to fully leverage the power of its brand and improve its equity. This process started with the founding of the Brand Equity Board and Global Brand Management (GBM), and has been invigorated with the introduction of management by brand as a corporate core process.

The key driver of this process is the president and CEO himself, who announced:

> The Philips brand is a significant company asset and its proper care and development is critical for the company to achieve its goal. Its addition as a corporate core process represents the clear intent of the board of management to re-emphasize the brand and its values in the company's approach to the market and to its stakeholders.

The Brand Equity Board was founded in mid-1999 when Philips determined there was a need for a cross-divisional entity to help enhance its brand equity and share best practices. It started with 11 members, representing each consumer product division, regional organizations, and corporate staff functions. The president and CEO is the chairman of the BEB.

The purpose of the BEB is to ensure that brand management strategy and policies are developed in concert with the organization and, consequently, have the full support of, and full deployment into, the organization and the businesses of the company.

The mission of the BEB is "to build premium brand equity for Philips." This will be accomplished by:

- developing the ways and means to create a balanced, cohesive, and relevant face to the market, and a deeper and more significant relationship with our stakeholders;
- creating networks, forging specific processes, and fostering discipline and synergies to leverage the power of the brand across Philips; and

• building and strengthening the Philips company culture through a stronger customer and market orientation.

Global Brand Management supports the board of management in developing brand strategy and managing issues around the Philips group portfolio of brands. It develops and monitors global brand standards and guidelines and challenges the businesses and the regions to set appropriate brand goals, contributing to raising the standard of marketing competence in the company.

GBM's mission is to: "Increase the value of the Philips brand by ensuring its development and protection, and encourage a stronger consumer/customer focus within the company."

GBM's objectives are:

1. *Brand strategy*: Through the creation of a brand platform, to set standards and goals for the development of the brand through corporate and product division initiatives.
2. *Setting global standards and targets*: GBM consults with the product divisions* and regions on developing appropriate marketing efforts to achieve brand objectives, advises the board of management when discrepancies exist, and develops plans to counteract them, if necessary.
3. *Competence building*: To build the company's overall marketing communication competence through training, sharing best practice, advising on key relevant personnel hires, and agency relationship management.
4. *Brand health reporting*: To hold quarterly brand health "barrel" reviews with the board of management. These are scheduled meetings between the brand and Philips' business groups/core corporate functions, with the purpose of reviewing progress on core strategic competencies.

REFERENCE

www.philips.com.sg/about/brand/visionofsimplicity/index.page

* There are various product divisions involved in the three main businesses of healthcare, lighting, and lifestyle products.

It is clear that many of the world's best brands take brand management extremely seriously, involving everything the business does. While existing and well-established brands such as Philips continue to work hard on their brand management, companies that are just starting to do branding will find that it often involves total organizational change, as Case Study 38 illustrates.

CASE STUDY 38: OPUS INTERNATIONAL GROUP PLC

Branding Means Commitment and Total Change

INTRODUCTION

OPUS International Group plc was formerly known as Kinta Kellas plc. The brand renaming was just one important part of a huge re-branding and repositioning exercise undertaken to create a powerful international brand.

Kinta Kellas plc was an industry leader in project management of large-scale transportation infrastructure and infrastructure development projects. Originally a tin mining company when it began operations in what was then Malaya in 1926, Kinta Kellas had a rich corporate history. It managed most of the huge infrastructure projects that put Malaysia on the world map, such as the North–South Highway and the 1998 Commonwealth Games stadium, among many others. As part of the huge U.E.M. World Group of companies, the reach of its professional and specialized consulting now extends beyond project management into facilities/asset management and development services for expressways, infrastructure, and the built environment.

But the heady days of huge projects required by the government have virtually gone in Malaysia. In 2004, Kinta Kellas, in an endeavor to move forward in a continually changing and sometimes turbulent operating environment, had to make urgent decisions about its future strategic direction in the face of the more challenging economic environment ahead, coupled with international liberalization and competition.

The group managing director, Suhaimi Halim, realized that the route to success in an ever-changing world, where parity rules, is branding. He understood that only a strong brand can provide the means of differentiation necessary for long-term survival and profitability, and that a strong brand name can be worth multiples more—in dollar terms—than the other tangible assets of the company.

Suhaimi said:

> Like many companies, we are faced with challenges that arise from shifting trends in the domestic market, the need to expand internationally, and a need to change our business accordingly. Whilst considering our response to these challenges, the opportunity arose to re-name our main company in Malaysia and link it with our fully owned subsidiary in New Zealand.
>
> We decided to take full advantage of this situation to change our whole business, but there had to be a focus for this, and we decided that the catalyst for change should be the brand. By this I mean we needed to develop a brand strategy that would drive all the changes necessary for us to be successful in the future.
>
> We knew that a brand-driven business means holistic change and that it would be no easy task. We have been working hard at this now for over a year, and are in the midst of changing mindsets, systems, processes, procedures, services, and communications. Nothing is to be excluded.
>
> It is a challenging and exciting time, but the brand implementation is already bringing benefits to us. We are determined that OPUS International Group plc will become a global brand name.

Kinta Kellas thus decided to seek out new strategies to retain its position as a leading provider of project management services domestically, and a leading supplier of road asset management services in New Zealand, where it had a 100 percent fully owned subsidiary called OPUS International Consultants Ltd, formerly a part of the government public works department. This meant that the company needed to be more efficient in its services and to accelerate its growth and performance, including introducing new and improved quality and added value services.

However, several challenges lay ahead that needed urgent attention.

THE BRAND IMAGE AND ARCHITECTURE CHALLENGES

Kinta Kellas had an image challenge to overcome if it was to forge greater growth and brand preference. Its name meant it was still perceived to some extent as a mining company, although it had achieved some degree of new brand awareness. There was a perception gap—both internally and externally—as to what Kinta Kellas had been and was now becoming. There was also another heritage factor—the shareholder U.E.M Group. Kinta Kellas had very specific targets, rather than the mass market, but the need still existed to develop trust in the company and an image driven more by emotional associations and less by rational factors.

There was also the issue of brand architecture. The parental image had some negative imagery, which had to be handled carefully. Additionally, the subsidiary company, OPUS, had achieved more awareness than the parent company. Consequently, there were brand architecture challenges to overcome, such as whether Kinta Kellas should grow via stand-alone brands or try to lift its image through associations with them. Would a Kinta Kellas endorsement add to or dilute other brand images, and what would be the financial consequences of the strategic alternatives?

The architectural strategy for managing such a combination of brands within the company were still unclear, and so these and other questions needed to be resolved urgently within the context of the international business strategy.

THE NAME ISSUE

In 2004, Kinta Kellas had to make the very important decision whether to change its name to support its intended corporate and brand strategies. Not only was it facing a domestic market that was moving away from large infrastructure projects, which required it to shift its business focus to managing assets as well as developing them, but it also had to move more into international markets. Its wholly owned New Zealand subsidiary, OPUS International Consultants Ltd., had already achieved a better business balance and a solid brand name in New Zealand and elsewhere.

It was decided that the Kinta Kellas brand name wouldn't travel well across markets and cultures, whereas "OPUS" would, and so the new organizational name "OPUS International Group plc" was adopted to replace "Kinta Kellas." This decision was to have many implications for all aspects of the business, not the least of which was brand communications. However, first, the new entity needed a brand platform on which to move forward that tied in a master brand to the New Zealand brand.

THE BRAND PLATFORM ISSUE

Importantly, the Kinta Kellas brand had no clear brand vision. Management realized both that a powerful brand vision connects the future of the brand emotionally with consumers across all markets and segments; and that true value lies in the emotional power of the brand itself, which leads consumers to pay price premiums and gives companies higher margins.

The brand platform needed to be reviewed, so that a brand personality (set of brand values) would support the new brand vision, and these two brand elements would be used to develop a strong brand culture. These elements are essential in a service organization for differentiation and building strong relationships with clients, suppliers, investors, and others.

Brand positioning statements would also be required to help create a communications strategy that would pull all the messages together consistently across all international markets, and develop brand awareness for the new brand name.

THE NEED FOR A COMPREHENSIVE BRANDING STRATEGY

In sum, Kinta Kellas needed a comprehensive brand strategy in order to defend and improve its business, market share, and profitability, and to expand internationally. It was agreed that this strategy should be driven by a powerful vision, supported by relevant brand values and a clear differentiation path via positioning statements.

The top management of the company also saw the need to undertake a clear review of the systems, processes, and culture that would enable the new brand promises to be delivered. The company's philosophy was that power brands drive everything in successful businesses, and management decided that Kinta Kellas would adopt this approach under its new name of OPUS International Group plc.

THE MAKING OF THE NEW OPUS BRAND

If a company doesn't know where it stands with respect to its brand image, then it is difficult to move forward, and so OPUS began its brand journey with a brand audit to assess its strengths and weaknesses.

The Brand Audit

As a part of the brand audit a selection of people from within the organization were interviewed, as well as a substantial number of external third parties, such as government officers, contractors, suppliers, clients, and others. The results were, in some ways, both expected and a shock. Positives and negatives were clearly identified in terms of how the brand's current image was perceived by various audiences. Interestingly, the company also received valuable feedback on where stakeholders' future expectations lay, and how its image could be improved.

The Brand Vision, Personality, and Positioning Process

All powerful brands have a brand vision that drives their business strategy. Following analysis of the interview research findings and a senior management workshop, the brand vision was agreed, along with a well-articulated and defined brand personality.

The Brand Personality

Many successful companies use carefully defined brand values to attract and retain customers. The aim of defining brand values in terms of a personality and its characteristic traits is to take the focus away from ordinary attributes and features, and move toward the type of relationship companies want to establish with the consumer, and which consumers wish to have with them.

The brand personality characteristics for OPUS were agreed as follows, with the meaning of the words defined in brackets. The brand personality contained both rational and emotional elements.

- Rational
  - **Innovative** (Creative, Resourceful, Entrepreneurial)
  - **Reliable** (Trustworthy, Dependable)
  - **Professional** (Competent, Knowledgeable, Expert)
- Emotional
  - **Friendly** (Warm, Approachable, Passionate)
  - **Versatile** (Adaptable, Flexible, Responsive)
  - **Helpful** (Understanding, Proactive, Sincere)

The more rational personality traits tended to be the brand strengths of the company, but it was seen to be weaker on the emotional side, which isn't surprising for a professional consulting business. The strategy, therefore, was to maintain the strengths and eliminate the weaknesses. However, the characteristic of *innovative* was regarded as essential for transforming the business and the brand image, so this trait attracted more focus when the brand implementation began.

BRAND MANAGEMENT STRUCTURE

The development of the brand as described above had to be inclusive, and required commitment from both the Malaysian and New Zealand sides. To this end, the vision, values, and positioning statements were subject to a process of iteration, with involvement from both sides via management workshops. But importantly, a structure was put into place that would ensure that everything to do with brand implementation was agreed, synchronized, and implemented in all geographical areas of the business.

Early on in the strategic thinking process, a brand management committee (BMC) was set up to facilitate this process and in anticipation of the tasks to be determined under the implementation program to follow. This was essentially a top management team, chaired by the chief executive, that took all the important decisions regarding brand implementation, and gained support from the board of directors where necessary.

As soon as the brand strategy elements were agreed across the companies, a brand working committee (BWC) was created to monitor the brand transformation and implementation over the next two years, to 2006. It reported to and received direction from the BMC regarding focus, priorities, and high-level decisions for brand execution.

Brand Implementation

While much of the task of implementing the new OPUS brand has already taken place, implementation is ongoing. The critical issue in enabling the repositioning of the brand is described by the general manager, group human resources and administration, Tunku Siti Raudzoh Tunku Ibrahim, as follows:

> Human capital is the key to any professional services brand, and at OPUS we are focusing very hard on training, development, and performance management systems that are linked directly to the brand.

> We have trained a pool of trainers so that everyone can understand not just what the brand means, but how they can impact on it in their everyday work. After all, everyone is a brand ambassador for the company, and they will be recognized and rewarded for performing well in this role. To help them, every employee, from the top management to the receptionists, has undergone training to represent the brand in a way that is relevant to their work, but consistent with our desired image.

...we have also renovated our reception area and staff working spaces to reflect the new brand personality. A new corporate visual identity is in place and the website has been revamped. We have a detailed public relations programme in place and each department has submitted plans for how they will bring the brand to life. We believe that a strong brand is the only route to sustainable success, and it is our people that will make it happen.

Below are a few of these activities.

Brand Action Planning

The first phase of brand implementation was to get senior management groups to work out action plans for executing the brand strategically across all business units. This involved a series of workshops with prioritized short- and long-term goals as the outputs.

These workshops were then taken down to the departmental level, with a similar process and outputs at a more functional and specific level. Concurrently with the workshops, a training-of-trainers program was designed and developed to explain the brand to all staff, and to help them think through how they could contribute in their jobs, both individually and in their teams.

Brand Training Handbook

A brand training handbook was produced for all staff, and used as a vehicle for training as well as information purposes. A trainer's guide was written for the trainers.

The trainers' programs for both Malaysia and New Zealand, and the roll-out, were completed in 2005, to coincide with the launch of the new brand name.

Induction and Orientation

The brand has been incorporated into the orientation and induction programs, so that all new employees are made aware of the importance of the brand and why they should reinforce it within their job scope.

Human Capital

OPUS recognizes that people must be recognized and rewarded for performing well on the brand values, just as they are with other important aspects of their work. This will reinforce the training initiatives and show employees that the company is taking its brand image seriously. This motivation is important in building the brand culture quickly.

The recognition of people who help make the brand come to life is important and can be achieved in many ways. OPUS has embarked on a scheme to recognize employees who have performed well on one or more of the brand values, which includes possibilities such as:

- role model recognition;
- nominations for awards;
- values performance certificates;
- an OPUS annual award for outstanding all-round brand performance; and
- team awards for certain important areas such as innovation.

Rewarding people in monetary terms by incorporating values performance into annual performance appraisal schemes has proved to be very effective, and it shows the seriousness with which the company is taking its brand-building task. Linking pay, increments, and promotions to the brand values via the annual appraisal scheme rewards people for their good performance on the brand values. It entails analyzing jobs at various levels, and possibly role model analysis, to determine what constitutes good and not-so-good performance on each value. While not easy to do, it certainly motivates employees and reminds them that the issue of branding is of great importance to the company's future.

With this in mind, OPUS has begun to devise ways in which it can incorporate the brand into its performance management scheme, in conjunction with other aspects of individual scorecards.

CORPORATE COMMUNICATIONS

With the introduction of a new brand name, inevitably there has to be a carefully designed and managed corporate communications strategy. This was the responsibility of the BWC, with the final green light given by the BMC, and it consisted of mainly corporate identity changes and a public relations plan.

Corporate Identity Manual

OPUS decided not to change its logo and to base its corporate identity on that of the New Zealand subsidiary; however, many changes were still required. A new corporate identity manual helped produce consistency across the companies and guidelines for all aspects of communication.

Public Relations Plan

An agency was selected and briefed to work with the BWC to produce an appropriate 12-month plan to take the company up to and beyond the brand name change. This included looking at all the target audiences that needed to be informed about the new brand and what it stood for, and why the re-branding had been carried out. As OPUS is an international group, the public relations plan had to take into account careful timing of announcements across markets, as well as events and media placement. The soft launch of the new brand was carried out in May 2005.

The OPUS brand is now well known, and has achieved its transformation, while the brand action plans continue to play a major role in the company's success.

The final case in this chapter shows how Acer has built its brand through a total brand management system that defines its brand anatomy.

CASE STUDY 39: ACER

Model of Brand Anatomy and Management

Acer has developed what it calls a total brand management (TBM) system. This mechanism was introduced, Acer's founder and chairman Stan Shih explained, because "we had not effectively and consistently conveyed our image to the general public," and "if you're not clear on the brand image you want to create, anything you do may conflict with that image and all effort is wasted."

ACER'S BRAND ANATOMY

The first step in the process was to develop the anatomy of the Acer brand, as shown in Figure 8.2.

Figure 8.2 Anatomy of the Acer brand

The mission for the Acer brand was defined as "breaking the barriers between people and technology." Acer has referred to this philosophy many times in the past in various ways (slogans, speeches, and so on), but it now became clearly defined. Following on from this statement, Acer developed three brand promises relevant to the mission, but intended for the brand's three major segments or customer groups. For the Original Equipment Manufacturer (OEM) group, it promised to be a reliable partner; for corporations, the promise was to be a company that they could depend on; and for individual consumers, the brand promised "easiness" in terms of convenience and simplicity.

A brand personality was chosen carefully to focus on five characteristics that would support the brand mission and promises, namely:

- dynamic;
- friendly;
- trustworthy;
- extremely creative; and
- very open.

Finally, Acer asked the question: "What is the value of the Acer brand?" This meant: "What value are we adding to the lives of partners, consumers, and customers through our brand?" The answers were:

- ease of use;
- dependability;
- innovation;
- concern for users; and
- good value for money.

Each step supported the previous stage. However, after applying and managing the brand in this way, the results were mixed. In the United States, especially, brand awareness wasn't prominent, which led to the question: "What exactly does Acer stand for?" Acer had a slogan, "We hear you," but it was thought that the message wasn't clearly understood and universally consistent. The company set out to build a brand culture by answering this question in a way that would bring the brand to life across all employees, channels, and customer groups. This process is summarized in Figure 8.3.

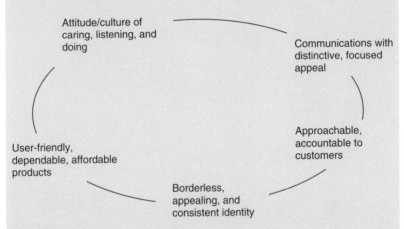

Figure 8.3 What is "Acer-ness"?

The full story of the Acer brand creation, development, and management is told in the book from which these diagrams and quotations are taken: Stan Shih, *Growing Global: A Corporate Vision Masterclass* (John Wiley & Sons, 2002).

Shih says that TBM was introduced and put on an equal footing with TQM (total quality management). "We stressed that just like product quality, brand management was everyone's responsibility. Beginning with me, every person in the company has to get involved in TBM." He continued: "Without effective brand management, it is very difficult to establish brand value." His words are a fitting summary of the message contained in this book.

This and the preceding chapters have dealt with generating and maintaining brand strength. The next chapter focuses on how brand managers might assess brand performance and strength.

Measuring Brand Success:

Market Research and Brand Valuation

It is vital to continuously track the effectiveness of your brand against the competition, especially when the stimuli to which consumers are exposed are constantly changing. I won't discuss here the many well-known ways in which brand effectiveness can be measured, as most readers will be aware of these. Instead, I will examine a few concepts that have more potential for use in effectively measuring brand success and for helping brand management to track brands differently and make better decisions about the future.

Continuous Tracking of Brand Performance

There are many items that can be tracked to help brand managers assess how their brands are doing in the marketplace, and what effect certain market interventions are having on their brand equity. For instance, purchasing, consumption, brand, and advertising awareness can be tracked against advertising spend, pricing policy, product launches, and in-store promotions. Also, tracking by demographic segments can enable brand managers to assess whether marketing campaigns are influencing the target consumer groups. Some companies also track their brand values and personality characteristics against the competition, to see whether they are gaining or losing ground. There are many available research methodologies that cover such areas of interest, such as BrandVision™, which can measure important variables such as "share of mind," "share of heart," and "share of sales."

Brand managers normally use all of these things as an ongoing part of their work. However, I would like to focus this discussion on how to track brand strength, which is of the utmost importance.

Brand Strength

The main purpose of measuring brand strength is to learn whether our customers are likely to remain with us. For many companies worldwide, measuring and increasing their brand strength is a key goal of their marketing efforts. However, most measures of brand strength only tell you how customers acted in the past, and not which brands they are likely to choose in the future. Research that measures past or current behavior alone can only tell us where we are; but to be truly actionable, we need to know where we are going.

The Conversion Model™ is one of the world's leading measures of brand strength. It is a psychological analysis of commitment to brands, incorporating measures of how to increase commitment and exploit weaknesses in the competition. Its diagnostic analysis allows brand managers to focus communication strategies on the most relevant consumers. Developed in South Africa in the late 1980s, the Conversion Model™ is now licensed worldwide. It was originally developed to understand religious conversion, and was expanded into politics and then business with enormous success in a wide variety of brand types.

There are two sides to the model: the strength of commitment and the balance of disposition. Through these measurements, the model provides a complete overview of a brand's position in the market.

Predictive Psychological Segmentation

The heart of the research is an immensely powerful psychological segmentation that can be used to assist many marketing decisions. The behavioral and/or attitudinal segmentation currently used by many marketers isn't enough, as these methods only tell you where you are.

The Conversion Model™ is predictive: it tells you where your brand and your market are going. By providing a full understanding of brand equity, it can also help predict swings in customer loyalty. Numerous validation studies have proved the power of this prediction. The model has:

- frequently identified shifts in the market before they actually took place;
- been rigorously validated through longitudinal studies in a variety of product categories and markets; and
- correctly identified, in numerous studies, which products or brands stood to lose or gain market share.

Complete Market Segmentation

The research provides data that fall into the following segments:

- The Entrenched—highly committed to using our brand, and won't switch in the foreseeable future.
- The Average—committed to our brand, but not as strongly as the Entrenched.
- The Shallow—not content, but waiting for a better alternative.
- The Convertible—discontented and actively seeking alternative brands.
- The Available—actively considering conversion, and may switch immediately.
- The Ambivalent—attracted to our brand, but need motivation to switch to us.
- The Unavailable—not interested in switching in the foreseeable future.

In other words, the Conversion Model™ successfully segments your market, giving you the ultimate edge, because you know:

- who to target to increase sales; and
- which brands pose the greatest threat.

AMI's PinPoint™ within Conversion Model™

Asia Market Intelligence (AMI) was founded in 1991. In March 2000, AMI joined media communications specialist Aegis plc, making it part of a global research and marketing consultancy network, which in turn was re-branded as Synovate. A unique AMI proprietary approach to the interpretation of the brand image data described above has been developed that provides actionable information on brand positioning and strategy.

The Analysis

AMI PinPoint™ analysis begins by grouping image attributes in terms of their relationship to the consumer. It then ranks these attributes in order of their relative importance in driving consumer preferences. The more important attributes can better discriminate the preferred brands from the non-preferred ones. It then standardizes the image data to identify the true strengths and weaknesses of each brand relative to its competitors. This removes the "familiarity bias" associated with both brands and image attributes. Standardized scores are calculated using prescribed formulas.

The second step in the research analyzes the true reasons for brand preference. Attribute importance measurement scores are calculated on a respondent-by-respondent basis, showing not only what is important to consumers but also the relative importance of these attributes.

The Strategic Output

There is a very clear visual output with this research model based on strategic matrices. For example, the matrix shown in Figure 9.1 is typical of one that a brand manager might get. The two axes of the matrix are the relative importance of the brand to the consumer and its relative performance compared to competitive brands. The output also provides several strategic recommendations based on what is important and where each brand's strengths lie. These may include enhancing a brand's performance or leveraging on its strengths.

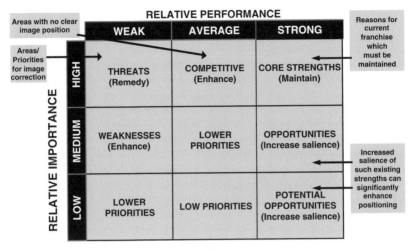

Figure 9.1   Strategic matrix interpretation

Source: Asia Market Intelligence.

Four Key Areas for Consideration

The output of the matrix can be condensed into four key areas for brand strategy:

1. *Competitive action (enhancement) strategy*: This is where the brand's performance is only average on attributes falling in this area. The brand manager might consider strengthening perceptions in order to solidify what is currently a weak image.
2. *Removing threats (remedial) strategy*: Here is an area where attributes are considered by consumers to be important and where the brand isn't performing well. Remedial action must be taken immediately, since this is a serious brand image weakness.
3. *Core strengths (maintenance) strategy*: Attributes in this area of the matrix are important to consumers. If the brand is currently performing well on these, then the recommendation is to take action to maintain these strengths, because they are the real reasons why consumers prefer your brand.
4. *Opportunities (increase salience) strategy*: This section is where the brand is performing strongly on the attributes that fall into this

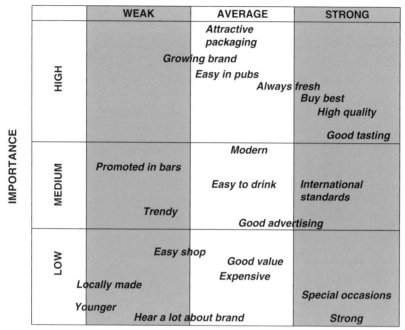

Figure 9.2 AMI Pinpoint™ analysis: An example from the beverage market

Source: Asia Market Intelligence.

quadrant, but which are relatively unimportant to consumers. The brand manager might be able to manage the perceptions of these attributes so that consumers see them as more important, and so increase brand strength through an improved positioning.

Brand Management Exercise

Figure 9.2 illustrates the use of the research in the beverage market. Have a look at it and decide what you would do with a brand that has this profile, taking into account the four key strategy areas indicated above.

Case Study 40 shows how research data derived from the above model was used to leverage customer profitability and satisfaction. As the case study shows, using the right kind of research methodologies for the problems you face as a brand manager can result in rapid and significant impact on the bottom line and lifetime value of customers. In this type of case, the matrix output from the research process adds value to brand management by suggesting strategic courses of action for different situations.

CASE STUDY 40: LLOYDS TSB

Tagging Customers for Increased Profitability and Satisfaction

BACKGROUND

The research methodologies described above were used to look at "committed" and "uncommitted," and "low-value" and "high-value," customers in the bank, and to resolve strategies for better customer relationship management, brand loyalty, and increased profitability. The bank was concerned about the leakage of business to competitor brands and decided to research this in order to discover the degree of "brand commitment" among its customer base.

THE RESEARCH

The bank produced a magazine that was sent out to its high-value customers each month. To ascertain the degree of "commitment" of these customers, a questionnaire was included that achieved a response rate of 10 percent from a base of 350,000 customers. The data revealed that the bank had both "committed" and "uncommitted" customers. The research showed that 20 percent of the "committed" customer group were likely to take up new product offerings that would result in a 9 percent increase in profitability over a six-month period. It also revealed that there was a large "uncommitted" group of customers, and although defections were expected to be limited, they would result in a decrease in profitability of 14 percent over the same time period.

1. Customer name	1. John Doe Enterprises
2. Customer ID no. and branch code	2. 10001/123456
3. Length of time as a customer	3. 6 years or more
4. Main business account is with	4. Retail Bank but has secondary
5. Overall satisfaction score out of 10	a/c at Bank B
6. Does Bank B perform better than us?	5. 7
	6. Yes, 9 out of 10
etc,	
13. In what areas are we giving	13. (3) Business manager does not stay
poor service (score out of 7)	in place for reasonable length of time
	(1) Business manager does not know
	and understand my business
	(1) A bank that doesn't make me
	feel valued as a customer
14. Overall level of commitment (1-4)	14. 4
15. Bank importance rating (1-10)	15. 10
16. Contact priority (1-40)	16. 40

Figure 9.3   An example of what the report could look like

Source: © Research Surveys (Pty.) Ltd.

Both sets of customer groups were analyzed using the Conversion Model™, and the database was "tagged" with their level of commitment. Figure 9.3 shows a typical customer report.

THE ACTION TAKEN

The Personal Choice Program was launched for the "committed" group in January 1998, with the aim of maintaining customer commitment and cross-selling products. The key features of this program were:

- Each customer was assigned a personal choice manager.
- Customized financial statements were provided.
- Customized money-management magazines were produced.
- Tailored products and services were offered.

The results were increased customer profitability from:

- lower levels of attrition;

- higher sales levels; and
- improved balances.

A program—unofficially called "Attempted Seduction"—was launched for the "uncommitted" group in September 1998 with the aim of eliminating service problems and responding better to individual needs. Profitable "uncommitted" customers were identified and sent a letter that said, "We know that you're unhappy…" and then assessed their:

- channel preference;
- interest in products and offers;
- life events tailored to financial needs; and
- open-ended opportunities to state their service problems.

The results after six months were as follows:

- willingness among members of the "uncommitted" group to consider new products rose from 24 percent to 66 percent; and
- product holdings increased by 5 percent.

REFERENCE

Asia Market Intelligence

Performance Tracking Using Brand Valuation

Brand valuations are increasingly being used as a management tool. The strategic use of brand valuation techniques is becoming more prevalent in many blue-chip organizations, allowing senior management to compare the success of different brand strategies and the relative performance of particular marketing teams.

Background

In the late 1980s, many investment analysts and fund managers were still basing their investment decisions on traditional measures of financial health, principally earnings per share, dividend yield, and balance sheet asset values. Such measures can fundamentally misstate corporate value.

The main impetus for acknowledging the value of brands, and other intangible assets, came from the corporate raiders and asset strippers of the 1980s who targeted brand-rich companies and paid significantly more than their net asset value. This resulted in huge "goodwill" values that had to be accounted for. Alarm bells rang in the boardrooms of many underperforming branded goods companies as directors realized there was a clear need for a method of accounting for brands that would recognize their true value in the balance sheet and avoid arbitrary write-offs that damaged investor perceptions.

A realization that the full value of brand-owning companies was neither explicitly shown in the accounts nor always reflected in stock market values, led to a reappraisal of the importance of intangible assets in general, and of brands in particular. This in turn raised the question of how such assets should be valued and disclosed. Although the accounting profession has only partially adapted to a world in which intangible assets are the main drivers of value, business leaders and investors have been quicker off the mark.

Despite volatile economic times, mergers and acquisitions continue, and brands continue to play a significant role in this activity. In 2000, French Telecom paid around US$30 billion for a mobile phone brand that had only been in existence for six years. Within its home market, Orange boasted higher customer acquisition, retention, and usage rates than its rivals—all key factors of a successful brand. Orange had achieved the magic ingredient that positioned it as a lifestyle brand. Instances such as this bring the value of specific brands into the public domain, but the bulk of intangible asset value remains "off balance sheet," and brands and other intangible assets contribute the bulk of shareholder value in many sectors.

In most stock markets around the world, approximately 72 percent of the value of companies is not reflected in published balance sheets. This percentage varies by sector, but it highlights the importance of intangible assets, of whose "unexplained value" brands form a significant part. Other intangibles such as patents, customer lists, licenses, know-how, and major contracts also play a role. Patents, for instance, are a major component of value in the pharmaceuticals sector.

Investors and business leaders have recognized that brands are major drivers of corporate value. Marketers are increasingly using brand valuation models to facilitate marketing planning; however, they should go one step further. Investors need and want greater disclosure of brand values and marketing performance. Marketers should play a lead role in ensuring that such information is adequately communicated to investors, rather than waiting for statutory disclosure requirements to catch up with reality.

Recent Developments

Over the last ten years, brand valuation has become a mainstream business tool used for the following purposes:

- merger and acquisition planning;
- tax planning;
- securitized borrowing;
- licensing and franchising;
- investor relations;
- brand portfolio reviews;
- marketing budget determination;
- resource allocation;
- strategic marketing planning; and
- internal communications.

A particular trend has been the increasing use of brand valuations as a tool to aid marketing management. The focus here is to increase the effectiveness of the marketing effort and aid brand management. A prime benefit in this regard is the fact that a brand valuation model is linked to the company's business model and provides a financial measure that is understood throughout the organization and by investors.

A well-constructed brand valuation pulls together market research, competitive data, and forecasts of future performance. This increases the understanding of the brand's value and its contribution to demand in each segment and identifies opportunities for leveraging the brand. A dynamic brand valuation model can be used for scenario planning purposes.

The ability to place a financial value on a brand within each key market segment isn't the only output of a valuation study. Other outputs include the following:

- Research into the drivers of demand yields information that aids a range of decisions, including portfolio planning and product positioning. It can help define the focus of the advertising message.
- An identification of causal relationships within the business model facilitates an increase in advertising effectiveness.
- The competitive benchmarking study that forms part of an assessment of the risk attached to future earnings provides a gauge of the brand's strength, in relation to competitors, from segment to segment.

Brand valuation is now commonplace, and some examples are discussed below.

The first example illustrates the use of a brand valuation to help resolve a specific issue. The impetus for the project had been the acquisition by a global financial services company of a number of new brands. This had resulted in a cluttered portfolio that required rationalization. The brand valuation was segmented by product and customer for all of the group's brands in the UK, Europe, Australia, Hong Kong, and the US. The project formed the framework to inform brand rationalization and brand architecture decisions.

In the case of a retail bank, a brand evaluation project was carried out in order to assess the contribution of the brand in the corporate, as opposed to the consumer, market segment. The study was also segmented by major product groups. Consumer research was commissioned to quantify the drivers of demand. The study impacted on the allocation of marketing resources between market segments and was applied to measure the effectiveness of marketing investment.

A global insurance company provides an example of a valuation initially carried out for a specific purpose, but that has now been repeated. In this instance, brand valuation and competitor benchmarking techniques were combined to determine the optimal global advertising investment behind the client's corporate brand. The results were used by senior management to set corporate advertising levels. The exercise has been repeated periodically by management in order to understand and monitor the effect of brand investment decisions on corporate brand value.

In the case of a listed food manufacturer, brand valuation was conducted in order to communicate the value of the company's main brand to analysts and investors. Management commissioned the study, as they believed the shares were undervalued and the company was vulnerable to takeover.

A major tobacco company illustrates the use of a brand valuation model on an ongoing basis. The corporate marketing finance team commissioned the construction of a brand evaluation model to monitor the performance of key client and competitor brands in local markets and at a global level. The brand valuation has been placed on the company's intranet and is supported by a manual that clarifies what information is required to be entered into the model and how the results can be used. The model is kept up to date by operating companies in approximately 60 countries. The data produced by the model informs local decision making as well as group planning.

Brand Economics

How do brands add value? In economic terms, the answer is simple: they impact on both the demand and supply curves.

On the demand side, brands enable a product to achieve a higher price at a given sales volume. Strong brands can also increase sales volumes and decrease churn rates. In some instances, price and volume impacts are achieved at the same time. An example, taken from *The Economist*, is of the GM Prizm and Toyoto Corolla in the US. These vehicles are virtually identical, coming off the same production line and having similar levels of distribution and service levels. However, the Corolla trades at an 8 percent premium and sells over double the volume.

Brands also establish more stable demand through their relationships with consumers, and this helps to establish barriers to entry. The relationship with consumers is due to both functional and emotional attributes. On the functional side, brands ensure recognition and further aid the purchase decision through a guarantee of quality. From an emotional perspective, they satisfy aspirational and self-expression requirements. This is most evident in the luxury and fashion sectors.

A further benefit of branding that has increased in importance in recent years is the ability to transfer the equity or values associated with a brand into new product categories. In order for brand stretching to be effective, it is necessary that the core values of the brand are image-based, rather than product-based.

While there are numerous examples of successful brands that have achieved significant price premiums or higher volumes, the impact of branding on the supply curve is often ignored. Brands tend to shift the supply curve downward, for the following reasons:

- greater trade and consumer recognition and loyalty, which results in lower sales conversion costs and more favorable supplier terms;
- lower staff acquisition and retention costs;
- lower cost of capital; and
- economics of scale achieved through higher volumes.

There is an increasing body of research indicating that successful brands add corporate value. There are, of course, examples of successful brands that have fallen from grace and branding initiatives that have failed. The challenge is to identify how your brand—or your client's brand—impacts on the business model, and to monitor whether strategies are successful in adding value to the brand.

Best Practice in Brand Valuation

A number of methods can be used to value brands. Cost-based brand valuations are rarely used, as the cost of creating a brand tends to have little relationship to its current value. Market-based comparisons are unsatisfactory as a primary method of valuing a brand, because of the scarcity of comparative data and the uniqueness of brands. However, where available, market comparisons are useful for testing primary valuations.

A more commonly used method is royalty relief. This approach is based on the assumption that if a brand has to be licensed from a third-party brand owner, a royalty rate on turnover will be charged for the privilege of using the brand. By owning the brand, such royalties are avoided. The royalty relief method involves estimating future sales and then applying an appropriate royalty rate to arrive at the income attributable to brand royalties in future years. The stream of notional brand royalty is discounted back to a net present value—the brand value.

Although the royalty relief method is technically sound, it provides little understanding of how and where the brand is creating value. It might, therefore, be an appropriate method of valuing a brand for balance sheet or tax purposes, but it will be of limited use to a marketing director wishing to leverage the value of a brand.

The economic-use method integrates consumer research and competitive analysis with the brand's forecast earnings. As such, it provides a foundation for brand management in addition to determining the value of the brand by market segment. As this method is of most interest to marketers, and is the most widely used means of brand valuation, it is discussed in more detail.

The Brand Finance methodology has been used by leading brand owners across the world and will be used to illustrate a marketing orientation valuation. A snapshot of this valuation framework is provided in Figure 9.4.

The focus is on the return earned as a result of owning the brand—the brand's contribution to the business, both now and in the future. This framework is based on a discounted cash-flow (DCF) analysis of forecast financial performance, segmented into relevant components of value. The DCF approach is consistent with the approach to valuation used by financial analysts to value equities and by accountants to test for impairment of fixed assets (both tangible and intangible) as required by international accounting standards.

For some purposes, market-based valuation or the royalty relief method of valuation may be possible. However, DCF valuation is the

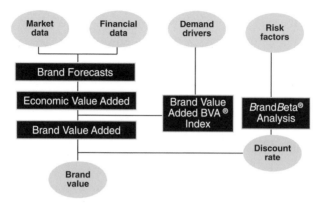

Figure 9.4 Brand Finance methodology

Source: Brand Finance plc.

most widely accepted approach to brand valuation and provides a greater depth of understanding the dynamics of the brand.

While brand valuations can be based on a multiple of historical earnings, it is clear that past performance is no guarantee of future performance and that investors base value judgments on expected future returns, rather than actual historical returns. However, historical results are crucial for an accrate valuation, mainly because they provide information and data relationships that help to forecast the future more accurately.

Valuations based on projected earnings are therefore the preferred approach by Brand Finance, with the caveat that forecasts must be credible. Where forecasts are credible, the valuation results are both robust and actionable.

A brand valuation study typically consists of four work streams:

- financial forecasts;
- Brand Value Added (BVA®)—analysis of the brand's contribution to demand;
- BrandBeta® analysis—determination of the risk attached to future earnings; and
- valuation and sensitivity analysis.

The BVA® section of the analysis can be extended to incorporate a study of causal relationships within the business model. This facilitates the development of a dynamic brand valuation model, as discussed later.

Prior to commencing these studies, however, it is necessary to decide on the most appropriate level of segmentation.

Segmentation

In applying the valuation framework, one of the first and most critical tasks is to determine the nature of the segmentation for valuation purposes. It is then important to identify how internal financial and marketing data, and external market and competitor data, can be obtained in a way that fits with the chosen segmentation. The principles behind effective segmentation for brand valuation purposes are as follows:

- homogeneous geographic, product, and customer groupings to ensure that the valuations are relevant to defined target markets;
- clearly definable set of discrete competitors in each segment to ensure that we are comparing apples with apples;
- availability of market research data to match the chosen segmentation; and
- availability of volumetric and value data for competitor brands to match the chosen segmentation.

There is little point in choosing a valuation segmentation based on an aggregation of product or customer groupings that obscures important underlying differences. Equally, there is little point in choosing a particular detailed segmentation against which it is impossible to obtain volumetric or value data to the appropriate level of detail. Without these it may be difficult, if not impossible, to estimate relative market shares and to compare performance and forecasts against competitors.

Much of the success of a brand valuation lies in the selection and planning of the relevant segmentation and the sourcing of suitable data. A dilemma in relation to customer segmentation is that below the broad categories lie many more specifically defined demographic, socio-economic, or psychographic sub-segments. The marketing and market research teams may well want to "drill" down to a more detailed level for new product development or communications planning purposes, while for practical reasons the valuation may need to be cut at a higher, more aggregated level. It is often impossible to sub-segment the financial valuation to the same level of granularity that may be desirable for a market-mapping segmentation. The brand valuation team therefore needs to ensure that the segmentation for the valuation cascades up from a more detailed underlying segmentation if one is used.

Another difficulty in relation to product segmentation is that volumetric or value measures for each product group may be difficult or impossible to obtain, particularly in less well-developed or well-defined product and service areas or countries. It is also common to find that, in some client segments, it is difficult to obtain reliable data for total market size, as competitor data may be unavailable. A pragmatic approach and a medium-term strategy to populate data gaps may be required, allowing subsequent years' valuations to have an increasing level of detailed comparative analysis.

The difficulties of selecting and populating the chosen segmentation with data have been noted to highlight the need for care and experience in planning and constructing the brand valuation.

Financial Forecasts

Typically, explicit forecasts for periods of three to five years are used for such valuations and should be identical to internal management planning forecasts. An important part of the brand valuation process involves ensuring that forecasts are credible.

Forecast Revenues

Macroeconomic Review

It is necessary to conduct extensive due diligence on each of the markets in which the brand operates to ensure the valuation takes into account all the macroeconomic factors likely to affect the level of demand for the brand. These could be technological, structural, legislative, cultural, or competitive. The brand valuation exercise needs to consider the likely trends for both volume and value for the market as a whole and for the brand being valued. This often involves detailed discussion between the brand valuation team and the internal competitor analysis, corporate strategy, market research, and marketing departments.

Microeconomic Review

It is necessary to consider the factors that have historically affected the performance of the brand in each of its markets. This can involve econometric modeling or some other form of statistical analysis of past performance to show how certain causal variables have affected revenues.

One of the key issues in terms of branding is to understand the causal relationship between total marketing spend, pricing, and sales results. It is equally important to understand the relative effect of different media on the overall level of sales. The task of the brand valuation team is therefore to ensure that brand and marketing factors are being accounted for properly in the modeling and analysis taking place, and that results are used to obtain the most appropriate forecast sales values.

In the same way that it may be desirable to use econometric analysis of past influences on sales, it may also be appropriate to use projective price elasticity research to predict the effect of price on sales. Price elasticity modeling of this type is typically based on large-sample quantitative research and is used to improve the accuracy of future sales forecasts. To the extent that this isn't already being done, Brand Finance recommends that it should be considered as an input to the brand valuation process to help refine forecast earnings.

Forecast Costs

It is also necessary to understand fully the basis on which forecast costs have been determined. The brand valuation team will need to confirm that the basis of cost allocation is sensible between each of the geographic, product, or customer segments on a current and forecast basis. The same principle applies to the allocation of capital to different segments and the resulting charges for capital made against the seg-mented brand earnings streams to arrive at forecast economic value added. Economic value added is the starting point for brand valuation. A proportion of the identified economic value added is ultimately attributed to the brand in the brand valuation calculation.

Calculating Brand Value Added (BVA®)

This is the heart of any valuation, as it determines the proportion of total economic value added to be included in the brand valuation. Having selected an appropriate segmentation and populated it with compara-tive volumetric, value, and market research data, we next need to identify, for each of the competitor brands under review, the extent to which the brand contributes to demand. This is done with trade-off analysis based on quantitative market research.

It is usual to identify first the key drivers of demand by reference to existing qualitative and quantitative research, or by means of manage-ment discussions. It is possible to reasonably estimate the relative importance of different factors in determining demand by means of detailed management workshops. However, it is preferable to eliminate the inherent subjectivity of this approach by using large-sample, cus-tomer-based research. It is ultimately more robust for justifying a financial valuation and more useful as a barometer of the relative importance of the different factors that drive sales demand. It is there-fore more usable as a line management decision-making tool, rather than simply as a valuation technique.

Drivers of Demand

Trade-off analysis can be conducted at a number of levels to identify the importance of the brand to the purchase decision from:

- one brand to another;
- one time period to another;
- one target audience sub-segment to another; and
- one product class to another.

Trade-off analysis is an invaluable, statistically robust means of attributing income to the brand in a brand valuation. In addition, it can be used for tracking the changing importance of different drivers in given markets, for planning resource allocation behind different drivers of demand, and for tracking the effect such resource allocations may have on the profile of factors affecting demand for the brand. It can also be used to assist in anticipating future demand.

Assessing Brand Risk

The final step in the brand valuation is to determine the appropriate discount rate to use in the DCF analysis. Brand Finance has developed an approach to discount rate determination that is a transparent adaptation of the capital asset pricing model. The appropriate discount rate is built up from first principles, as follows:

- Discount rate = [BrandBeta$^®$ adjusted cost of equity × (proportion of equity funding)] + [cost of debt × (proportion of debt funding)]
- BrandBeta$^®$ adjusted cost of equity = risk-free rate + (equity risk premium × sector beta × BrandBeta$^®$)

The 10 years' risk-free borrowing rate in the geographic market under review is the starting point. The equity risk premium is the medium-term excess return of the equity market over the risk-free rate. This can be obtained from investment data providers and a number of risk evaluation services. So, too, can the sector beta, which is used to determine an average implied discount rate for all brands in the sector under review.

This sector-specific discount rate is finessed to take account of the relative strength of different brands in the given market. Brand Finance calls this "BrandBeta$^®$ analysis" and bases it on 10 key criteria for which data are usually available and which in its view represent the best indicators of risk. The generic list of BrandBeta$^®$ attributes used by Brand Finance is shown in Table 9.1. It must be stressed that these attributes are evaluated in each instance to ensure that the most appropriate grouping of risk measures for a specific sector is identified.

Table 9.1 A standard BrandBeta® scoring template

Attribute	Score
Time in the market	0–10
Distribution	0–10
Market share	0–10
Market position	0–10
Sales growth rate	0–10
Price premium	0–10
Price elasticity	0–10
Marketing spend	0–10
Advertising awareness	0–10
Brand awareness	0–10
Total	0–100

Careful planning will be required to define which competitors need to be monitored and evaluated, and in which sectors. There may also be a need to change the competitor set over time if the focus of the business shifts into new areas.

A score of 50 implies that the brand offers average investment risk in the sector under review and therefore attracts a BrandBeta® of 1. This means that the discount rate used in the valuation will be the average composite rate for the sector. A score of 100 implies a theoretically risk-free brand, which would be discounted at the risk-free rate. A score of 0 implies a particularly weak brand that doubles the equity risk premium.

The review of data for the BrandBeta® analysis provides invaluable insights into the competitive position of the brand in its market and acts as a useful focus for a balanced scorecard for the brand. Where available, perceived quality of brands is a strong alternative to simple "brand awareness" in the BrandBeta® scorecard. The scorecard is data-driven, transparent, and produces supportable discount rates.

Point-in-Time Valuation

The result of the foregoing analysis is a branded business value for each segment identified. The branded business value expresses the full net present value of the intangible earnings in each segment. In addition, the valuation team produces a detailed competitive review with risk scoring and a robust estimate of the contribution the brand makes in each segment. This is used to derive a value for the brand alone within the total value of the branded business. Also produced is a sensitivity analysis indicating the impact on value of altering certain key assumptions.

An important philosophy behind a brand valuation exercise is that the model should become a simple and comprehensible rallying point for the whole brand team, not a sophisticated model for the initiated only.

Dynamic Brand Evaluation

A point-in-time valuation methodology discussed thus far provides a robust point-in-time brand valuation model drawing directly on financial, analytical, and marketing research activities that either are, or should be, in place already. In a sense, it merely brings together existing measures and processes in a coherent way. It is therefore a suitable way of producing valuations on a periodic basis by and for internal management. It is often preferable to create a static valuation model, and then increase the sophistication of the model and introduce a scenario planning capacity.

This is the purpose of a dynamic brand valuation model: to incorporate causal relationships into a brand valuation model; to use the model to carry out scenario planning in order to select the most appropriate strategy; and then to track the impact of the selected strategy. Such a model can be used for considering and comparing the level of marketing investment behind the brand in different segments. It can be used for flexing key assumptions on the basis of hypotheses and testing the value impact of changes to brand activities. It will show where brand and corporate value is being created and destroyed, together with the intermediate measures that cause the growth or decline.

Econometric modeling and BVA® research are used to identify historic and predictive cause-and-effect relationships between marketing inputs and sales volumes. Both these and market assumptions can be built into a dynamic brand evaluation model in such a way that the likely impact of marketing actions on short-term profitability and long-term value can be established.

Such a tool sounds like the marketing holy grail; however, it must be remembered that the predictive ability of the model will only be as good as the research that has been used to determine the causal relationships. Even in the absence of ideal research, we have found that the process of estimating cause-and-effect relationships and assessing the sensitivity of the business model to changes in these assumptions can be extremely useful.

Before we take a look at our final case study, it will be useful to consider other brand valuation methodologies than those discussed above, as the outcomes can vary considerably.

Other Brand Valuation Methodologies

Two other well-known brand valuation methodologies are those developed by Interbrand and Millward Brown.

Interbrand

Interbrand, a division of Omnicom, is a branding consulting firm. Founded in London in 1974 as Novamark by John Murphy, a former employee of Dunlop, Interbrand has developed into a full-service branding consultancy with 40 offices in 25 countries. Annually, Interbrand and *Business Week* publish "The 100 Top Brands." Interbrand's approach, which is a method limited to big, high-profile brands, uses a three-year weighted average of profit after tax. Only those factors that relate directly to the brand's identity are considered. Thereafter, the multiplier is attached to the calculation. The multiplier takes into account seven components of brand strength: market, stability, leadership, trend, support, diversification, and protection.

Millward Brown

Created by one of the world's leading market research companies, London-based Millward Brown, the BrandZ Study provides what is believed to be a highly accurate methodology. Unlike the Interbrand approach, which focuses on large brands, the BrandZ methodology works for smaller, lower-profile brands. It is based on the combined effects of historical financial data as well as consumer studies. The basis of this approach is something called "voltage," which is a brand's potential to grow its market share in the future.

Comparison of Methodologies

Some variance should be expected given that there are differences in the valuation methodologies used by each agency. Interbrand and Millward Brown both use an "earnings split" approach, which calculates brand value as the net present value of the proportion of a company's forecast future earnings that are directly attributable to its brand. However, each uses different sources for the forecast future earnings and the estimation of what proportion of earnings are brand related. In contrast, Brand Finance uses a royalty rate approach, which estimates what a company would have to pay out in royalties if it were licensing its brand from a third party. This approach starts with a sector average royalty rate that is then adjusted up or down according to the strength or weakness of the individual brand.

Comparison of Brand Rankings

Here is a comparison of the 2007 and 2008 rankings of the world's most valuable brands by Interbrand, Millward Brown, and Brand Finance.

Table 9.2   Brand value, 2008: Interbrand/Millward Brown/Brand Finance

Company	Interbrand (US$m)	Millward Brown (US$m)	Brand Finance (US$m)	Factor*
Apple	13,724	55,206	21,779	4.02
Porsche	4,603	21,718	5,569	4.72
ING	3,768	15,080	10,046	4.00

* Highest brand value divided by lowest brand value

Table 9.3   Brand value, 2008

Company	Interbrand (US$m)	Millward Brown (US$m)	Brand Finance (US$m)
Google	25,590	86,057	43,085
Apple	13,724	55,206	21,779
GE	53,086	71,379	36,123
McDonald's	31,049	49,499	21,812
Microsoft	59,007	70,887	44,501
HSBC	13,143	18,479	35,456
Coca-Cola	66,667	58,208	45,441
IBM	59,031	55,335	37,949
Marlboro	21,300	37,324	23,705
Pepsi	13,249	15,404	24,813
BMW	23,298	28,015	17,215
Oracle	13,831	22,904	9,513

The first two publish a Top 100 list, while the latter publishes a Top 500 list. There are 53 brands that appear in common between the three lists across both years. Each of these valuation methods can result in dramatically different estimates of the value of individual brands—by as much as a factor of four.

Putting the highly volatile financial sector aside for the moment, valid arguments may be put forward about why the estimates of the value of the brands of high-growth companies such as Apple and Google might vary considerably. But it is harder to rationalize why the value of Coca-Cola should vary from US$45 billion to US$67 billion depending on whose 2008 ranking you read.

The most troubling aspect of valuation studies is the lack of agreement between the major agencies about whether the value of individual brands is increasing or decreasing from year to year. For example, for 40 percent of the brands that were common to the three rankings in both years, they disagreed about whether their value had risen or fallen over the previous year. To illustrate the different outcomes resulting from their methodologies, Table 9.4 compares the percentage change in brand value for a number of leading brands between 2007 and 2008.

Table 9.4 Change in brand value, 2008 vs. 2007 (percent)

Company	Interbrand	Millward Brown	Brand Finance
AIG	−6	21	2
American Express	5	7	−11
AXA	−4	50	6
BMW	8	9	−4
Budweiser	−2	9	6
Chanel	9	15	−47
Disney	0	5	−15
eBay	7	−13	−19
Ford	−12	−13	17
Gillette	8	20	−1
Goldman Sachs	−3	45	44
HSBC	−3	6	6
ING	−3	31	−1
JPMorgan	−6	15	42
Marlboro	0	−5	−12
McDonald's	6	49	−9
Mercedes	9	1	−11
Morgan Stanley	−16	1	−18
Samsung	5	−7	−16
Starbucks	7	−25	−10
UPS	5	−4	5
Yahoo!	−9	−13	8

Notes on Methodology

Interbrand (Extracted from Firm's Website)

Our valuation approach is a derivative of the way businesses and financial assets are valued. It fits with current corporate finance theory and practice. There are three key elements and they are detailed below.

Financial Forecasting

We identify the revenues from products or services that are generated with the brand. From these branded revenues we deduct operating costs, applicable taxes, and a charge for the capital employed to derive the economic value that is generated by all tangible and intangible business assets of the branded business. Economic value added (EVA) is a value based management concept and is a generally accepted principle to measure the ability of a business to generate returns over and above its invested capital. Based on reports from financial analysts, we prepare a financial forecast and calculate the EVA of the branded business.

Role of Branding

Since EVA includes the returns for all assets employed in the business, we need to identify the earnings that are specifically attributable to the brand. Through our proprietary analytical framework, called Role of Branding, we can calculate the percentage of EVA that is entirely generated by the brand. In some businesses, e.g. in fragrances or packaged goods, the Role of Branding is very high—as the brand is the predominant driver of the customer purchase decision. However, in other businesses (in particular, B2B) the brand is only one purchase driver among many, and the Role of Branding is therefore lower. For example, people are buying Microsoft not only because of the brand, but because the company has an installed base of 80 percent of the market and it would be extremely difficult for most users to switch their existing files to a new software platform. In the case of Shell, people buy not only because of the brand, but also because of the location of the gas stations. For each of the brands (and categories) we have assessed the Role of Branding. The Role of Branding is derived as a percentage. Thus, if it is 50 percent, we take 50 percent of the EVA as brand earnings. If it is 10 percent, we only take 10 percent of the EVA.

Brand Strength

To derive the net present value of the forecast brand earnings, we need a discount rate that represents the risk profile of these earnings. There are two factors at play: first, the time value of money (i.e. US$100 today is more valuable than US$100 in five years because one can earn interest on the money in the meantime); and second, the risk that the forecast earnings will actually materialize. The discount rate represents these

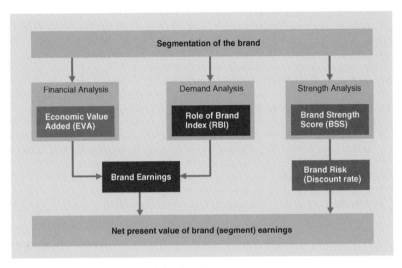

Figure 9.5   Segmentation of the brand

factors as it provides an asset-specific risk rate. The higher the risk of the future earnings stream, the higher the discount rate will be. To derive today's value of a future expected earnings stream, it needs to be "discounted" by a rate that reflects the risk of the earnings actually materializing and the time for which it is expected. For example, US$100 from the Coca-Cola brand in five years requires a lower discount rate than US$100 from the Fanta brand in five years, as the Coca-Cola brand is stronger and therefore more likely to deliver the expected earnings. The assessment of brand strength is a structured way of assessing the specific risk of the brand. We compare the brand against a notional ideal and score it against common factors of brand strength. The ideal brand is virtually "risk free" and would be discounted at a rate almost as low as government bonds or a similar risk-free investment. The lower the brand strength, the further it is from the risk free investment and so the higher the discount rate (and therefore the lower the net present value).

Millward Brown (Extracted from Firm's Website)

Millward Brown Optimor applies an economic approach to brand valuation, and uses a methodology similar to that employed by analysts and accountants. The brand value published is based on the intrinsic value of the brand—derived from its ability to generate demand. The dollar value of each brand in the ranking is the sum of all future earnings that brand is forecast to generate, discounted to a present day value. Given the high volatility of financial markets over the past 12 months, the brand value is in some cases high relative to current market capitalization, reflecting true value rather than current market swings.

The Data Sources

CUSTOMER OPINION   The secret ingredient is WPP's BrandZ database, based on an annual quantitative brand equity study in which consumers and business customers familiar with a category evaluate brands. Since BrandZ's inception over 10 years ago, more than one million consumers and business-to-business customers across 31 countries have shared their opinions about thousands of brands. It is the most comprehensive, global, and consistent study of brand equity.

FINANCIAL PERFORMANCE   Financial data is sourced from Bloomberg, analyst reports, Datamonitor™ industry reports, and company filings with regulatory bodies. Financial models are then prepared for each brand that link brand perceptions to company revenues, earnings, and ultimately shareholder and brand value. The BrandZ Top 100 values market-facing brands, i.e. brands which directly generate revenues and profits through the sale of goods and services to customers. Corporate brands such as Procter & Gamble, Unilever and Nestlé, which have significant value especially with the investment community, are not included in the ranking.

The Valuation Process

BRANDED EARNINGS: WHAT PROPORTION OF A COMPANY'S EARN-INGS IS GENERATED "UNDER THE BANNER OF THE BRAND"?   First, the branded earnings are identified. For example, in the case of Coca-Cola some earnings are not branded Coca-Cola, but come from Fanta, Sprite, or Minute Maid. Once identified capital charges are subtracted, this ensures only value above and beyond what investors would require any investment in the brand to earn is captured: the value the brand adds to the business. This provides a bottom-up view of the earnings of the branded business.

BRAND CONTRIBUTION: HOW MUCH OF THESE BRANDED EARNINGS ARE GENERATED DUE TO THE BRAND'S CLOSE BOND WITH ITS CUSTOMERS?   The portion of these earnings driven by brand equity is called "Brand Contribution": the degree to which brand plays a role in generating earnings. This is established through analysis of country-, market-, and brand-specific consumer research from the BrandZ database. This guarantees that the Brand Contribution is rooted in real-life customer perceptions and behavior, not spurious "expert opinion": in some categories, brand is important—luxury, cars, or beer, for instance. In categories like motor fuel, on the other hand, price and location play a very strong role. Furthermore, as markets develop, consumer priorities and the role of brand may change.

BRAND MULTIPLE: WHAT IS THE GROWTH POTENTIAL OF THE BRAND-DRIVEN EARNINGS?   In the final step, the growth potential of these branded earnings is taken into account. Both financial projections and consumer data are analyzed. This provides an earnings multiple aligned with the methods used by the analyst community. It also takes into

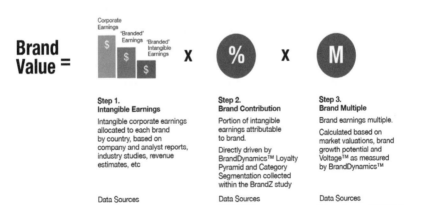

Figure 9.6   MIllward Brown brand valuation model

account brand-specific growth opportunities and barriers. To capture the weaker economic outlook, all projections have been validated using IMF economic growth forecasts. The Brand Momentum™ indicator that indicates each brand's growth is based on this evaluation. It is presented as an indexed figure that ranges from 1 to 10 (10 being high).

Many companies now use brand valuation to track the success of brand management, using methodologies such as those detailed above. The final case study is that of the giant food and beverage company Diageo, which uses brand valuation to continuously track performance, and so give management strategic and operational control over the group's most valuable assets.

CASE STUDY 41: DIAGEO

Performance Tracking

Prior to its merger with Guinness to form Diageo, Grand Met had a portfolio of brands including names as prominent as Smirnoff, Baileys, Häagen-Dazs, Green Giant, and Burger King.

In 1988, Grand Met shocked the financial world by including its acquired brands as intangible assets on its balance sheet. Being so rich in name brands, it was little surprise that senior management appreciated their importance to the long-term health of the organization and wished to reflect this in the company accounts. The 1988 balance sheet included brands with a cost of £608 million.

To the board of Grand Met, the fact that a series of expensive and high-profile acquisitions might not have been included in the accounts seemed an absurd contradiction and would have left the company perilously undervalued.

An anomaly remained. Only acquired brands were included on the balance sheet, despite the obvious value to Grand Met of its internally generated brands. Similarly, early valuations were based on historical earnings multiples, a method not currently seen as accurately reflecting the true worth of a brand.

Grand Met's response to this problem, and evidence of a real bridge being built between marketing and finance functions, was the introduction of its "brand equity monitor." The purpose of this wasn't to place a historical value on a brand, but to give management an idea of the performance of brands. The factors measured couldn't be measured in purely profit and loss terms, and the monitor included both economic, consumer, and perceptual measures of performance, which together formed a subtle and responsive mechanism for tracking both brand health and, if necessary, financial brand value.

The process has been extended from its early beginnings, and Diageo now monitors a number of key financial and marketing drivers to establish the level of brand equity. These drivers focus management's attention on gaining customer awareness, loyalty, market share, and the brand's ability to charge a price premium. It is this premium which communicates the value of a brand to the company's stakeholders.

There are a number of checks used by Diageo to assess the trends in brand equity. A sample of these measures includes awareness, advertising spend, market penetration, and share of display. Management is able to gauge the relative health of brands from a flow of consistent and reliable data. The fact that the vast majority of this data will never be included in the company accounts is irrelevant; it provides, instead, a degree of strategic and operational control over the group's most valuable assets.

Conclusion

Throughout this book I have stressed that brands drive business in the new world. Only by allowing this to happen can companies achieve true consumer-centricity. The other side of this "coin" is that, while companies may initially create them, brands are built and "owned" by customers, with companies merely having custody of them. It is therefore vital that brands understand their consumers. Brand management has now changed in its emphasis; it isn't so much about persuading consumers to prefer your brand, but more about understanding consumers so well that you can give them a brand that really adds value to their lives. The brand has to become a part of them.

With this in mind, brand managers need to concentrate on things that move people's souls, and these aren't found in the rational world. *Emotion* is the key to gaining consumer acceptance, friendship, and lasting loyalty, and yet so many companies still choose to ignore this fact. Simply put, rationally based branding doesn't work in a world where parity is the norm. Functional product differences, for example, will become even more trivial. This isn't to say that a brand's promise need not be based in quality, service, innovation, and ethics; on the contrary, all great brands must have these attributes. But it is more than that. Passion is playing a much more important role in consumer buying behavior than ever before. Brands must listen to, respond to, and support the fast-changing needs of consumers. In fact, attitude is becoming a defining factor in brand performance.

Connected to this message is the debate as to whether brands are good for people and countries, and what the future looks like for branding. I believe the route to corporate success in the future will be found in developing brands that show more care. By this I mean that the "winning brands" in the foreseeable future will be those that demonstrate not just social responsibility, but a genuine willingness to care for people and the world in which we live. Some brands are already doing this, and are passionate about how they can contribute to the well-being of humanity. Some brands merely give lip service to this subject, and others don't bother at all.

This is what I mean by "winning brands." There needn't be a correlation between a powerful brand and an absence of the "human touch." The great brands of the future will be those that can demonstrate both market power and worldly compassion. Great brands will be like great people—those whom we respect for their humility, leadership, compassion, leading-edge thinking, and the trust they place in consumers. Brands that reach such heights will, in return, be a part of the lives of millions, admired for what they are and what they do. What brands actually do for people, and what people love and care for, will become a much more important determinant of success. Emotional proactivity will be a critical success factor for brand management.

This forecast, when taken together with all of the topics I have covered in this book, means that the role of brand management is vitally important and changing rapidly. The best brand managers of the future will be those that can run businesses, understand and care for consumers, constantly force innovation yet maintain top quality, balance profit with social responsibility, and motivate thousands of people to work for them happily. Indeed, this is why the world's top corporate executives are now those that are proficient in brand management and marketing skills.

The demand for additional skills in the repertoire of brand managers will increase significantly as a result of these changes. Professional knowledge and skills will no longer be enough. The top brand managers of the future will need to be special people, with a diverse array of knowledge, skills, and attitudes. The good news is that skilled brand managers are now in great demand all around the world, and there are many opportunities to work in this exciting and very dynamic field. One thing is for sure: you will never be bored when managing brands!

In the Toolkit that follows, I have compiled questions, lists, and thoughts that I hope will assist those given the responsibility for managing brands.

Good luck with all your branding initiatives, and keep in touch with our website for additional ideas: www.temporalbrand.com.

Paul Temporal
October 2009

Appendix
Your Brand Management Toolkit

This toolkit is designed to help you with your overall brand management process. It is not exhaustive, but covers the following key areas:

1. Questions on the brand as a business
2. A general brand audit questionnaire
3. Building brand personality—creating a personality and test questions
4. A question guide to the brand positioning process
5. Customer relationship management—guidelines and benefits
6. An advertising diagnostics checklist
7. A sample statement on brand strategy for investor relations
8. A brand scorecard: The top 12 traits of the world's strongest brands—do you have them?

1. Questions on the Brand as a Business —

The key questions you have to answer before you start to build and/or set plans for managing your brand are:

- What business is my brand in?
- What is the vision for my brand?
- What consumer insights can I use to help answer the first question?
- Has my brand business got its basis in the emotional sphere?

- What personality and attitude (character) does my brand have?
- Does the brand character match that of my target audience?
- How can I improve the emotional relationship between my consumers and my brand?
- What are the implications for the future development of my brand?
- Are projects and business activities that don't add value to the brand allowed or not?
- How does my company ensure that proper brand guardianship takes place?

2. A General Brand Audit Questionnaire

This audit is a general one that is used merely to take a snapshot of what is happening in your brand world. It doesn't deal with specifics—those come in the following sections—but serves as a reminder of the things you have to keep an eye on. Such questions should be asked once or twice a year. It also includes questions on OEM activities, as many companies get caught out, especially in recessionary times, because they have focused their efforts on building other people's brands and not their own.

A. Corporate Brand Questions

- When is the corporate brand name used?
- Where is it used?
- How is it used? On its own? With products? On what basis? Where are you on the continuum between true corporate branding and absolute product branding?
- What determines the usage of the corporate brand name when subsidiaries/alliance partners are involved?
- What is the vision of the company?
- Is this the same as, or different from, the brand vision? How do they relate?
- What are the core values of the company?
- What are the brand values?

- Do either sets of values conflict?
- Does the culture represent the values?
- What are the current consumer perceptions of the brand, and how do these differ by market/segment?
- What are your alliance partner's perceptions of the brand?
- Does the brand have a strategic competitive advantage compared to your competitors?
- What are the current brand images (consumer perceptions) of the major competitors in each market/category/segment?
- What are the desired consumer perceptions of the brand? Do these vary by market/category/segment?
- What are the opportunities and threats facing the brand in each market/category/segment?
- Is there an obvious opportunity to stretch the brand into a different market/category/segment?

a. Product/Sub-Brand Questions

- What is the current brand architecture, and is it appropriate?
- How do product and/or sub-brands relate, if at all, to the master brand?
- What are the strengths and weaknesses of each product/sub-brand?
- Do any of them have a strategic competitive advantage or a unique selling proposition?
- How do they compare against the main competitor brands in terms of brand image?
- Does this differ by market/segment? If so, how? How are categories changing, and what effects are these having on your brands?
- Is your emphasis on own brands or OEM?
- What determines whether or not a product is marketed as an OEM brand?
- How are new product brand names chosen?
- What is the decision-making procedure for bringing a new product to market?
- How are pricing decisions made?
- How well are your channels representing your brands?

- Are there any obvious gaps in the different categories that you could fill with a new or existing brand?
- Are you tempted to extend any of your brands?
- Have you pre-tested with consumers whether they will accept the extension?
- Is your brand still in touch with its target audience? Will it continue to be if you extend it?
- Has its image shifted negatively or positively? Will it shift with an extension?
- Are you evolving the brand in line with market changes while staying true to its personality?
- Is competition eroding its position?
- Does it need repositioning or revitalizing?
- Will consumers accept a new positioning?
- What investment do you need, and what returns can you expect from a revitalization process?
- If you need to "kill" a brand, can you cope with the fallout?
- Will you just reduce investment in the brand and let it die naturally, or will you need to delete it as quickly as possible?

b. Marketing, Advertising, and Promotion Questions

- What percentage of turnover is spent on advertising and promotion (A&P)?
- How is this split between advertising and promotion?
- How much goes to customer relationship management (CRM)?
- How does this compare to the main competitors?
- What determines how much is spent on each brand in each market/category/segment?
- Is there a corporate marketing communications plan?
- Are there marketing communications plans for each product/ sub-brand?
- Are you providing your agency with proper positioning and communications briefs?
- Is the agency providing you with an integrated approach to brand communications?

- Have you tried co-branding, and has it been successful? Why or why not?

c. Additional Questions

- What new joint ventures/strategic alliances/changes to the current organizational structure are envisaged?
- How is the brand management function organized? Does it need strengthening?
- Is it intended to change the proportion of OEM business? If so, when, and by what proportion, in which markets?
- What new products/brands are to be introduced in the short and longer term?
- What are the brand strengths and weaknesses of each subsidiary/strategic alliance?
- List the brands in order of priority, from highest to lowest value in each market, taking into account gross profit and volume sales.

3. Building Brand Personality

A. Creating a Personality

Your brand's personality can be created in two main ways:

- Create a list of personality characteristics, say 20 or 30, and then narrow these down to the three to seven most important ones you want your brand to have. These might include some that your brand already has or some you want it to have. In other words, some may already be brand strengths, and some weaker aspects of the brand you wish to be perceived as owning. This is a common way to create a personality for a brand that is being revitalized or repositioned. It needs consensus among all who can influence the brand inside your company, and you may have to work very hard on the elements your brand doesn't yet possess. This may take time, but it will be well worth the effort.

- Match the brand characteristics to those of your target audience. Here, you must rely on market research to tell you what these characteristics are.

B. Test Questions

Test questions used to gain agreement on how your brand might relate to people can include the following:

- What would your brand be if it were a holiday destination?
- What would it be if it were an animal? A film star? A car?
- What brands of clothing would it wear if it were an actual person?
- What kind of place would it live in?
- What would its lifestyle be like?
- What kind of friends would it have?
- If it went out to a restaurant, what food would your brand eat, in what kind of ambience?
- If you had to introduce your brand to a friend, what would you say?
- If you had to write an obituary for your brand, what would you say?

These questions are not only useful for testing the consistency of brand management thinking, but can be also be used in focus group discussions to see whether the personality is clear, and with agencies to determine what should and shouldn't appear in their creative execution.

4. A Question Guide to the Positioning Process

This comprehensive set of questions will help you through all aspects of the positioning process.

Step 1: Taking a Good Look at the Market

- How fast is the market growing?
- What level of competition is there, and where is it coming from?
- Who are our main competitors for each of our brands?
- What segments exist in the market are we interested in?
- Where are the growth opportunities? Which segments are growing faster than others, and why?
- Why do customers come to/leave us?
- Why do they go to each of our competitors?
- What are our priorities for business growth?

Step 2: Understanding Our Present Image and Position

- How do people (employees and customers) see us at present?
- What are the strengths and weaknesses of our current brand image?
- How does our image compare with those of our key competitors?
- What is our position relative to the competition on a consumer perceptual map?
- How close or far away from the consumer ideal preferences are we and the other players?
- What strategic opportunities are there to move into spaces or gaps that consumers would appreciate, and yet haven't been filled?
- Can we do more research to add precision to these views of consumer perceptions?

Step 3: Developing Positioning Alternatives

- What is our desired position and image?
- What space do we want to move into in the mind map of consumers?
- What strategy, or combination of strategies, do we think are best suited to achieving our goal?

- How will we explain what we stand for in terms of our personality, and what makes us both different from and better than the main competitors?
- Are the options sustainable in the long run, or will they only afford us a short-term differential advantage?

Step 4: Creating the Final Positioning Statement

Now it is time to write the final positioning statement, which is framed in consumer language as a statement of how precisely we want consumers to think about us.

- What business or product class are we in?
- Who is our target audience?
- What benefits are we offering them?
- Why are we better than and different from the competition?

Above all, this desired position and image we wish to create in people's minds must be credible, believable, relevant to them, and capable of being delivered.

Step 5: Adapting to the New Position—Delivering on the Promise

- Do we have to develop a new product or adapt existing ones?
- Do we have to change our service standards?
- Do we have to change our visual identity or product packaging?
- Do we have to change our brand name(s)?
- Do we have to change our corporate culture?
- Do we have to adjust our pricing or distribution policies?
- What will be our communications strategy once all these things are in place?
- What is our communications plan?
- Do we have a good online strategy to complement the offline communications strategy?

Step 6: Monitoring Success—Have We Achieved the Brand Image We Want?

This last step is very important, as we may have to adjust what we offer, our communications, or even our position, if the market situation changes or the perceptions, needs, and wants of the consumers evolve. Monitoring image and positioning means constantly evaluating every one of the steps mentioned above. If this isn't done, there is a real danger that we will lose touch with the market and, importantly, consumer feelings and perceptions about us. Image building is a continuous process and requires continuous feedback from all quarters. There is no room for complacency, and corporate graveyards are littered with failed businesses that never understood the thoughts of those people who really counted. Images are fragile, delicate things that must be given care and attention. They exist only as thoughts and feelings, and temporarily occupy positions in people's minds. Without constant reinforcement and improvement, they will lose their importance, and be replaced by other stronger images. The positioning process builds strong images, but it is careful management of the positions created that sustains them.

5. Customer Relationship Management— Guidelines and Benefits

A. What Is CRM?

- CRM represents a fantastic opportunity for anyone wishing to build a corporate brand, because it helps the rapid build-up of both brand equity and brand value.
- Additionally, it creates differentiation and helps grow market share, and by so doing builds the financial value of the brand.
- CRM helps build brands *quickly*. It accelerates both the learning curve about the customer, and the development of the brand—customer relationship. It is the future of brand building.

- CRM is all about collaborating with your customer. It is concerned with creating the classic win–win situation, where you add value to your customer's daily life, and he or she gives you loyalty in return.
- Not all customers are equal. The Pareto principle (80:20 rule) nearly always applies to any business situation, where approximately 80 percent of your profits come from 20 percent of your customers.
- The purpose of a CRM program is to recognize the best customers and hold on to them. It also has the aim of transforming lower-value customers into higher-value ones.
- Effective CRM is about applying the knowledge you hold about your customer every time he or she interacts with you, in such a way that you add value to your product or service, strengthening the emotional bond between the customer, your brand, and your company.
- CRM isn't a fantastic new technique that has been created for the new millennium. It was being practiced way back in the days when mom and pop stores proliferated.
- Many CRM programs take the form of points-based loyalty schemes; however, generally speaking, points-based schemes do little to improve the loyalty of customers.
- CRM isn't something that can give impact to your business overnight. The real payback will come over time, but it will be real, and it will be permanent.
- I have yet to come across a single organization or business that wouldn't derive real benefits from CRM.
- CRM allows you do the unthinkable: to benefit your customer and yourself at the same time.

B. How CRM Works

CRM works by:

- Creating a continuous communication loop between your organization and your customer.
- Getting to know the customer.

- Using existing customer data.
- Asking the customer what they want from you.
- Establishing the unlocked potential.
- Creating the knowledge.
- Reusing the knowledge time after time.
- Having CRM in your company will give you a large number of benefits, including:
  - Helping you to build your brand image.
  - Attracting new customers.
  - Selling more to your current customers.
  - Shielding your customers from approaches by your competitors.
  - Increased returns on brand investment.
  - Stronger and cheaper customer acquisition rates.
  - Increased customer referrals.
  - Lower rates of brand defection.
  - Expressing brand personality.
  - Increasing staff loyalty.
  - More effective use of A&P budgets.
  - Better understanding of the business cost drivers.
  - More effective, relevant product design.
  - Reduced research needs.
  - Increased profits and brand value.
  - Adding value to investor relations.
- Companies that focus on developing a strong relationship with their customers will obtain twice the sales growth of those that don't.
- Those same companies can expect to receive six times the return on equity of those that don't build a bond with their customers.
- Far and away the main reason for customers leaving is that companies don't talk to them, and they feel unwanted or badly treated.

Adding value to your brand really means that it has to do one or all of the following:

- It saves customers money.
- It saves them time (time equals money).
- It saves them hassle (offers a quicker/more efficient service).
- It customizes products or services specifically to customer needs.

C. Implementation Steps

- The key question for every manager every day is: What are you doing today to add value to your customers' lives?
- In the new-style company, it isn't the brand or product manager who is most important—it is the "customer manager."
- Segmentation has always been a key element of any marketing strategy and is vital to the branding process. The better-defined the target, the more effective your brand strategy is likely to be.
- Installing your CRM program is a great chance to "spring clean" your processes. Remove tasks being performed each day that add no real value to either your customers or your organization.
- Set up a pilot program and monitor its impact.
- Prepare in advance for roadblocks to your CRM project.
- Work through your financial justification for your project as soon as possible.
- Don't neglect your internal marketing.
- Reuse current initiatives wherever possible.
- Find a project champion.
- Make sensible use of outsourcing to speed up your project.
- Plan your migration strategy while your pilot is running.
- The three golden rules before starting your CRM program are:
  - Develop clear objectives.
  - Make things easy for the customer.
  - Be realistic about what you can achieve.

D. Profitability of Customers

- You must establish the profitability of your customers.
- How does the Pareto principle apply to your customer base? Is it 80:20 or 90:10?

- Your money should be seeking out customers who:
  - buy from you regularly;
  - have bought from you recently;
  - are making a significant contribution to your company profits;
  - are recommending your product or service to friends and colleagues; and/or
  - have significant development potential.

You need to build a profile of your most profitable customers: who they are; where they live; what they do for a living; their family background; their lifestyle.

Your next priority is to look at the second-most profitable group. Who is in this group and fits the profile of your most profitable customers? What are they doing differently that means they are not so profitable for you? How can you use your marketing skills via CRM to change their habits?

Plug your information gaps by talking to your customers by any means available to you.

The hub of any CRM initiative must be your marketing database. Without it, you cannot hope to harness the information you hold about your customers.

Look at the recency, frequency, and value of your interactions with your customers, and use this to prioritize your CRM activities.

When you build your program, include tiers to create recognition and to motivate customers within the program to perform in such a way that they reach the next level of value to your company.

6. An Advertising Diagnostics Checklist

This is a basic framework for evaluating advertisements/storyboards put forward to you by agencies. Sometimes (in my experience, *always*) advertising agencies get carried away with their creative ideas. Some of these may be outstanding, but some may be way off strategy, and as a brand manager it's your call. You must be disciplined and tough to take on the pressure of agency persuasion. Here are some useful reminders of the kind of things you should be focusing on, instead of the "smoke and mirrors" the agencies sometimes produce in their efforts to gain revenue. Above all, try to be totally objective, even though your job and/or the brand's success depends on your judgment. Put yourself in the shoes of the target consumer. Have a mental picture of them, or some hard data that gives you an understanding of who they are and what they are like.

A. First Reaction

- What is your immediate response to the agency's presentation?
- Is there a central message or idea?
- Will it be noticed?
- Will it be received and enjoyed?
- Is it entertaining?
- Is the idea capable of sustaining a long campaign?

B. Consumer Response

- What will the consumer take out? (Not what the agency has put in.)
- What key messages are there from the brand's positioning?
- Does the brand personality come across adequately?

C. Visuals: Look at These Very Carefully with Your Colleagues

- What impact do the visuals have on you?
- As an entity, is it on brand or not?
- If you feel it is, does the opening shot set the stage and attract?
- Will the people remember the brand and not the ad?
- Is the situation interesting to consumers?
- Can they identify with it—the style, story, mood, effects?
- Is it too gimmicky or quirky?
- Is there a story? Is the story believable?
- Is it simple and easy to understand?
- Will it stand out from the clutter?

- Is the tone right? (e.g. not patronizing)
- Is it durable, or will people get tired of it very quickly?

D. Words: Read These Two or Three Times

- Do the words support the pictures?
- Do they fit with the brand personality?
- Are they of interest to the consumer?

E. Check for Total Understanding

- Does the whole represent your vision of the brand and the way it should relate to consumers?
- Does the advertisement attract the heart, as well as the head?

7. A Sample Statement on Brand Strategy for Investor Relations

This statement is a typical media release intended for investors under circumstances when a company is either involved in a campaign for listing, or when trying to change the perceptions of investors in the light of repositioning activities. It is corporate by nature, for obvious reasons. It is fictitious and can be modified to suit different occasions and circumstances.

Company X believes in the value of brands, and in their worth as strategic business assets. Developing and managing our brands is a business priority, and will fulfill our vision.

In the industry we belong to, we believe that only the strong brands will survive in a profitable way. Whilst operational effectiveness is necessary, it does not serve to differentiate a company in a crowded market. We believe that competitive strategy is all about being different, and that branding brings about that difference.

Company X has embarked on a program of activity to build a powerful corporate brand, and leverage on the significant competitive strengths that the company has. With a corporate reputation for being passionate, professional, innovative, and loving in the minds of consumers and partners, Company X intends to generate further brand awareness and loyalty at all levels of the value chain by enhancing the presence of the corporate brand in all market communications.

At present, a significant amount of our business has been created through the branding of our individual products as opposed to corporate branding, and we have done very well. However, a recent brand audit has revealed substantial opportunities to further enhance the image of the parent brand. Whilst product branding is clearly an important feature of the overall business profile, a carefully introduced corporate master brand will add further consistency, trust, and confidence across all our offerings. It will add strength to individual brands and produce synergy across all our communications. Moreover, it will avoid the need for costly duplication of advertising and promotional resources, particularly when new brands are introduced, as they will be in the future.

The company believes that brands are strategic assets in their own right and is fully aware of the value that can be attached to brand names. Presently, a brand strategy project is nearing completion that will produce a "blueprint" guide to the building of Company X brand equity and value, both corporate and product.

8. A Brand Scorecard: The Top 12 Traits of The World's Strongest Brands—Does Your Brand Have These Attributes?

Throughout this book I have referred to best practices in brand management. These are now summarized in a brand scorecard. You will find it helpful to discuss and rate your brand(s) on these attributes, from both an internal and external perspective. Be honest and *especially* look from the outside in—through the eyes of the consumer. Working hard on all of these attributes will ensure brand success. Ignoring any of them will leave your brand(s) with unfulfilled potential, and a degree of vulnerability. It is also worth mentioning that the attributes are intertwined, and changes in one may bring about changes in others.

The world's most powerful brands have the following attributes in common:

1. They have a vision of their own.
2. They develop emotional capital.
3. They are well differentiated (positioned).
4. They are highly consistent in adherence to their values.
5. They always remain relevant to consumers, and balance consistency with change in an evolutionary manner.
6. They are not diluted by poor brand architecture.
7. They use multi-channel market communications and have adequate financial support.
8. They always deliver the highest quality and value for money, as defined by the consumer.
9. Their perceived value to users is always high, and this is reflected in pricing policy.
10. They always deliver on their promises, and provide a great brand experience.
11. They are monitored and guarded meticulously by their brand managers, and/or the brand management structure.
12. They increase in value and equity year on year.

Index